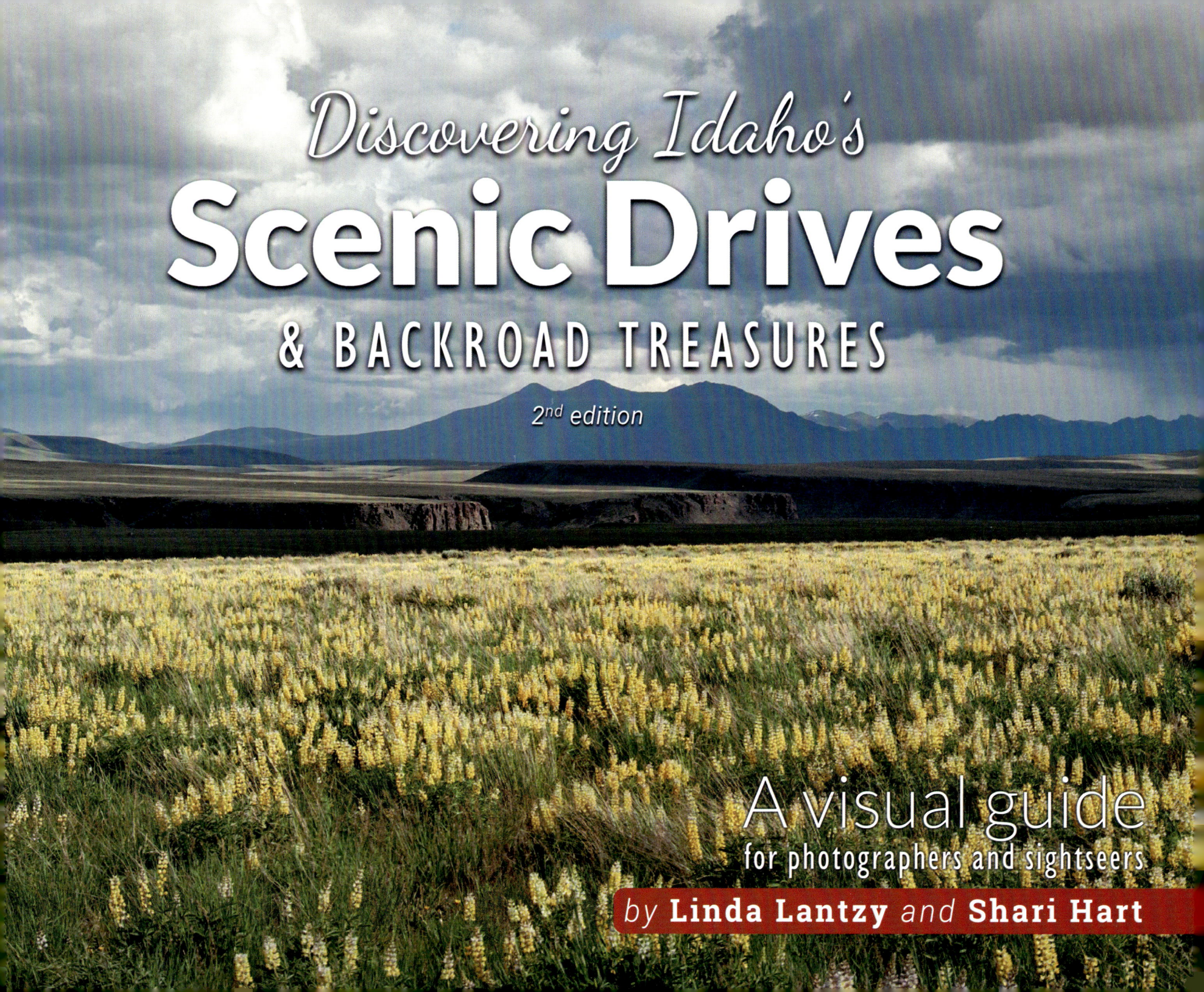

Author and Photographer: Linda Lantzy | Idaho Scenic Images
Author and Photographer: Shari Hart | Wind and Sage Photography
Designer: Kyle Lantzy | Lenzi Forge
Editor: Ken Levy | Ken Levy Media

Photography and Text © 2021 Linda Lantzy and Shari Hart
Design and Layout © 2021 Kyle Lantzy

All rights reserved. No portion of this book, either text or photographs may be reproduced, distributed or transmitted in any form or by any means, including photocopying, recording, or other electronic or mechanical methods, without the express written consent of the authors, except in the case of brief quotations embodied in reviews and certain other non-commercial uses permitted by copyright law.

The authors, designer, editor and publisher disclaim any liability for damage, injury or death caused by following the routes or engaging in the activities outlined in this book.

Second Edition May 2021
Library of Congress Control Number: 2021908921
ISBN # 978-0-9985669-5-5

First Edition August 2019
Library of Congress Control Number: 2019905761
ISBN # 978-09974118-8-1

Created in the United States.
Designed and Printed in Canada
Published by Idaho Scenics Publishing - Hayden, Idaho

To order additional copies visit Idahoscenics.com

Cover Image: Fall color in the Caribou Mountains of Eastern Idaho on Route 30.
Title Page Image: Lupine on the China Creek Road in route 42.

www.lenziforge.com   www.idahoscenics.com   www.windandsagephotography.com   kenlevymedia.com

Disclaimer

Important notes and disclaimers: Always read and understand the Notes and Cautions sections before embarking on any route.

Most route directions begin at the nearest town. Driving times and distances are approximate. The maps in this book are meant only to provide a general location of each photo or sightseeing opportunity and are not intended for navigation. We have chosen not to include GPS coordinates in this book, but instead are providing scannable QR codes that you can use on your digital device as you travel. Map points provided in the book and via QR codes online are also approximate. Our routes are easy to follow by the directions given, but we recommend you travel with a GPS and detailed maps of your area. We recommend the Idaho Road and Recreation Atlas from Benchmark Maps. It is highly recommended to have an assistant reading the route to you as you travel.

Always be prepared for rapid, unpredictable weather changes. Roads often wash out, rocks can pop tires and other vehicle damage is possible without your full attention. Snow and ice can make travel treacherous and some areas impassable. Most of the routes in this book are suitable for 2 wheel drive vehicles. Occasional sections may recommend all-wheel drive. Leave the trailers and RVs home, or at a base camp.

Be alert! Activities described in this book come with a certain degree of danger. Cliffs, drop-offs, and steep terrain are all potentially deadly. Crossing roadways should be done with extreme caution. Wildlife can be unpredictable, and their sudden appearance on a blind curve or darting out of a forest should be anticipated. Idaho is home to cougars, moose, bears (both grizzly and black), rattlesnakes, wolves and a variety of other dangerous animals. Be mindful of this when hiking. This is not a hiking guide. Please obtain hiking guides before your planned outings.

Be prepared! You should always start each route with a full tank of gas; bring plenty of water and food and other emergency supplies. Some routes are on forestlands and require you bring an axe, shovel and bucket. Make sure all campfires are dead out.

The photographs in this book were collected over many visits to each area by trained and experienced photographers and are only intended as references. There are no guarantees of what you may see or capture. This will depend on weather conditions, time of day, season, equipment and your own vision and skill.

These routes were developed based on concentrations of photogenic opportunities within a relatively close proximity to each other. In no way is it meant to say there are not other photo or sightseeing opportunities within the state. We realize not all items will be of interest to all travelers. Photo and sightseeing interests vary from person to person, but we have done our best to document potential subject matter.

Remember, time changes all things. Buildings fall, vehicles get moved, autumn colors are more pronounced one year over another, wind strips leaves from the trees, wildflowers that are abundant one year may be non-existent the next. Water levels rise and fall with the seasons. Roads get closed. Rivers re-route themselves. Snow conditions are increasingly unpredictable.

The authors, designer, editor and publisher disclaim any liability for damage, injury or death caused by following the routes or engaging in the activities outlined in this book.

Sunset at Stanley Lake, route 48

Acknowledgments

A huge thank you to all who helped make this book possible including our many photographer friends, facebook followers, attorney and print representative. We couldn't have done it without your support, help, encouragement, guidance, skills and belief in us.

A special thanks to editor and friend Ken Levy, proofreader Debbie Mitchell, designer and son Kyle Lantzy, husbands, Ted Lantzy and Gordon Hart, Linda's parents; Sharon Erickson and the late Marvin Erickson.

Thanks To Our Sponsors

Northern Routes

1. The Gathering Place
2. Rusty Moose
3. Moose Knuckle
4. Hotel Ruby Sandpoint
5. Evan's Brothers Coffee Roasters
6. Michael D's Eatery
7. Harrison Creamery
8. The Snake Pit
9. Main Street Bistro

North Central Routes

10. The Monarch Hotel
11. Moscow Bagel
12. The Pie Safe
13. Hearthstone Bakery
14. Super 8 Grangeville
15. River Dance Lodge
16. Hearthstone Lodge
17. White Bird Summit Lodge

Central Routes

18. River Rock Cafe
19. Salmon River Motel
20. My Father's Place
21. Gramma's Family Restaurant
22. Awesome Burger
23. The Village at North Fork
24. The Stagecoach Inn
25. Rise & Shine Espresso
26. Lower Stanley Country Store

Eastern Routes

27. Connie's Restaurant
28. Big Hole Bagel
29. The Snake River Roadhouse
30. Cedar Bay Marina and Cafe
31. Caribou Gem
32. Cody's Gastro Garage
33. The Ranch Bakery

South Central Routes

34. Picabo Angler
35. Silver Creek Hotel
36. Sammy's Mini Mart
37. Smoky Mountain Pizzeria
38. The Prairie Inn
39. Tracy General Store
40. T and T Cafe'
41. Mountain View Barn
42. The Rogerson Store

Southwestern Routes

43. Papa Kelsey's Pizza and Subs
44. Bruneau One Stop
45. Dan's Ferry Service
46. The Y-Stop Country Store and Restaurant
47. The Bowling Alley, LLC
48. Two Rivers Grill

Table of Contents

Title Page	I
Copyright Page	II
Disclaimer	III
Acknowledgements	V
Come Discover Idaho	2
Things You Should Know	3
Photographer Rights	4
Idaho Geology	5
How To Use This Guide	7

Northern Region
Introduction	9
Route 1 - *Purcell Trench and the Eastern Selkirks*	11
Route 2 - *Purcell Mountains and the Moyie River*	15
Route 3 - *Priest Lake and the Selkirk Mountains*	19
Route 4 - *Pend Oreille Lake and the Cabinet Mountains*	23
Route 5 - *Sagle and Pend Oreille River Loop*	29
Route 6 - *State Parks and Lake Views*	35
Route 7 - *The Coeur d'Alene River and Lake Loop*	41
Route 8 - *The North Fork and Silver Valley*	47
Route 9 - *Route of the Hiawatha*	53

North Central Region
Introduction	59
Route 10 - *Barns and the Palouse*	61
Route 11 - *Palouse and the Clearwater River Canyon*	67
Route 12 - *Waterfalls and the Clearwater Mountains*	71
Route 13 - *Clearwater River*	75
Route 14 - *Camas Prairie and Winchester*	79
Route 15 - *Whitewater and the Bitterroot Mountains*	85
Route 16 - *The Clearwater River North Fork*	91
Route 17 - *White Bird and Hells Canyon*	95
Route 18 - *Salmon River and The Seven Devils Mountains*	99
Route 19 - *Gospel Wilderness and Hells Canyon*	103

Central Region
Introduction	107
Route 20 - *Roseberry and the Salmon River Mountains*	109
Route 21 - *Snowbank Mountain and Lakes*	115
Route 22 - *Dunes Rivers and Canyon Views*	119
Route 23 - *The Bitterroot and Salmon River Mountains*	125
Route 24 - *The Salmon River and Pahsimeroi*	129
Route 25 - *Beaverhead and Lemhi Mountains*	133
Route 26 - *Land of the Yankee Fork*	139

The Lemhi Mountains, as seen on route 25

Eastern Region
- Introduction.........143
- Route 27 - *Dunes to Caldera*.........145
- Route 28 - *Teton Valley and Mountain Views*.........149
- Route 29 - *South Fork of the Snake River*.........153
- Route 30 - *Palisades and Caribou Mountains*.........157
- Route 31 - *Chesterfield and Oneida Narrows*.........161
- Route 32 - *Cub River and Bear Lake*.........167
- Route 33 - *Bannock Range and the Arbon Valley*.........171

South Central Region
- Introduction.........175
- Route 34 - *Craters of the Moon and Picabo Valley*.........177
- Route 35 - *Black Magic Canyon and Big Wood River*.........183
- Route 36 - *Lost River, White Knob and Pioneer Mountains*.........189
- Route 37 - *Sawtooth and Boulder Mountains*.........193
- Route 38 - *Little City and the Camas Marsh*.........201
- Route 39 - *City of Rocks and the California Trail*.........207
- Route 40 - *Waterfalls and Snake River Canyon*.........213
- Route 41 - *Rock Creek Canyon and the South Hills*.........219
- Route 42 - *Salmon Falls Dam and Three Creek Road*.........223
- Route 43 - *Thousand Springs and the Snake River*.........229

Southwestern Region
- Introduction.........225
- Route 44 - *Bruneau Dunes and Owyhee Backcountry*.........237
- Route 45 - *Silver City and the Owyhee Mountains*.........241
- Route 46 - *Reservoirs and Canyons of the Boise Mts*.........245
- Route 47 - *Owyhee Foothills and Leslie Gulch*.........249
- Route 48 - *Payette River and the Sawtooths*.........253

A Day in the Life.........259
A Hike to Mt. Harrison.........262
Behind the Scenes.........263
Coupons.........264

Take a drive down Balanced Rock Grade on route 42

Trout Springs Road along the Owyhee Backcountry Byway, Route 44

Come discover Idaho...
Its scenic drives and backroad treasures.

Idaho..far more than visions of potato fields as far as the eye can see. Beyond those fertile farmlands lies the vast photographic potential of towering peaks, sagebrush deserts, evergreen forests, pristine rivers, deep canyons, idyllic waterfalls, lava flows and beautiful lakes, all created by a plethora of geological events that shaped these magnificent wonders. Not so long ago, people added their own photographic charms to the landscape, via remnants scattered along pioneer routes and the homesteads of early settlers.

Many of these wonderful sights and photographic opportunities can be found just off the interstate. Some locations, however, are far less obvious, and may include old barns, abandoned antique vehicles and pioneer cabins, along with the iconic landmarks and landscapes that are not to be missed...if you know where to look.

We invite you to share in our beloved Idaho.

The view from Lower Stanley on route 26

Things You Should Know

As with any human endeavor, landscape photographers strive to get the most out of their experience. This requires the awareness, respect and courtesy of letting others also get the most out of theirs. We don't want others inadvertently walking into our frames, disturbing wildlife or vegetation, or loudly shouting in the relative solitude we find in nature. We are good stewards of our surroundings and leave as little impact as possible on the places we visit.

Below are some guidelines we hope you'll follow on your excursions. They cover general rules, interactions with your environment and others, and your rights as a photographer. Keeping these in mind will keep your experience as pleasant and stress-free as possible.

- Stay on trails whenever possible. Vegetation such as wildflowers, and wildlife habitat, can be damaged or destroyed by walking off into delicate pristine areas. Avoid hiking on soggy, muddy trails to ease the impact of erosion.

- Practice "Leave No Trace." Take only pictures, leave only footprints. Don't litter, and pack out everything you pack in.

- Do Not Trespass. Respect private property at all times. On public lands, areas marked "closed" are closed either for your protection, for vegetation regeneration or both. Keep out.

- Give wildlife plenty of space. Don't bait wildlife. Failure to comply with either of these can be harmful to the animal and yourself, and can lead to stiff fines.

In short, be a good role model as a photographer and a citizen. Educate others by your actions.

When you find yourself photographing in the presence of others:

- Be kind and courteous to other photographers and non-photographers. They have as much right to be there as you do.

- Give other photographers some space! Don't set up right next to someone who is already set-up. Find your own angle or wait until they leave the spot to shoot there yourself. Remember to let others have the same opportunities you want for yourself.

- Silence is golden. Help maintain solitude in both wild and not-so wild natural places. Many photographers seek solitude and peace when creating images, and shouting, constant chatter and incessant interruptions can adversely affect the creative process.

- Always be aware of other photographers' set-ups and carefully avoid walking into their frames. If you're uncertain, ask. Cooperation and patience are keys.

- If you are photographing from the roadside, park appropriately. Do not block the road or prevent other photographers from setting up.

- If you are at a location and a photography workshop arrives, remember you have as much right to be there as they do. Never let a workshop instructor intimidate you into leaving.

- In short, a little respect goes a very long way. Striking up a friendly conversation with other photographers helps build rapport and, quite frequently, lasting friendships.

Photographer Rights

There are common misconceptions regarding permissions and rights to photograph by both photographers and the general public. When in doubt, getting permission from a landowner is a courtesy.

- You can photograph just about everything while on public land, including people, without permission. Military installations, TSA security checkpoints and power-generation facilities are off limits. Otherwise, you can publish any image made on public land.

- Photographing private property from public space (ie. public roads or public road right of ways) is allowed.

- Entering or photographing from private property is not allowed and you can be prosecuted. Businesses and public buildings are considered private property and their photography policies should be respected.

- In most cases, unless you are breaking the law, police cannot confiscate your equipment or memory cards, and cannot force you to delete your photos.

Source: photographylife.com. For additional information, visit The Photographer's Right, at krages.com/phoright.htm

The White Cloud Mountains as seen on route 26

Idaho Geology
a Convergence of Wonders

By Idaho Public Television (used with permission)

Being a geologically "active" region gives Idaho's landscapes an extra crispness. A lot has happened to the land in Idaho in just the last 15,000 years. Glaciers have moved. Ice has melted. Volcanoes have erupted. Earthquakes have adjusted the elevations of mountain peaks. All around Idaho, the evidence of these events is so fresh that it seems like they happened yesterday.

At Craters of the Moon in southern Idaho, for example, where magma poured from fissures in the earth's crust only 2,000 years ago, it is likely that Native Americans might have watched from the nearby hills. After the magma cooled, what they saw is what we see today--uneroded cinder cones, craters, endless fields of lava that look as if they rolled across the land yesterday.

Continental and alpine glaciers, the legacy of the last ice age, were grinding away on Idaho mountains as recently as 10,000 years ago. Glaciers created over 500 cirques in the high mountains of Idaho. A cirque is a form remaining at the head of a glacial valley where glacial erosion removed big blocks of rock from a mountain and quarried it out. Shallow cirques appear as wet meadows today, while the deeper ones with bowl-shaped floors may contain lakes.

Above the cirques are the scoured and rugged remains of the rock left behind. Glaciers gave central Idaho the spectacular skyline of the Sawtooth Mountains. Not enough time has passed for gravity to pull down the horns and aretes (jagged peaks and ridges) or moderate their vertical walls, or round off their sharp edges.

The Salmon River Canyon as seen on route 19

As the glaciers pushed their load of gravel and debris down the valleys, they piled up lateral and terminal moraines (ridges made up of boulders and gravel) along the sides or out in front. Lodgepole pine forests grew on the moraines (which contain a fair amount of clay and silt), but not enough time has passed to cover up the rocks and boulders completely. The glaciers shaped the valleys they moved through.

The swift violence of Idaho's magma eruptions, glacier carving, and earthquakes is a reflection of what is happening more slowly deep below the earth. Continental drift, plate tectonics, the hot spot — these theories become very convincing when you look around Idaho.

A heavy ocean plate collided with a continental plate about 65 million years ago, sinking below the lighter continental plate. The crustal material heated up to become molten magma. The magma formed into plumes that moved upwards towards the earth's surface. Plumes that arrived at the surface erupted as volcanoes; the ones that didn't are called batholiths.

The center of Idaho is a huge batholith complex called the Idaho Batholith — a huge mass of granite. The material that sat above the pluton as it rose toward the surface was lifted up like a turtle on the back of a hippopotamus emerging from the bottom of a river. Mountains formed. In central Idaho, these mountains are in varying stages of erosion, but mostly the exposed rock is the granite of the pluton. The "turtle" eroded away long ago.

As the plutons rose toward the surface, the outside edges cooled first. Hot gases and liquids became trapped inside and were forced to occupy less and less space as the cooled "rind" of the pluton became thicker and thicker. Finally, the pluton cracked from the pressure, and the gases and liquids shot out the cracks. These too cooled and became the veins so familiar to anyone visiting the mountains. The veins contain gold, silver, lead, zinc, cobalt, copper, and many other rare minerals.

South of the Idaho Batholith is a crescent-shaped flatness brought about by the passage of Idaho over a "hot spot." Imagine a candle sitting on a table. Pass a piece of white paper over the candle slowly enough to turn the paper brown. Now imagine a tectonic plate — a large piece of the earth's crust — passing slowly over an intense source of heat coming from the mantle below. The heat melts the crust, burns it up, and weakens it. Magma squeezes up through fissures and spreads out over the land, filling up stream valleys and erasing the pre-existing topography.

The legacy of the hot spot is Idaho's "flat spot," more properly called the Snake River Plain, the brown streak on the piece of white paper. The "burned" crust is from 50 to 70 miles wide and 400 miles long. The lava rock at the western end of the crescent is the oldest. At the eastern end, Yellowstone boils and bubbles with hot water and gases taking their heat from that candle below. If the hot spot theory is right, the tectonic plate will keep moving westward a few millimeters a year, and its path of destruction will eat into Wyoming and Montana.

The Snake River is another crescent that crosses southern Idaho. It carved its way through the many layers of lava and interbedded sediments that accumulated during the quieter millennia of geologic time. The water from the aquifer, the Snake River, and the rich volcanic soil of the plain gave modern human settlers a rich heritage upon which to build "permanent" settlements.

River carving goes on all over Idaho, of course, one of the more constant and visible processes of geologic change. Whether geologic events are sudden like earthquakes or slow like the progress of tectonic plates, they have produced one of the best places in the world to see them all at work.

City of Rocks on route 39

How to use this guide

Regions: We have divided the state into 6 regions. Each region has between 5 to 10 routes to follow for a total of 48 routes. Each route has a basic map with designated points of interest that correspond with items found in the text. These basic maps can be supplemented with an online map accessed by a QR code.

QR Codes: QR Codes, like the one to the right, are supplied with each of our route maps and are found throughout the book. These codes can be scanned with your smartphone using a QR Code reading app, allowing you quick access to a detailed on-line map, or other useful websites. Simply focus your phone's QR Code reader on the code and the link will appear. Tapping on the link will take you to a Google Map of the route, making it easy to navigate and locate points of interest. Alternatively, you can manually type the web link (provided below each QR code) into your favorite web browser. There are many routes that will have intermittent internet access via a cellular data plan, and some routes that will have none. If you wish to look over the route's online map, it may be best to do so prior to departure.

idahoscenics.2.vu/home

Online Maps: The online maps associated with this book only provide approximate locations of each point of interest. Some pinpoints may display an image of the location or feature extra information when selected. Keep in mind that some routes will not have internet available, so be sure to download the relevant offline maps in your Google Maps app prior to departure. Scan this code for access to the complete list of all route maps.

idahoscenics.2.vu/maps2

Navigation: Most route directions start at the town nearest to that particular route. You'll want a companion to read directions to you, rather than try to read and drive. Mileages reset when reaching each stop or point of interest. Helpful tip: reset your odometer trip setting to 0 after reaching each destination point. A GPS for saving locations, and a map of the area, could come in handy.

Routes: Routes vary from just a few hours driving time to overnight trips. All driving times are estimates and do not include any stops you may choose to make. Routes are numbered in no particular order, After each route we offer suggestions for which route you should take next.

Fees: Many routes include fee areas such as state parks, national recreation areas, trailheads, hot springs, and day-use areas. While we have done our best to inform you of such fees in the Notes and Cautions section of each route, fees may change or could be added after publication.

Notes and Cautions: Always read this section provided before each route, and heed the cautions given regarding road conditions, seasonal closures, vehicle recommendations, wildlife habitat, fees and any other insight we may provide. Remember to always check current weather and road conditions before setting out on any route. Storms, road construction, the aftermath of wildfires and other hazards can alter or prevent access to any location.

Photography Tips: We have included helpful information and advice for each route regarding best time of day to visit certain locals, suggested lens focal lengths, and useful filters. Our routes are designed to get you to many of the key points of interest in time for the best light (morning and evening), and to place you in optimum locations for photography.

Hikes: Most hiking opportunities are less than 1 mile. A couple of them are longer hikes. Obtain a trail map locally if in doubt.

Sponsors and Coupons: Directions to nearby route business sponsors are included with each route. We encourage you to patronize these friendly businesses for dining, lodging and other amenities. Most have provided a coupon for your use. If you don't wish to remove perforated coupon pages, ask the business to sign or stamp your coupon at the time of use.

Photo Location: Most photos in this guide feature a numbered icon that corresponds to a point on the route's map, and also corresponds with a number in the route's directions. Images that contain a (♦) icon feature miscellaneous scenery that you may find along the route.

Updates and Help: Visit the website to the right to view updates and changes to the book as they become available, and to submit corrections if you find a mistake. This web page also provides answers to frequently asked questions and other helpful information.

idahoscenics.2.vu/help

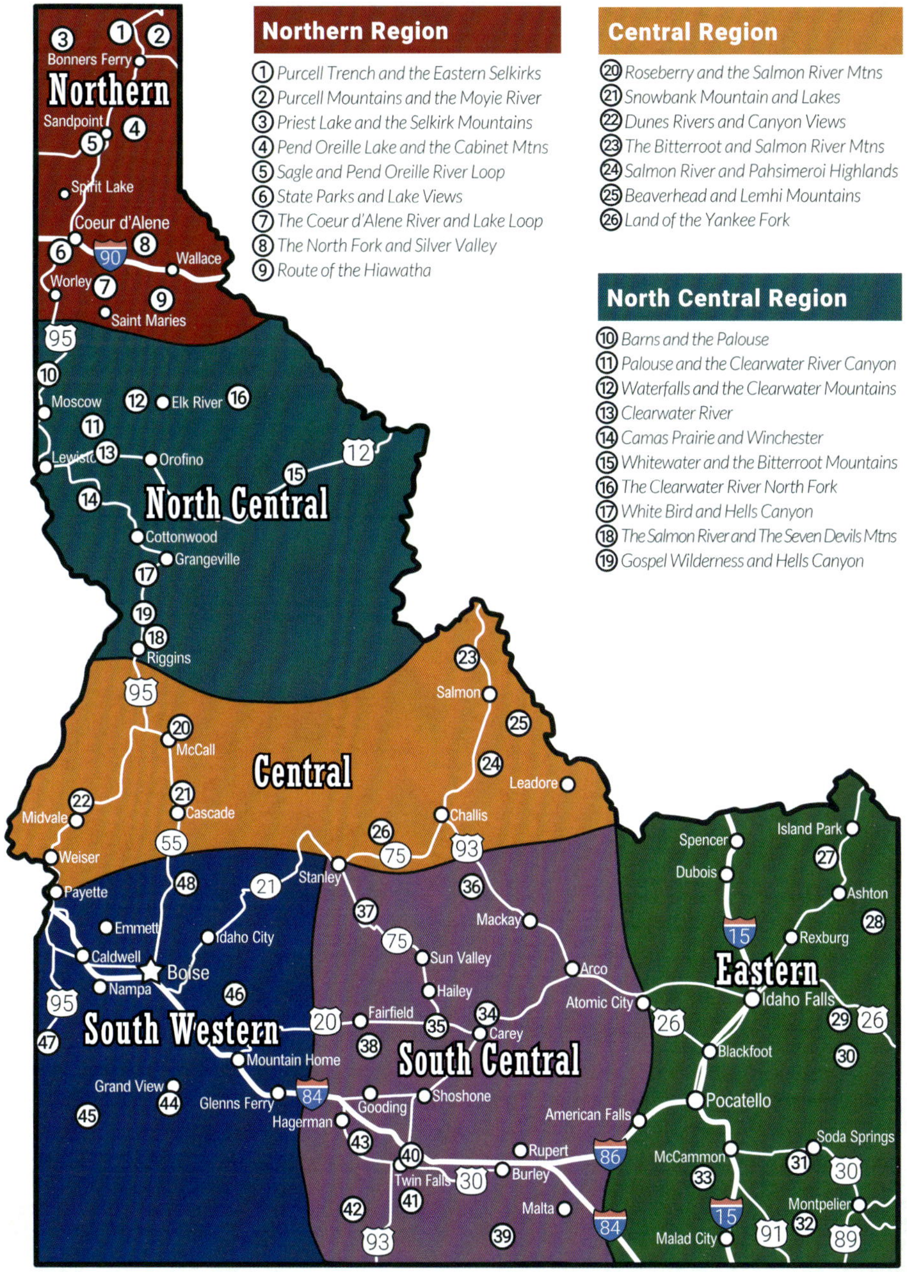

Northern Region
1. Purcell Trench and the Eastern Selkirks
2. Purcell Mountains and the Moyie River
3. Priest Lake and the Selkirk Mountains
4. Pend Oreille Lake and the Cabinet Mtns
5. Sagle and Pend Oreille River Loop
6. State Parks and Lake Views
7. The Coeur d'Alene River and Lake Loop
8. The North Fork and Silver Valley
9. Route of the Hiawatha

North Central Region
10. Barns and the Palouse
11. Palouse and the Clearwater River Canyon
12. Waterfalls and the Clearwater Mountains
13. Clearwater River
14. Camas Prairie and Winchester
15. Whitewater and the Bitterroot Mountains
16. The Clearwater River North Fork
17. White Bird and Hells Canyon
18. The Salmon River and The Seven Devils Mtns
19. Gospel Wilderness and Hells Canyon

Central Region
20. Roseberry and the Salmon River Mtns
21. Snowbank Mountain and Lakes
22. Dunes Rivers and Canyon Views
23. The Bitterroot and Salmon River Mtns
24. Salmon River and Pahsimeroi Highlands
25. Beaverhead and Lemhi Mountains
26. Land of the Yankee Fork

Eastern Region
27. Dunes to Caldera
28. Teton Valley and Mountain Views
29. South Fork of the Snake River
30. Palisades and Caribou Mountains
31. Chesterfield and Oneida Narrows
32. Cub River and Bear Lake
33. Bannock Range and Arbon Valley

South Central Region
34. Craters of the Moon and Picabo Valley
35. Black Magic Canyon and Big Wood River
36. Lost River, White Knob and Pioneer Mtns
37. Sawtooth and Boulder Mountains
38. Little City and the Camas Marsh
39. City of Rocks and the California Trail
40. Waterfalls and Snake River Canyon
41. Rock Creek Canyon and the South Hills
42. Salmon Falls Dam and Three Creek Road
43. Thousand Springs and the Snake River

South Western Region
44. Bruneau Dunes and Owyhee Backcountry
45. Silver City and the Owyhee Mountains
46. Reservoirs and Canyons of the Boise Mts
47. Owyhee Foothills and Leslie Gulch
48. Payette River and the Sawtooths

DISCOVERING IDAHO
Book Group

Join our Facebook group for book updates and to share photos from your Idaho travels!

idahoscenics.2.vu/fb

Moonset on Moon Pass, route 9.

Northern Region

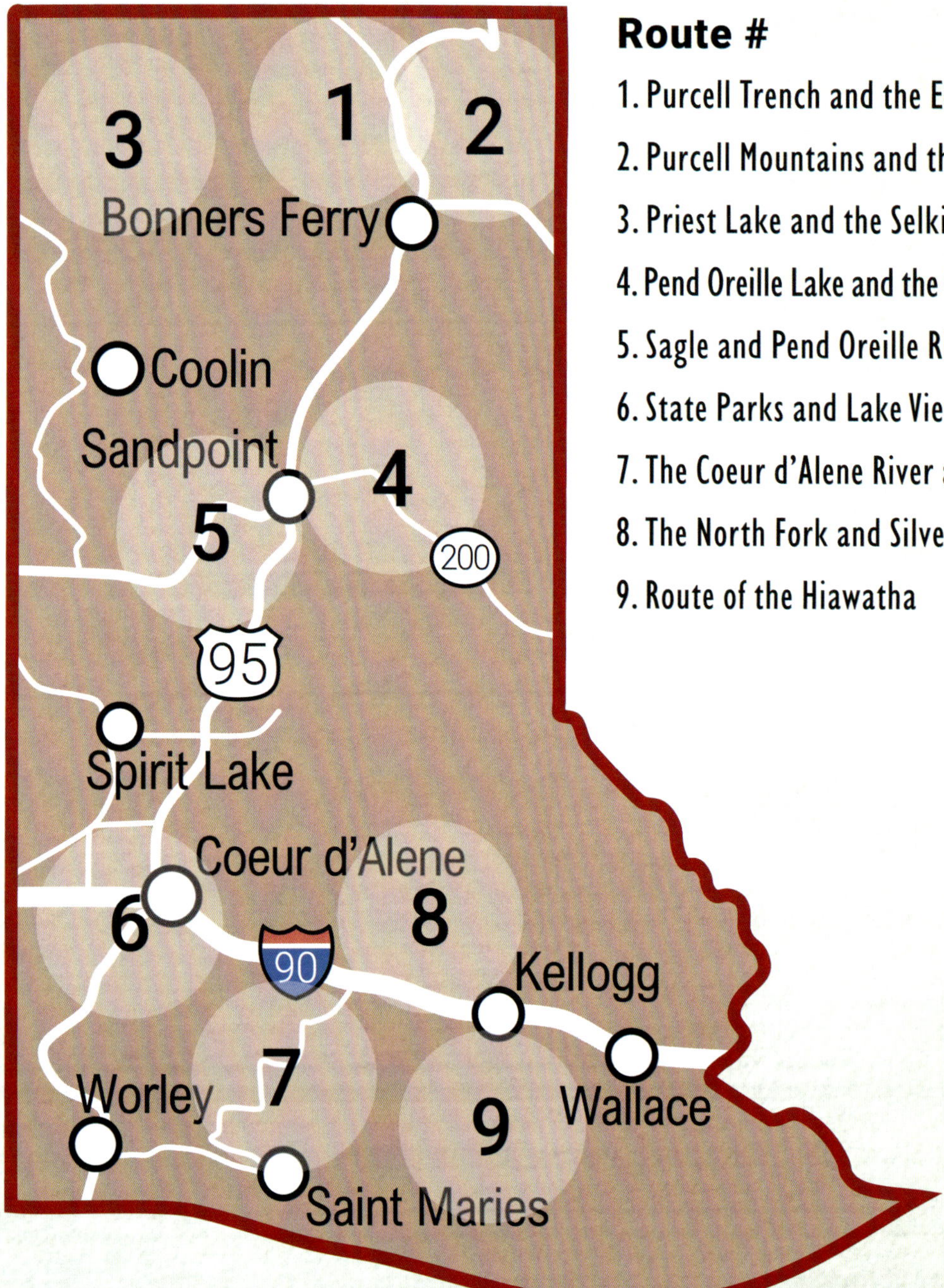

Route #

1. Purcell Trench and the Eastern Selkirks
2. Purcell Mountains and the Moyie River
3. Priest Lake and the Selkirk Mountains
4. Pend Oreille Lake and the Cabinet Mountains
5. Sagle and Pend Oreille River Loop
6. State Parks and Lake Views
7. The Coeur d'Alene River and Lake Loop
8. The North Fork and Silver Valley
9. Route of the Hiawatha

Welcome to Idaho's Northern Region

Stretching from the Bitterroot Mountains, across glacier-carved valleys to the Selkirk Range, these routes take us through the magical paradise of North Idaho. You'll find alpine lakes and hidden waterfalls, and winding rivers draining the snowpack from forested peaks. Discover the evidence of the homesteaders who settled here in the mid-1800s, including the Cataldo Mission, Idaho's oldest standing building, and several others that add to the region's distinct flavor. Missionaries and members of the Coeur d'Alene tribe built the Cataldo Mission of the Sacred Heart between 1850 and 1853. The Selkirks are geologically older than the Rocky Mountains, of which the Bitterroots cover nearly 5,000 acres.

Trestle Creek on route 4 meanders through autumn color.

Sunset over Lake Pend Oreille can be viewed on route 4.

Purcell Trench and East Selkirks

Route 1 ◇------------▶ Bonners Ferry West and North

This Route at a Glance:

Estimated Driving Time: 4 hours

Highlights: Waterfalls, Mountains, Lakes, and Barns

About This Route: This route explores the eastern edge of the Selkirk Mountains and the Purcell Trench, west and north of Bonners Ferry. Carved by ice-age floods, this valley now flows with the Kootenai River. Waterfalls cascade from the steep eastern slopes of the Selkirks. A few early 1900's barns and buildings dot the landscape.

Notes and Cautions: This route is mostly gravel interspersed with sections of highway. In winter many of the gravel sections will be inaccessible. Be mindful of private property. Exercise extreme caution at Myrtle Falls as falling would be deadly. This is grizzly bear territory, so remember to pack bear spray if you intend to do any hiking.

Directions

We start our travel from Bonners Ferry, taking Riverside Street west to the **Kootenai Wildlife Refuge (1)**. The one-way refuge loop is a great place to photograph sunrise. Watch for wildlife; this is a good location to spot moose and migratory birds. The loop road is approximately 4 miles and begins just beyond the refuge headquarters. The loop is not maintained in winter. Back at Riverside St., turn right and loop back to the refuge headquarters and park in the lot across the road. Less than a ½ mile hike (one way) will take you across the scenic **Myrtle Creek (2)** and to **Myrtle Creek Falls (3)** after a short steep climb. Use caution! The falls will be right in front of you over a steep drop off.

For a slightly longer hike to 2 beautiful waterfalls, turn right out of the parking lot and continue south on Westside Road for 2-3 miles. Turn uphill (right) on Snow Creek Road and find the trailhead to Upper and **Lower Snow Creek Falls (4)** about 2 miles on the left. The trail splits after ¼ mile. The longer but gentler trail goes to the right and reaches upper and more impressive **Snow Creek Falls (5)** in 1 mile.

Continue to a high mountain lake in the Selkirk Range. This will likely add 1-1/2 hours to your route and is only recommended in mid-summer to mid-autumn and with all wheel drive. Proceed west on Snow Creek Road for 8 miles and bear left, crossing a bridge over the creek. Continue for 6 miles and turn right just as you start descending **Ruby Pass (6)**. The lake will be reached in about 2 miles. This road can get rutted and muddy in bad weather. There is a boardwalk for views of **Roman Nose Lake (7)**. Upper Roman Nose Lakes can be reached by hiking from the trailhead located here.

Return to Riverside Street and after crossing the bridge over Deep Creek take a left into the boat ramp parking lot. Here you'll find river access and great autumn color views along **Deep Creek (8)**. Follow Riverside Street back to Bonners Ferry, then go north through town and continue north until you reach the junction of Highway 95 and Highway 2. Just beyond here on the west side of the highway is **The Gathering Place; Sharon's Country Store and the Bread Basket (9)**. They serve a variety of delicious pastries and

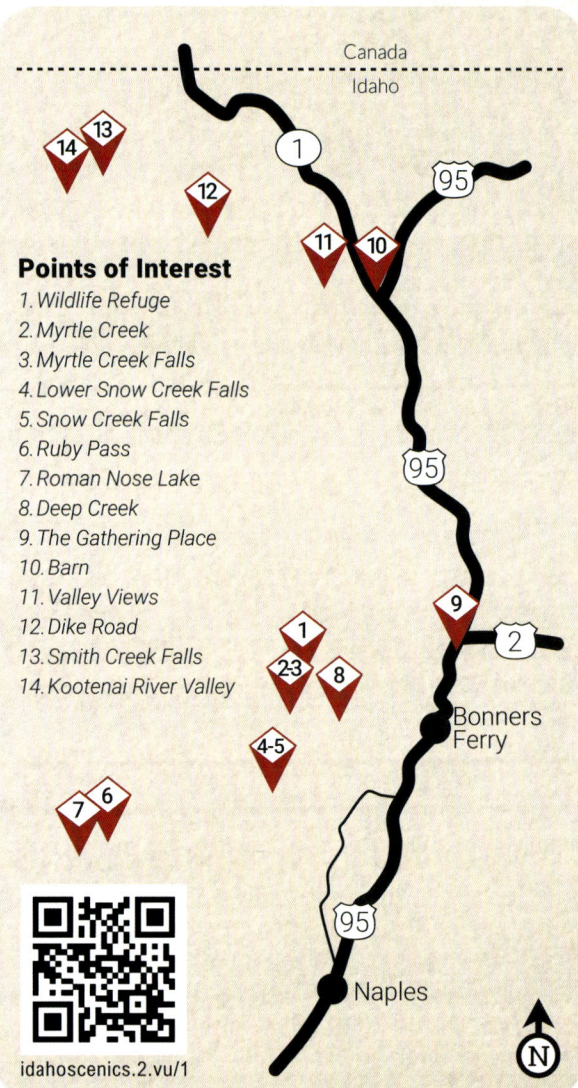

Points of Interest
1. Wildlife Refuge
2. Myrtle Creek
3. Myrtle Creek Falls
4. Lower Snow Creek Falls
5. Snow Creek Falls
6. Ruby Pass
7. Roman Nose Lake
8. Deep Creek
9. The Gathering Place
10. Barn
11. Valley Views
12. Dike Road
13. Smith Creek Falls
14. Kootenai River Valley

idahoscenics.2.vu/1

Directions Continued

one of the best breakfasts in North Idaho. Stop in for a rich cup of coffee or espresso mixed drinks, a full meal or just snacks, or deli meats and cheeses for the road. In the summer they also have a fruit stand.

Continue north on Highway 95 another 12 miles and take a left (northwest) on Highway 1, then a right on Pioneer Road. There is a photogenic **barn (10)** with a Selkirk Mountain backdrop within a mile on the left. Return to Highway 1.

Continue northwest on Highway 1 for 1 mile and take a left (west) on Copeland Hill Road. Cross the river and turn right (north) on Westside Road. Westside Road winds its way along the base of the **Selkirk Range with views out over the valley (11)** and the meandering Kootenai River. In 3 miles take a right on Kerr Lake Road (Parker Creek Road). Here you'll find views over the river along the **dike road (12)**. Return to Westside Road and turn right (north). After another 5 miles you'll cross Smith Creek. **Smith Creek Falls (13)** are just upstream. In one mile West Side Road splits into Smith Creek Road and Boundary Creek Road. Stay left (west) on Smith Creek Road and follow for just over three miles to find a viewpoint over the **Kootenai River Valley (14)**. It's a good spot to catch the last rays of daylight touching the Purcell Mountains.

Photography Tips

An ultra-wide angle lens is desirable at Myrtle Falls. Both Upper and Lower Snow Creek Falls can be shot with wide to mid telephoto lenses. Wear water shoes and cross the creek, if flow allows, for better compositions. Both of these falls will be in full sun by mid morning as they face east. Overcast days may be best, or a visit later in the day as the sun falls into the western sky. Smith Creek Falls is on private property but can be seen from the road after crossing the creek. If you can walk upstream when the water flow is low, you are not trespassing. Otherwise shoot with a telephoto lens, late or early in the day.

Up Next: Routes 2, 4, or 5

This Route's Sponsor

The Gathering Place
510752 US 95,
Bonners Ferry, ID
(208) 267 4100

SHARON'S COUNTRY STORE · THE BREAD BASKET · 3-MILE PRODUCE STAND

Purcell Mountains and the Moyie River

Route 2 ◇------------▶ Bonners Ferry East and North

This Route at a Glance:

Estimated Driving Time: 3-4 hours

Highlights: Barns, Waterfalls, Rivers, and Lakes

About This Route: We'll travel through the Purcell Mountains and cross into Montana for another waterfall opportunity. This route features North Idaho's highest waterfall, and one of Idaho's highest bridges. We'll also visit pristine lakes, a raging river and more quaint, old buildings.

Notes and Cautions: The roads on this route are pavement and maintained gravel except in winter when gravel roads may not be plowed. Exercise extreme caution at Moyie Falls as falling would be deadly. Bear spray is recommended for hiking in grizzly bear territory. This route includes a ¼ mile hike (one way) to Copper Creek Falls and short walk along Gillon Creek. Robinson Lake sits in a bowl and requires a short but moderately steep walk to the docks.

Directions

From Bonners Ferry go north and turn right (east) on District 2 Road just after crossing the Kootenai River bridge. Watch for nice views of the **valley and mountains (1)**. In 1.5 miles you'll see a **white barn (2)** on the left followed shortly by a lone tree in a field on the right. In 1.7 more miles there are **3 old barns (3)** together on the right. Return to Highway 95 and turn right (north). Go about 3 miles to the junction with Highway 2 and turn right (east) for about 8 miles, then turn right (south) just past the Moyie Store on Roosevelt Street. Take the first left, and an immediate right on Railroad Street. Take the first left again and then another left to Canyon View Road (Old Highway 2). Go under Highway 2 and arrive at the viewpoint for **Moyie Falls (4)**. The best views are from the road about halfway down the grade. You are also below the **Moyie Bridge (5)**, the second highest bridge in Idaho at 464 feet. Here you can choose to continue east for a barn photo op and Yaak Falls in Montana, by adding about an hour to your route (or skip to the next paragraph). Return to Highway 2 and turn right (east). In about 6 miles, turn left (north) on Herman Lake Cutoff Road. There is a nice barn with **fence and silo (6)** on your left after about a mile. Turn right and follow Old Highway 2 back to the highway, watching for an **old truck (7)** in a field on the right. At Highway 2 continue left (east) for 1 mile. You are in Montana now. Turn left (north) on NF Road 508. Watch for an old cabin on the left and then the **Yaak Falls (8)** pullout on the right, just beyond the Yaak campground.

Backtrack to Highway 2 and return to Idaho. Cross the Moyie River Bridge and watch for Meadow Creek Road (NF Road 34) on the right (north) in about 4 miles. Turn here and stay right at the first intersection within .5 mile. You'll pass **Dawson Lake (9)**, within a few miles where you can see beautiful reflections on a calm day. There are **several barns (10)** and an old cabin about 6.5 miles from the intersection. In 2.5 more miles the pavement ends. You'll reach the first of the **Moyie River (11)** crossings in 2 miles. The river is also photogenic. Keep left just over the bridge and follow NF Road 34 along the river. The pavement begins again in 2.5 miles. Find the Feist Creek Restaurant and Lodge on the right, a great lunch spot with its own private **Feist Creek Falls (12)** on Feist Creek, after 4 miles on pavement.

At Highway 95, continue north 2-3 miles, crossing the Moyie River. Take an immediate right (east) on NF 2517. Find the parking lot

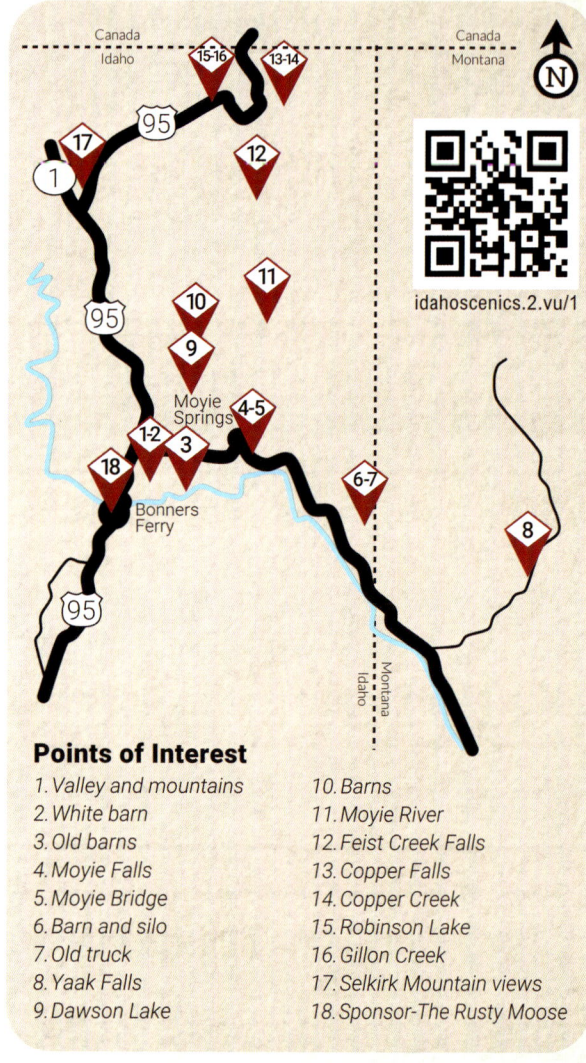

Points of Interest

1. Valley and mountains
2. White barn
3. Old barns
4. Moyie Falls
5. Moyie Bridge
6. Barn and silo
7. Old truck
8. Yaak Falls
9. Dawson Lake
10. Barns
11. Moyie River
12. Feist Creek Falls
13. Copper Falls
14. Copper Creek
15. Robinson Lake
16. Gillon Creek
17. Selkirk Mountain views
18. Sponsor-The Rusty Moose

Photography Tips

Copper Falls will be in full shade until late morning, as it faces north and is in a narrow chasm. It needs an ultra-wide angle lens to fit the entire falls. Morning or early evening are best at Robinson Lake. If you start this route by mid morning you should end with an evening view over the Kootenai River Valley (depending on how many stops you make and the time of year).

This Route's Sponsor

The Rusty Moose Tavern and Grill
7211 Main St, Bonners Ferry, ID 83805
(208) 267-1950
therustymoosetavern.com

See page 264 for coupon

Directions Continued

and trailhead for **Copper Creek Falls (13)** in 2 miles. This short .3-mile trail leads to a fenced viewpoint for North Idaho's tallest waterfall at 225 feet. Explore the lower trail to find photo opportunities on **Copper Creek (14)**.

Return to Highway 95 and turn left (south). Watch for the signed road to **Robinson Lake (15)** Campground. This scenic little fishing lake is worth a quick stop, as is the walk along the trail by **Gillon Creek (16)**. This can be found on the left as you enter the campground. Back on Highway 95, turn right (southwest). You'll pass a log barn on the left at 5 miles. Continue 4 more miles to a large pull off on the right for views of the **Selkirk Mountains and Kootenai River Valley (17)**.

Bonners Ferry is about 16 miles ahead. Turn right on Main Street, then stay left. You'll find this route's sponsor **The Rusty Moose Tavern and Grill (18)** at the end of the block on the left.

The Rusty Moose Tavern and Grill is located in the heart of downtown, this family friendly establishment offers a wide variety of favorites including ice cream and espresso, burgers, sandwiches, wraps, and salads...huckleberry desserts too. Their dinner menu offers wild Alaskan sockeye salmon, quality steaks, pastas, pizza, burgers and more. They have local brews and old favorites on tap and by the bottle as well as wine. "Stop in...you'll be glad you did".

Up Next: Routes 1, 3, or 4

Priest Lake and the Selkirk Mountains

Route 3 ◇------------------▶ Priest Lake Area

This Route at a Glance:

Estimated Driving Time: 6 hours

Highlights: Mountain Vistas, Waterfalls, and a Fire Lookout Tower

About This Route: Surrounded by forests and nestled among the peaks of the Selkirk Range, regal Priest Lake is Idaho's crown jewel. Boasting tournament-sized fish, the lake is surrounded by ample hiking trails and great camping locations. You'll find several waterfalls, a slick-rock river slide and some of the largest and best-tasting huckleberries anywhere among these slopes. We'll marvel at the expansive views of this snow-lover's paradise from an old fire lookout, and see a sunken shipwreck.

Notes and Cautions: This is a full-day adventure, from sunrise to sunset with hikes, in between. In winter, most gravel roads offer snowmobile access only. Waterfalls are both about ¼ mile hikes. The slick rock slides are about 2 miles. This is grizzly bear and moose habitat. Hike with bear spray and make noise. We visit two units of Priest Lake State Park, both requiring day-use fees. Bring your swimsuit and water shoes in late summer.

Directions

Starting in Priest River, travel north on Highway 57 about 26 miles to Outlet Bay Road and turn right. In less than .5 mile, turn left on NF Road 237 (also known as W. Lakeshore Road and Westshore Road) Follow north along the lake shore about 3.5 miles. Pick a spot to park and access the shoreline for views of sunrise over the **Selkirk Range (1)**. Alternately, continue 1.5 miles to Hills Resort and park in the restaurant lot. You can photograph sunrise from their **public beach (2)**.

Continue north on W. Lakeshore Road until it intersects with Kalispell Bay Road and turn right (east). For a short hike with a view over the lake at Indian Rock turn right (east) on Kalispell Bay Road and continue to its end in less than 2 miles. Follow Kalispell Bay Road Back to Highway 57 and turn right (north).

You'll be passing **Bismark Meadows (3)** on the left in one mile. This area can be filled with wildflowers in late spring/early summer. Bismark Meadows is spring grizzly bear habitat, so be alert and don't venture far into this area. Continue north on Highway 57 for 15 miles through the community of Nordman. The pavement will end, and it becomes NF 302. You will see a sign for the **Roosevelt Grove of Ancient Cedars (4)** and the Stagger Inn Campground. Park at the trailhead for **Granite Falls (5)** and explore the cedars and the creek. The lower view of Granite Falls is better for photographs and is only about .1 mile, but you can hike to the upper viewpoint for more options.

Back on NF 302 turn left (north). In less than a mile, **Playa Lake (6)** on the left, has a rock wall on the far side that reflects in the water on a calm day. In autumn, continue up Granite Pass for **golden western larch (7)** and views looking back into Idaho. Retrace your route to the Roosevelt Grove/Stagger Inn signage, then measure about 3 miles. Take a gravel road on the right (west) and cross the creek. Here you will find the somewhat odd **"Shoe tree" (8)**. Someone burned it in recent years, but it still makes for an interesting view. Return to Nordman and go south 14 miles, then turn left (east) on Dickensheet Highway Follow about 5 miles.

Points of Interest
1. Lake and mountain views
2. Beach
3. Bismark Meadows
4. Cedar grove
5. Granite Falls
6. Playa Lake
7. Granite Pass
8. Shoe tree
9. Sponsor-Moose Knuckle Burgers and Brews
10. Hunt Creek Falls
11. Shipwreck
12. Lionhead Creek
13. Lake Views
14. Views
15. Views
16. Sundance Lookout

idahoscenics.2.vu/3

Directions Continued

You'll find **Moose Knuckle Burgers and Brews (9)** at the intersection of Cavanaugh Bay Road just south of town. The Moose Knuckle is family friendly atmosphere! We have indoor seating as well as seating on our "hot spot" spectacular patio in the summer! We are known for the best burgers around the lake and smoke all our own meats! The menu includes affordable meals from BBQ, juicy burgers, pizza, salads and sandwiches! We also have a variety of microbrews, beer and wine!

Turn left on Cavanaugh Bay Road, which eventually becomes East Shore Road. After about 7 miles take a right uphill before crossing Hunt Creek. Turn left in less than a mile into a large undeveloped camping area. Follow the road across the field as it turns to the right (east) and goes into the trees. Park or continue as far as you are comfortable driving. The road gets small and rough. Park and walk the rest of the distance (less than ¼ mile) to **Hunt Creek Falls (10)**. The falls is very photogenic, but it can be difficult to get a good angle. Be very careful near the edge of the precipice.

Return to West Shore Road and turn right (north). Go about 16 miles to the Lionhead Unit of Priest Lake State Park. Enter the day-use area and pay the day-use fee (unless you have an Idaho State Park pass).

The sunken shipwreck (11) of the Tyee II-a steamboat that carried passengers, mail, freight and towed logs up and down the lake during the first half of the 20th Century-will be found just off shore at the day-use area. You may also find photo opportunities by walking the Nell Shipman Nature Trail along Lionhead Creek within the park boundaries.

Exit the park and turn left, then right. Follow Lionhead Creek Road, staying left at the Y, for about 5 miles. Photo ops can be found by walking along **Lionhead Creek (12)**. For a mid-late summer hike to the slick road waterslides, cross the creek at the parking area and follow the trail about 2 miles. Return to East Shore Road and turn left. In 11 miles enter the Indian Creek unit of Priest Lake State Park. Make your way to the day-use area for **lake views (13)**.

Back on East Shore Road turn right. In 10 miles turn left on Lee Lake Road and, in 1 mile stay right on NF19. Travel 4.8 miles, staying left at each intersection. At 4.8 miles turn right to go uphill. The road steepens and becomes rougher. In 2.3 miles you'll arrive at gorgeous views of Priest Lake and the **Selkirk Mountains (14,15)**, tour the **fire lookout (16)** and enjoy an Idaho mountain sunset. Make your way back to Coolin or Priest River.

Photography Tips

Granite Creek and Hunt Creek Falls will both be in the shade until mid morning. Granite Creek will be in the shade again in the evening. It slides down a narrow chasm and is best viewed from mid-stream below the falls.

This Route's Sponsor

Moose Knuckle Burgers and Brews
10 Cavanaugh Bay Rd,
Coolin, ID 83821
(208) 443-2222 | mkcoolin.com

See page 264 for coupon

Up Next: Routes 4 and 5

Pend Oreille Lake and the Cabinet Mtns
Route 4 ◇----------------------▶ Sandpoint to Clark Fork

This Route at a Glance:

Estimated Driving Time: 5 hours

Highlights: Views, Barns, Waterfalls

About This Route: Start your day by watching sunrise from Schweitzer Mountain before heading out to visit two waterfalls in the Cabinet Mountains and gorgeous views of Lake Pend Oreille, with a few barns along the way. We'll finish this route with another exceptional vista point overlooking the lake, with views of the Selkirk, Coeur d'Alene and Cabinet Mountains available.

Notes and Cautions: Begin this route early to watch sunrise over Lake Pend Oreille or midday to arrive in time to watch sunset at the end of the route. Both locations are great viewpoints. The middle of the route takes you to two different, short waterfall hikes. Neither will be accessible in the winter or early spring. The roads are slightly bumpy but mostly good gravel. The sunset vista point up Johnson Creek Road is moderately washed out and higher clearance vehicles are recommended. Char Falls is viewed from a dangerous precipice. Use caution. The Cabinet Mountains are also grizzly territory. Hike with bear spray and make noise.

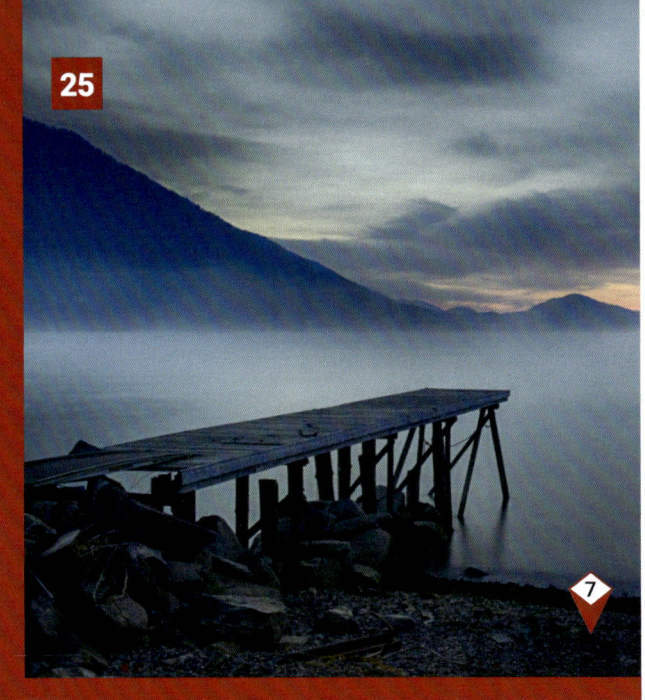

Directions

From Highway 95 in Ponderay (north of Sandpoint). Turn west on Schweitzer Cut Off Road. Proceed straight through the roundabout. In .5 mile turn right (north) on Boyer Road In .8 mile turn left on Schweitzer Mountain Road. There's a large pullout on the left just before a switchback in 6.5 miles. Here you'll have a great view over Sandpoint, Lake Pend Oreille and the **Cabinet Mountains (1)**. Return to Boyer Road. watching for great winding road shots along the way.

Turn left at Boyer Road. In .5 mile turn right on W. Bronx Road. In another .5 mile turn left on Highway 95. Follow Highway 95 north 2 miles and turn right on Selle Road. In 2 miles turn left on Center Valley Road. There is a **barn (2)** on the right in .6 mile. In one more mile there is a distant barn on the left. In .5 mile, turn right on Center Valley Road and in another .5 mile turn left on Center Valley Road. In 1 mile turn right on Colburn Culver Road and, in .9 mile you'll cross a bridge with views of the Pack River. In 2 miles turn left on Grouse Creek Cutoff Road In .5 mile look back for a barn view. In 1.1 miles turn right on Grouse Creek Road (NF 280). In 1.8 miles you'll cross **Grouse Creek (3)**, which can be exceptionally beautiful in the winter. In 1.5 miles stay right. In 1.6 miles turn right on a small, two-track road. You'll arrive at the trailhead for **Grouse Creek Falls (4)** in .1 mile. Return to Colburn Culver Road.

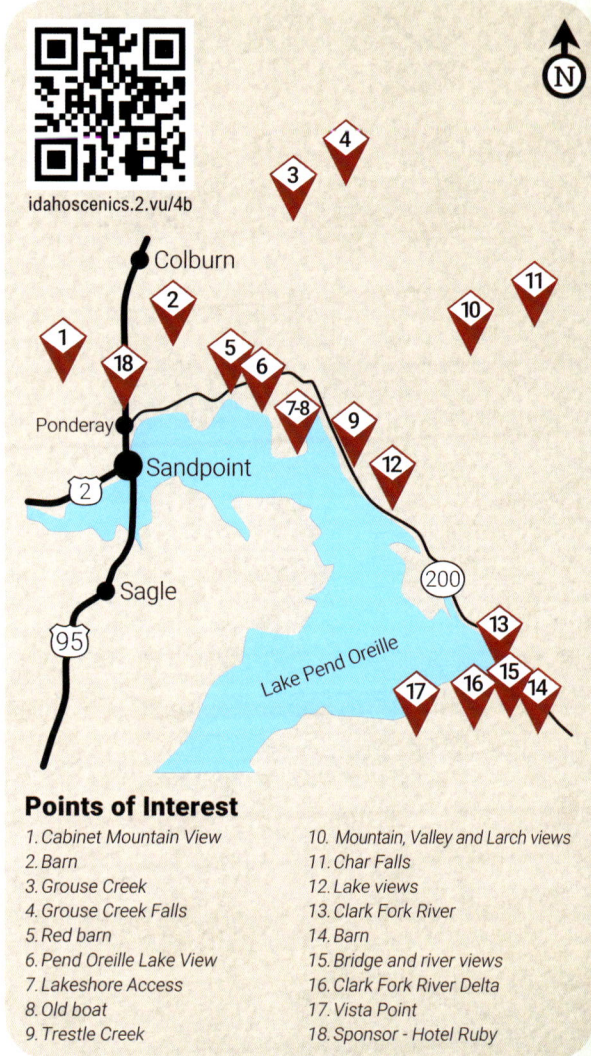

Points of Interest

1. Cabinet Mountain View
2. Barn
3. Grouse Creek
4. Grouse Creek Falls
5. Red barn
6. Pend Oreille Lake View
7. Lakeshore Access
8. Old boat
9. Trestle Creek
10. Mountain, Valley and Larch views
11. Char Falls
12. Lake views
13. Clark Fork River
14. Barn
15. Bridge and river views
16. Clark Fork River Delta
17. Vista Point
18. Sponsor - Hotel Ruby

Turn left on Colburn Culver Road. A river crossing with views of Schweitzer Mountain can be seen in 2.5 miles. In 2 more miles turn right on Jacobsen Road. There is a red barn on the right in .6 mile. Make a U-turn, then turn right on Hickey Road. In .9 mile there is a **red barn (5)** on the right. Turn left on Highway 200, then right on Sunnyside Cutoff Road.

Directions Continued

There is a barn on the right in .2 mile. In .9 mile turn right then left on Sunnyside Road. There is a barn on the left in .4 mile, followed by trailhead parking on the right. This trail takes you to **Pend Oreille Lake (6)** views. In .3 mile there is a parking area on the left for public lake access on the right. In another 1.8 miles there is more public **shore access (7)**. Just beyond this a **dilapidated boat (8)** on private property can be seen roadside. In winter, turn around here and retrace your route to Highway 200 and go right until the junction with Sunnyside Road in .8 mile. Otherwise, in .7 mile stay right. In 3.8 miles turn right onto Highway 200. A large pullout on the right provides lake views in 5 miles. In .2 miles turn left on Trestle Creek Road (NF 275). In .4 mile take a two-track on the right to a primitive day-use area. Park here and walk upstream a short distance to beautiful **Trestle Creek (9)** views.

Continue on Trestle Creek Road. In .8 mile another small pullout on the right provides more creek access. In 4 miles stay left. Watch for mountain, valley and **larch (10)** views in autumn over the next 6.5 miles. Turn right on NF 275. In .5 mile stay left. In 3 miles

Directions Continued

there is a nice viewpoint. In .4 mile turn right on Lightning Creek Road (NF 419). In .7 mile take a small, rough road to the left. You'll arrive at the trailhead in .5 mile. This .2 mile trail takes you to the multi segmented **Char Falls (11)**. Return to Highway 200. Turn left on Highway 200. A right turn will take you to Trestle Creek Recreation Area in .3 mile. This is a nice picnic spot. Back on Highway 200, continue east 2 miles to an overlook on the right. In .3 mile turn left, then stay right on W. Main Street. In .7 miles turn left on Main Street. You'll find more **lake views (12)**. In .4 mile turn left, then stay right in .3 mile. Turn right on Centennial Boulevard. In .2 mile turn left on Highway 200. There is a lake access on the right in 4 miles. In 1 mile turn right onto Driftwood Yard Road. Follow to the end in less than 1 mile for views of the Green Monarch Mountains and the **Clark Fork River (13)** as it joins lake Pend Oreille. Return to Hwy 200 and turn right. In 4 miles turn right on N. Stephens Street and follow it across the Clark Fork River Bridge. In less than 1 mile you'll find a **barn (14)** on the right. Make a U-turn, then turn left just before the bridge on Johnson Creek Road There are numerous bridge and **river views (15)** over the next 2.7 miles.

Photography Tips

We like this route best for autumn color, which peaks around the second week of October. Waterfalls will have better flow in early to mid summer. A solid neutral density filter and polarizer can help slow your shutter speeds for those velvety water shots at the falls. Grouse Creek Falls may require wading the river for the best views in mid to late summer. Do not attempt if the water is too high. Mid to late October is great to see the western larch put on a golden display in the Cabinet Mountains. Several of the barns require a mild telephoto.

Directions Continued

Stay left on Johnson Creek Road (NF 278). In .9 mile there's a nice view over the **Clark Fork River delta (16)**. In 2.9 miles turn right on Vista Point Road and arrive at the **vista point (17)** in 1.6 miles, on the east end of Lake Pend Oreille. This is an excellent sunset location. Return to Clark Fork then travel 24 miles west on Highway 200 back towards Sandpoint. Turn right on Kootenai Cutoff Road. In .7 mile turn right (north) onto Highway 95. You'll find our route sponsor, **Hotel Ruby Sandpoint (18)** on the right.

On your visit to the Gem State, book a room at Hotel Ruby Sandpoint and enjoy the new pool, hot tubs, ski waxing room, sunning patio and dog run! Relax in one of the hot tub rooms and enjoy their complimentary continental breakfast to get you started. They are pet-friendly and 100% non-smoking. Meeting space is available and free Wi-Fi access keeps you connected.

This Route's Sponsor

Hotel Ruby Sandpoint
477255 US-95, Ponderay, ID 83852
(208) 263-5383
hotelrubyponderay.com

See page 264 for coupon

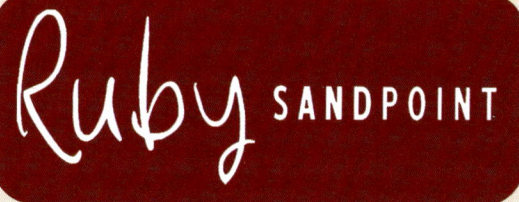

Up Next: Routes 5 and 2

Sagle and Pend Oreille River Loop

Route 5 ◇--▶ Sandpoint South

This Route at a Glance:

Estimated Driving Time: 4 hours

Highlights: Lake and river views, barns

About This Route: There's a lot going on in this small loop route just south of Sandpoint. Begin by watching sunrise over Lake Pend Oreille from a little-known beach. You'll find views over the lake and the Cabinet Mountains, visit Albeni Falls Dam and Round Lake and discover several barns in between. Finish your day with sunset over Lake Pend Oreille from another vantage point.

Notes and Cautions: Start early for an excellent sunrise location on Lake Pend Oreille. There's optional hiking at several locations. A few of the roads to the hiking trails will not be accessible in winter. Park carefully along roadways and be respectful of private property. Round Lake State Park requires a day-use fee.

Directions

From the south end of Sandpoint's long bridge, proceed 2.9 miles to Sagle Road and turn left. In 1.2 miles stay right on Talache Road, and in 2.7 miles stay left. The pavement ends in 2 miles. Stay straight in another 2 miles. In .5 mile arrive at Talache Landing lake access for a great sunrise view over **Pend Oreille Lake (1)**. Retrace your route, watching for an **old boat (2)** at the first intersection. In 5.5 miles from the lake access turn left for access to **Shepherd Lake (3)**. This small fishing lake has nice tree-lined reflections when calm. There is a lakeshore trail on the left in .5 mile. In 1 mile turn right on Sagle Road.

In just under 6 miles stay right on Garfield Bay Road and in .8 mile keep left. There is a nice **lake access (4)** with boat launch on the right in .4 mile. There is an undeveloped beach access in .2 mile. Turn left on Garfield Bay Cutoff Road in .1 mile.

This optional side trip takes you to a couple different lake viewpoints and hiking trails. In .3 mile turn right on Green Bay Road, which is rough and not maintained for winter travel. Skip to the next paragraph to avoid this section. In 1.3 mile stay left then stay right in 1.9 miles. Arrive at the trailhead parking and picnic area in

Points of Interest
1. Pend Oreille Lake
2. Old Boat
3. Shepherd Lake
4. Lake Access
5. Pend Oreille Lake View
6. Barn with Truck
7. Wildflower Area
8. Cabinet Mtns and Lake Views
9. Structural Remains
10. Pend Oreille Bay Trail
11. Marina
12. City Beach
13. Sponsor - Evans Brothers Coffee Roasters
14. Dover Trail and Bridge
15. Public Access
16. Barn
17. Barn
18. Albeni Falls Dam and Train Bridge
19. Bridge and River Views
20. Barn
21. Round Lake
22. Barn
23. Lake Viewpoint

idahoscenics.2.vu/5b

Directions Continued

0.4 mile. A short walk to the picnic area will get you a partially obscured view over **Lake Pend Oreille (5)**. A longer hike will get you better views. Return 2.2 miles and turn left on the road to Green Bay Campground. A moderate descent down the hillside trail will get you views of the shoreline cliffs. Return to Garfield Bay Cutoff Road and turn right.

There is a moderately distant barn on the corner. There's an old cabin on the left in 1 mile. In .9 mile turn right on Sagle Road. There is a very photogenic barn with an **old truck (6)** in front in 1.5 miles. Park carefully. This is well marked as private property, so only observe from the road. In 1 mile turn right on Glengary Bay Road. Gamlin Lake will be on your right. At the far end there is trailhead parking. This easy trail wanders through the forest and then emerges into a spring **wildflower area (7)**. There is also an old vehicle with some trees growing through it in the vicinity of the trail. Glengary Bay Road dead-ends in about 1 mile.

Retrace your route to Sagle Road and turn left. There is a church and cemetery on the left in about 2 miles. In 1.2 miles turn right on Sky Meadow Road for another optional side trip in summer or fall, or proceed to the next paragraph. Travel up Sky Meadow Road .8 mile, staying left at the Y. Sky Meadow Road then becomes NF 2642. Watch for views over Lake Pend Oreille and the **Cabinet Mountains (8)** over the next 5 miles. At the end of the road, hike the short trail for additional views over the lake and Sandpoint including the long bridges. Return to Sagle Road and turn right.

Stay straight on Sagle Road for 6.6 miles. Turn right on Hwy 95. In 4.8 miles exit right into Sandpoint. In .6 mile turn right on Bridge Street and, in .2 mile turn left on Sandpoint Avenue. Stay straight past the resort and arrive at access to the Pend Oreille Bay Trail. Take a short walk to view **structural remains (9)** off shore. This is a great **autumn color (10)** trail. On your return make a quick stop at the **marina (11)** by turning left on Dock Street. At Bridge Street turn left to explore the **beach area (12)**. Return to First Ave and turn right. Round the corner to the left onto Cedar Street and turn left on 5th Avenue. In .1 mile turn right onto Church Street. You'll find **Evan's Brothers Coffee (13)**, this route's sponsor ahead on the right.

Evans Brothers Coffee was founded in 2009 by brothers Rick and Randy, over long rides on Schweitzer Mountain's Chair 6. Since that time, EBC has won national recognition including two Good Food Awards and a Top 3 America's Best Coffee House. They focus on creating a

Directions Continued

connection to the coffee itself, traveling directly to origin, to source the best coffees and strengthen relationships with their producer and farmer partners.

In addition to providing coffee on a wholesale basis to many of the area's top restaurants and cafes, Evans Brothers operates a café by its roastery in Sandpoint, along with a new café in downtown Coeur D'Alene. You will find the area's best baristas offering exceptional coffees dripped to order, a full espresso menu, rotating specialty drinks, organic burritos, empanadas, and vegan pastries. Follow on Instagram and Facebook to learn about upcoming events.

Turn left onto North 6th St and then right onto Highway 2. In 3 miles turn left at Dover onto Roosevelt Avenue. In ¾ mile, turn right on Lakeshore Avenue. You'll arrive at trailhead parking on the right in less than 1 mile, just before the road ends. Here you can walk to **views of the Pend Oreille River and a bridge (14)** over an inlet. Return to Highway 2 and turn left.

There is another river view spot on the left in 3 miles. In 2 miles turn left on Riley Creek Road. In 1 mile stay straight to a **public access area (15)** with docks and benches. Retrace your route .2 mile and turn left on Riley Creek Road. Arrive at the Riley Creek Recreation's day use area for swimming, picnicking, fishing and river views. Return to Highway 2 and turn left. In 5 miles turn left on Thama Drive. You'll find a nice **barn (16)** on the left. Return to Highway 2 and turn left. In 2.5 miles turn left into the Mudhole Recreation Area. Here you can see a view of a nice bridge over the Priest River. Proceed 2.2 miles through the town of Priest River to a **barn (17)** on the left. Park safely off the highway. In 2.7 miles turn left and visit the Albeni Falls Dam. There is also a **train bridge (18)** over the Pend Oreille River to be seen here. Return to Highway 2 and turn left. In 2 miles you'll cross the river. Turn left at the stoplight on State Avenue. In 2 miles turn left on Albeni Cove Road. In .3 mile turn right. In 1.5 miles you'll arrive at the day use area. Walk to views of the **train bridge and river (19)**. Heading out of the recreation area, turn left on Blackthorn Road. In .7 miles turn left on Old Priest River Road.

In 5 miles stay straight on Dufort Road. In 8.6 miles an old car can be seen on the left. There is river access in 4 miles, with some interesting old pilings and a heron rookery across the highway to the north.

Photography Tips

Waves crashing against rocks are a great time to slow your shutter speed by trying a neutral density filter. Use a wide and telephoto lens on Lake Pend Oreille for different perspectives. A polarizing filter is great for accentuating reflections in the smaller lakes. Start this route early- about 45 minutes before sunrise-to arrive for potential pre-sunrise color over the Monarch Mountains.

This Route's Sponsor

Evans Brothers Coffee Roasters
524 Church St.
Sandpoint, ID 83864
(208) 265-5553
www.evansbrotherscoffee.com

See page 264 for coupon

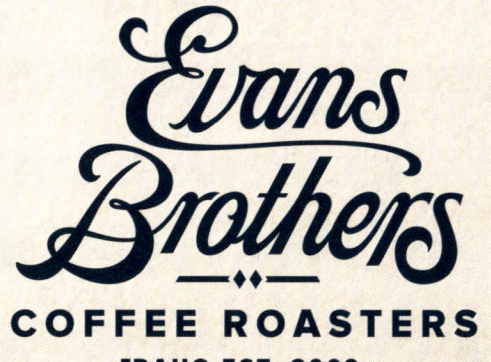

Up Next: Route 3 or 4

Directions Continued

In .1 mile there's an **old barn (20)** on the left. Watch for a tractor and old cabin on the left in 1 mile. In 2.7 miles turn right into Round Lake State Park. Take a walk around the lake on the nature trail, fish, swim or view the **tree line reflecting in the water (21)**. Leaving the park, turn right on Dufort Road. In 2 miles turn left to Highway 95. In 5.5 miles turn right on Bottle Bay Road. In .3 mile there's an **old barn (22)** on the right. Cross the railroad tracks and stay straight. In less than 1.5 miles you'll find a great sunset **viewpoint (23)** over the lake.

State Parks and Lake Views

Route 6 ◇------------▶ Plummer to Bayview

This Route at a Glance:

Estimated Driving Time: 4 hours

Highlights: Lake Views, Barns, Dam, and Bridges

About This Route: Lake views, lake views and more lake views. Throw in a couple of barns, lime kilns, marinas and some scenic bridges to complete this route. We'll start the day by watching sunrise over the southern end of Lake Coeur d'Alene at Heyburn State Park, then wind our way north, visiting Post Falls Dam and the north shore of scenic Lake Coeur d'Alene. We'll take you to one of the areas most photogenic barns and finish our day in the quaint town of Bayview on Lake Pend Oreille.

Notes and Cautions: You will need a state park pass for both Heyburn and Farragut state parks on this route. For your safety, stay inside the fence at Post Falls Dam. Respect private property. This route includes travel through the town of Coeur d'Alene, which makes a good base for several routes, but our route only features scenic drives and photo opportunities. Bring your binoculars for trying to spot mountain goats above Lake Pend Oreille. Not all roads in Farragut State Park are maintained in the winter.

Directions

Starting in Plummer, travel east on Cedar St. (Highway 5) for about 6.5 miles. Turn left (north) on Chatcolet Road into Heyburn State Park and turn left immediately. Follow the road along the lakeshore for about 2.5 miles to a parking area. Walk either way on **Trail of the Coeur d'Alene's (1)**. Going left will take you over the **old train bridge (2)** over Lake Chatcolet. Return to Plummer and turn right (north) on Highway 95 for 24 miles then turn right (east) on Putnam Road. In .5 mile keep right on Tall Pines Road. In .5 mile turn right on S. Lofts Bay Road. Immediately cross the **marsh area (3)** of Mica Bay, which features nice views, especially in morning and autumn.

Return to Highway 95, turn right (north) and proceed 7 miles to a boat launch on the left with a short **boardwalk (4)** trail system. This is a nice walk, especially in autumn. Continue on Highway 95 for another .5 mile. Just after crossing the bridge over the Spokane River turn right (south) on Northwest Boulevard. In .5 mile turn right on W. River Avenue. Stay straight through two roundabouts, then enter Rosenberry Drive along the lakeshore (or park and

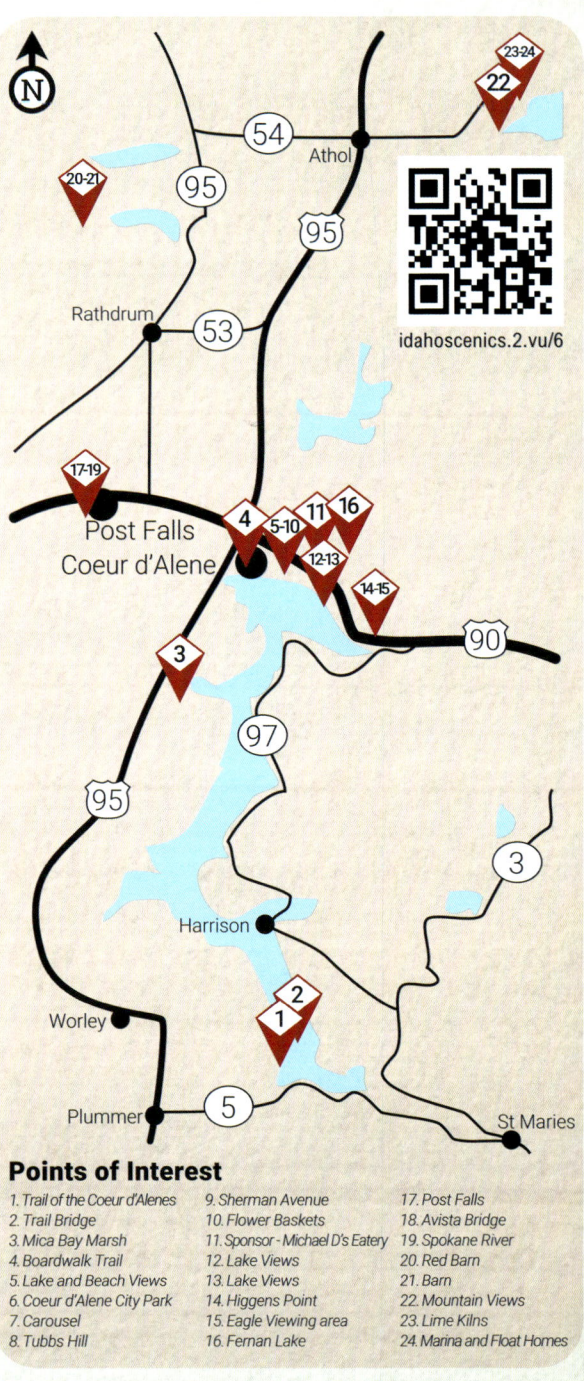

Points of Interest

1. Trail of the Coeur d'Alenes
2. Trail Bridge
3. Mica Bay Marsh
4. Boardwalk Trail
5. Lake and Beach Views
6. Coeur d'Alene City Park
7. Carousel
8. Tubbs Hill
9. Sherman Avenue
10. Flower Baskets
11. Sponsor - Michael D's Eatery
12. Lake Views
13. Lake Views
14. Higgens Point
15. Eagle Viewing area
16. Fernan Lake
17. Post Falls
18. Avista Bridge
19. Spokane River
20. Red Barn
21. Barn
22. Mountain Views
23. Lime Kilns
24. Marina and Float Homes

Directions Continued

walk). This is a one-way single lane road with lake and **beach views (5)**. Drive slowly. Turn left (north) on Park Drive then right on W. Fort Grounds Drive. Park on the right for **Coeur d'Alene City Park (6)** and **carousel access (7)**.

Make a U-turn then turn right on Park Drive and follow to W. River Ave. Turn right onto Northwest Boulevard and follow through downtown as it turns to Sherman Ave. At Third St. turn right and follow straight into the below grade parking. From here you can walk around **Tubbs Hill (8)** or down **Sherman Ave (9)** for quaint views of this small city. There are beautiful **hanging flower baskets (10)** lining the streets all summer. Return to Sherman Avenue and turn right. Follow east until you almost reach the Interstate.

Turn right on E. Coeur d'Alene Lake Drive. You'll find this route's sponsor, **Michael D's Eatery (11),** on the right. Serving breakfast and lunch to locals and visitors alike for over 20 years, with hundreds of great reviews, they won't let you down. Conveniently located as you take a drive along the north shore, stop in for breakfast, brunch or lunch.

Continuing on Coeur d'Alene Lake Drive watch for stunning **lake views (12, 13)** anytime of year. This scenic lake drive dead

Directions Continued

ends in about 5 miles at **Higgins point (14)**, which is prime **eagle watching (15)** from mid-December to mid-January. The short trail at the end gives better views of the lake and eagles. Return to Sherman Avenue and turn right (east) for more lake viewing, follow Sherman Avenue under the interstate. After driving a couple of blocks through residential neighborhoods the road becomes **Fernan Lake (16)** Road. Follow it all along the shoreline and maybe spot some herons near the end. This is a great fishing and canoeing lake.

Return to Fernan Village and turn right onto the Interstate 90 on-ramp. In 10 miles take Exit 5 to the right. Turn left (south) on Spokane Street and right (west) on W. 4th Avenue until it ends. Here you will walk a ¼ mile to views of the **Post Falls (17)** and the old **Avista Bridge (18)** over the **Spokane River (19)**. Follow 4th Avenue across Spokane Street until it reaches Seltice Way. Cross Seltice Way and enter the onramp for Interstate 90 going east. In one mile take Exit 6 for Highway 41. Turn left (east) on Seltice Way and left (north) on Highway 41.

Go 7 miles to Rathdrum. Turn left on Highway 53, then right to continue on Highway 41. In 5 miles take a left (west) on W. Twin Lakes Rd. Follow for about 5 miles.

Photography Tips

A pre-sunrise start will let you watch sunrise over Lake Coeur d'Alene. Use a polarizing filter to accentuate any reflections in the lakes. A long telephoto will be necessary for any mountain goat images.

This Route's Sponsor

Michael D's Eatery
203 E Coeur D'Alene Lake Dr,
Coeur d'Alene, ID 83814
(208) 676-9049
www.michaelds.com

See page 264 for coupon

Directions Continued

You'll see the large **red barn (20)** of the Easterday Ranch on the left and another **barn (21)** behind it if you follow the road a little farther. Return to Highway 41 and turn left (north). In 5 miles turn right (east) on Highway 54. Follow 12 miles through the town of Athol and under Highway 95 to a roundabout. Stay straight (slightly northeast). In 2.5 miles stay straight on Locust Grove Road/Blackwell Circle Drive. Take the first right on Crossover Road. Turn right on S. Shore Rd. for access points to Buttonhook Bay and Beaver Bay for **mountain views (22)** and stop to look for mountain goats on the cliffs across the bay, or go left to the boat launch (Launch Road and Sunrise Day Use Area). Back on South Shore Road, turn right and follow to Macdonald Point view area. Return to Highway 54 and turn right (northeast). In 1 mile enter the town of Bayview. Turn right on Scenic Bay Road/East Pier Road. Park and view the **lime kilns (23)**, **marina (24)** and float homes on Scenic Bay of Lake Pend Oreille. Return to Highway 95 and go south to Coeur d'Alene or north to Sandpoint.

Up Next: Route 5 or 7

Coeur d'Alene River and Lake Loop

Route 7 ◇------------▶ Chain Lakes to Wolf Lodge Bay

This Route at a Glance:

Estimated Driving Time: 3 hours

Highlights: Forest Views, Lake Views, Barns, Mossy Creek

About This Route: Start the day by watching sunrise in the Coeur d'Alene District of the Idaho Panhandle National Forest. The Coeur d'Alene River meanders its way through a maze of small lakes as it makes its way to Lake Coeur d'Alene. We'll visit a couple of nice old barns, then wind our way north along the Lake Coeur d'Alene shoreline. Stops include Beauty Creek, a hidden oasis of green in spring and early summer. Take a hike up Mineral Ridge for some of the best views of the lake, and finish with sunset on Wolf Lodge Bay.

Notes and Cautions: Some highway sections are winding and steep. Beauty Creek Road is very rough and being in a narrow canyon, remains covered in snow most years until early May.

Directions

From Coeur d'Alene head east on I-90 to Exit 28 (4th of July Pass), cross the freeway and turn right (east) on NF Road 3098. Stay on 3098 for 3 miles (Mason Saddle) until you have a view over the **forest valleys (1)** to the east. This is a great place to watch the sunrise in summer and fall. Return to Interstate 90 and proceed east.

Exit I-90 at Exit 34 (Rose Lake) and go south. Turn right (west) on Highway 3 and go 1.5 miles to the turn off for Rose Lake. The fishing access with **dock (2)** is in 1.4 miles. Return to Highway 3 and go right. In

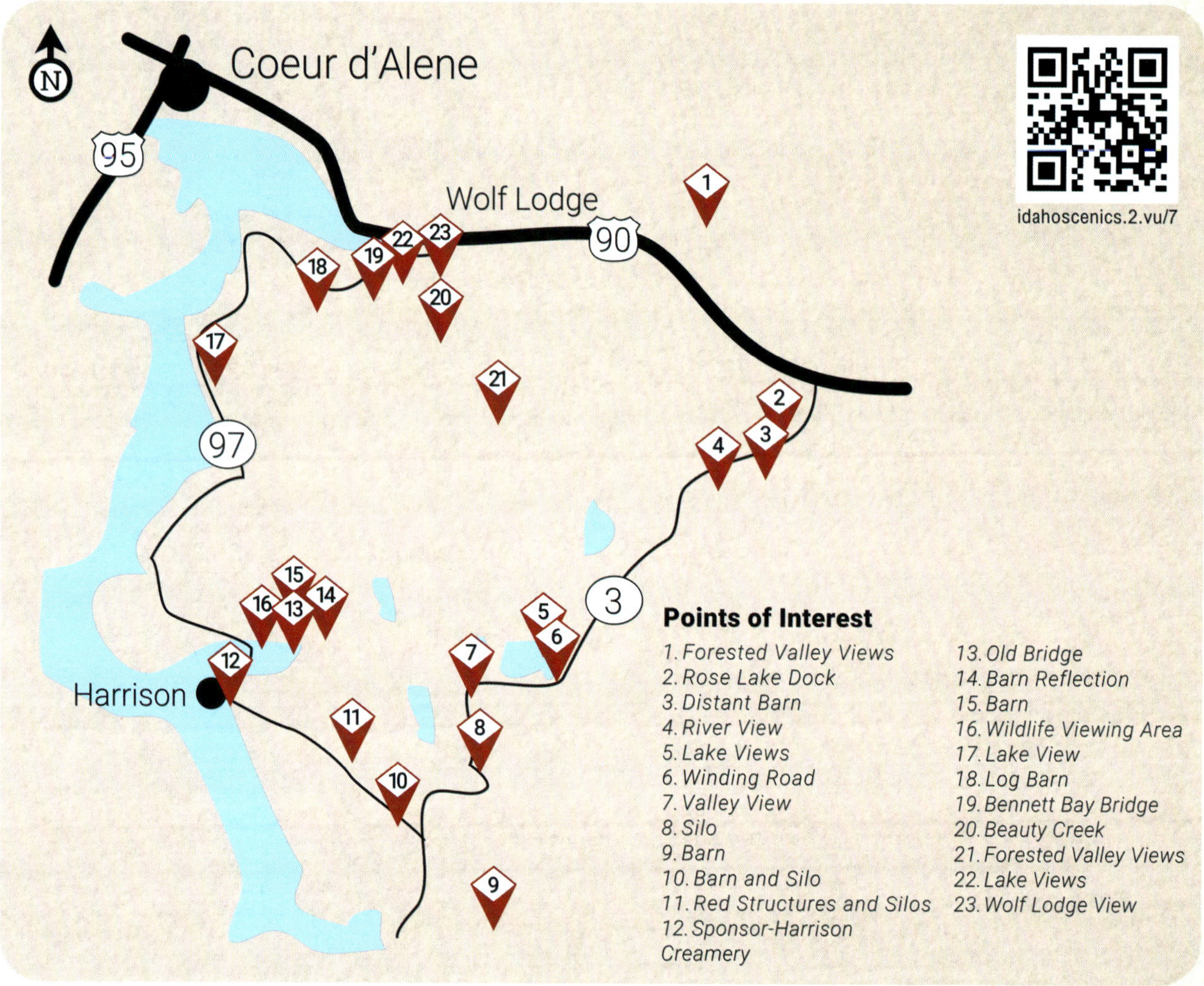

N
Coeur d'Alene
95
Wolf Lodge
90
97
3
Harrison
idahoscenics.2.vu/7
Points of Interest
1. Forested Valley Views
2. Rose Lake Dock
3. Distant Barn
4. River View
5. Lake Views
6. Winding Road
7. Valley View
8. Silo
9. Barn
10. Barn and Silo
11. Red Structures and Silos
12. Sponsor-Harrison Creamery
13. Old Bridge
14. Barn Reflection
15. Barn
16. Wildlife Viewing Area
17. Lake View
18. Log Barn
19. Bennett Bay Bridge
20. Beauty Creek
21. Forested Valley Views
22. Lake Views
23. Wolf Lodge View

5

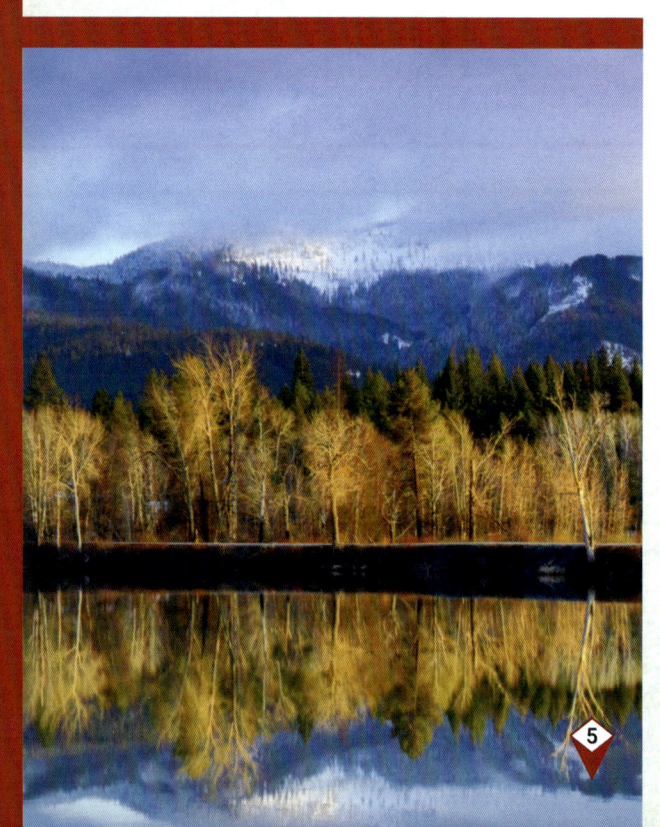

.9 mile a small pulloff on the left gives you a distant view of a **barn (3)** on the other side of a pond. In 1.9 miles, park on the right and carefully cross the highway for a beautiful view back up the **river (4)**. In .9 mile turn right on Killarney Lake Rd. In .3 miles, a barn sits against the hill in the distance. Continue the three miles along the tree lined road until you reach the boat launch on the left. Return to Highway 3 and turn right. In 1 mile there is a river access on the right. In 2.7 miles a quaint farm scene is on the left. Continue to Rainy Creek Road in 2 miles. Turn right (west) on Rainy Creek Road and follow to the intersection with Medimont Road. Turn left (east) and park for **lake views (5)** on both sides of the road. Continue on Medimont

Directions Continued

Road for about a mile until it rejoins Highway 3. In the autumn, the tree-lined, **winding road (6)** just before the highway makes a nice road shot.

Turn right on Highway 3. You'll pass Cave Lake in .7 mile, which is a good spot to return to someday for a sunset. In 2 miles a designated scenic viewpoint provides a **valley view (7)**. In two more miles a lone **silo (8)** remains on the left. You'll reach Highway 97 in about 4.5 miles. Turn left (south) and go .5 mile to Hells Gulch Road. Turn left and proceed 3 miles to the intersection with Deep Creek Road. Here you'll find a beautiful **barn (9)** with an old weathervane. Return to Highway 97 and turn right (north) and return to the junction with Highway 3. At the intersection bear left and continue on Highway 97. Watch for another barn with **silo (10)** on the right in less than 1 mile. This is a public access area and you are welcome to enter the fenced area.

In .5 mile turn right on Gem Road, then left on Sunrise. There are some red structures and **silos (11)** on the left. Turn right on Bell Canyon Rd., then left on Van Dusan in 1 mile. There are some old buildings on the right before the corner. Turn left on Skyline and right on Highway 97. In 1.5 miles a pulloff on the left gives you lake views.

Continue on Highway 97 to the town of Harrison in .5 miles. You'll find our route's sponsor on the left as you enter town. **Harrison Creamery and Fudge Factory (12),** located in the heart of historic Harrison, ID is a seasonal, charming, old fashioned ice cream shop. They offer 35 flavors of ice cream and serve it anyway one would like, cones, handcrafted shakes and malts, sundaes, and "date-worthy" banana-splits, crafted to order. They have gluten-free, sugar-free, and non-dairy options. They also feature home-made pies, cookies and brownies. Their operating months are May until mid-October: check their Facebook page, Harrison Creamery & Fudge Factory, for days and times as they vary during the season.

In 1.5 miles after crossing the highway bridge, turn right on Blue Lake Rd. In 1.4 miles a nice **old bridge (13)** comes into view. This would make a photogenic fall scene. You'll pass a river access on the right. In .2 mile a distant **barn (14)** reflects in the lake on a calm day. In .5 mile stay left then left. There is a barn on the right. Drive along the lakeshore for another mile until

Directions Continued

you reach an nice old **barn (15)** followed by a cabin. Turn left. In 1 mile there is a **wildlife viewing area (16)**. This area fills with a pink foliage in summer. You'll reach Highway 97 in less than 1 mile. For lakeshore access continue straight across the highway on E. Harlow Point Road. Return to Highway 97 and turn left (north) as it hugs the east shore of Lake Coeur d'Alene in many areas. This is a narrow, winding highway prone to many deer crossings, especially in the twilight hours. Pullouts are few and far between. Be careful parking.

In 3 miles there's a small barn on the left. In 6 more miles, a view of Carlin Bay. Continue 3.3 miles for Lake access and a gorgeous **view (17)** to the south. In 6 miles turn right on Burma Road and park immediately on the right. There is an old log **barn (18)** here. Continue on Highway 97. Watch for the Beauty Bay trail on the left (west) side of the road in 1.5 miles. This short, accessible trail takes you to a viewpoint overlooking Beauty Bay and the **Bennett Bay Bridge (19)**. Continue left (north) on Highway 97 as it descends to Lake Coeur d'Alene. Turn right on Beauty Creek Road immediately after crossing the bridge at the base of the hill. This road is bumpy and narrow as it follows **Beauty**

Photography Tips

A variety of focal length lenses can be utilized on this route. You'll want a telephoto in particular if you stop to view eagles in early winter. A wide angle is useful for landscapes and a wide to mid range zoom lens works well on beauty creek where you will also want a polarizing filter. Water shoes can also be helpful.

Creek (20) and enters a narrow canyon that is coated in lush green mosses in spring and after summer and autumn rains. You'll find access to the creek in about 2 miles for some great creek photography. Optionally, continue up Beauty Creek Road for about 5 miles to Beauty Creek Saddle for views over the **forested valleys (21)**.

Return to Highway 97 and turn right (north). In less than 1 mile you'll arrive at the trailhead for Mineral Ridge. Some of the best **views over the lake (22)** can be found by hiking the left branch of the trail for about 1 mile uphill. This is a 3-mile loop trail; you can opt for the more gradual route by going to the right at the junction. Trail maps can be found at the trailhead.

Turn right back onto Highway 97. Very small pullouts on the right over the next mile provide options for eagle viewing in December and January. In 1 mile find the large pull-out on the left. Carefully make your way down to the lakeshore for a nice sunset shoot over **Wolf Lodge Bay (23)**. I-90 is just ahead. Go left to Coeur d'Alene or right to Kellogg.

This Route's Sponsor

Harrison Creamery and Fudge Factory
206 S Coeur d'Alene Ave,
Harrison, ID 83833
(208) 689-9241
harrisoncreamery.com

See page 266 for coupon

Up Next: Routes 6 or 8

The North Fork and Silver Valley

Route 8 ◇------------------▶ Kingston to Wallace

This Route at a Glance:

Estimated Driving Time: 4 hours

Highlights: Bridges, River, Mission, Waterfalls, Autumn color

About This Route: We'll find photogenic waterfalls, a cedar grove, the Cataldo Mission and some picturesque barns on this route, which follows the North Fork of the Coeur d'Alene River. The North Fork travels through the Coeur d'Alene Mountains, fed by myriad tributaries draining the western slopes of the Bitterroot Range. End your day with sunset light at an alpine lake.

Notes and Cautions: Forest Service roads are mostly closed in winter. The last 6 miles into Fern and Shadow Falls can be rough; there are sections with concrete paver beams that are bumpy but allow water to pass through along creek beds. Fern Falls is encountered within ¼ mile and then the trail gets rougher and steeper as you approach and reach Shadow Falls within .5 mile. Moose are commonly seen along the trail to Fern and Shadow Falls. Do not approach wildlife! Settlers Grove is an out and back trail of 3.3 miles through 500-year-old cedars. It is also a popular moose hangout.

Directions

From eastbound Interstate 90, take Exit 34. Turn left, crossing the interstate and then right (east) on Canyon Road. In 2 miles there is a nice barn on the right. In one more mile turn left (north) on E. Hardy Loop, then turn left on Hardy Creek Road. There are **two barns (1)** on the left within a mile.

Return to Canyon Road and turn left (east). Follow to Dredge Road and turn right. Follow across Interstate to the **Cataldo Mission (2)**. Both the outside and **inside (3)** of the Mission are worthy photography subjects. There are beautiful autumn **river views (4)** past the Mission at the boat ramp.

Retrace your route to the Canyon Road and turn right. In one mile you'll pass a beautiful grove of **white-barked trees (5)** on the left that can be stunning in mid-October. Turn left (north) on CCC Road and pull off to the

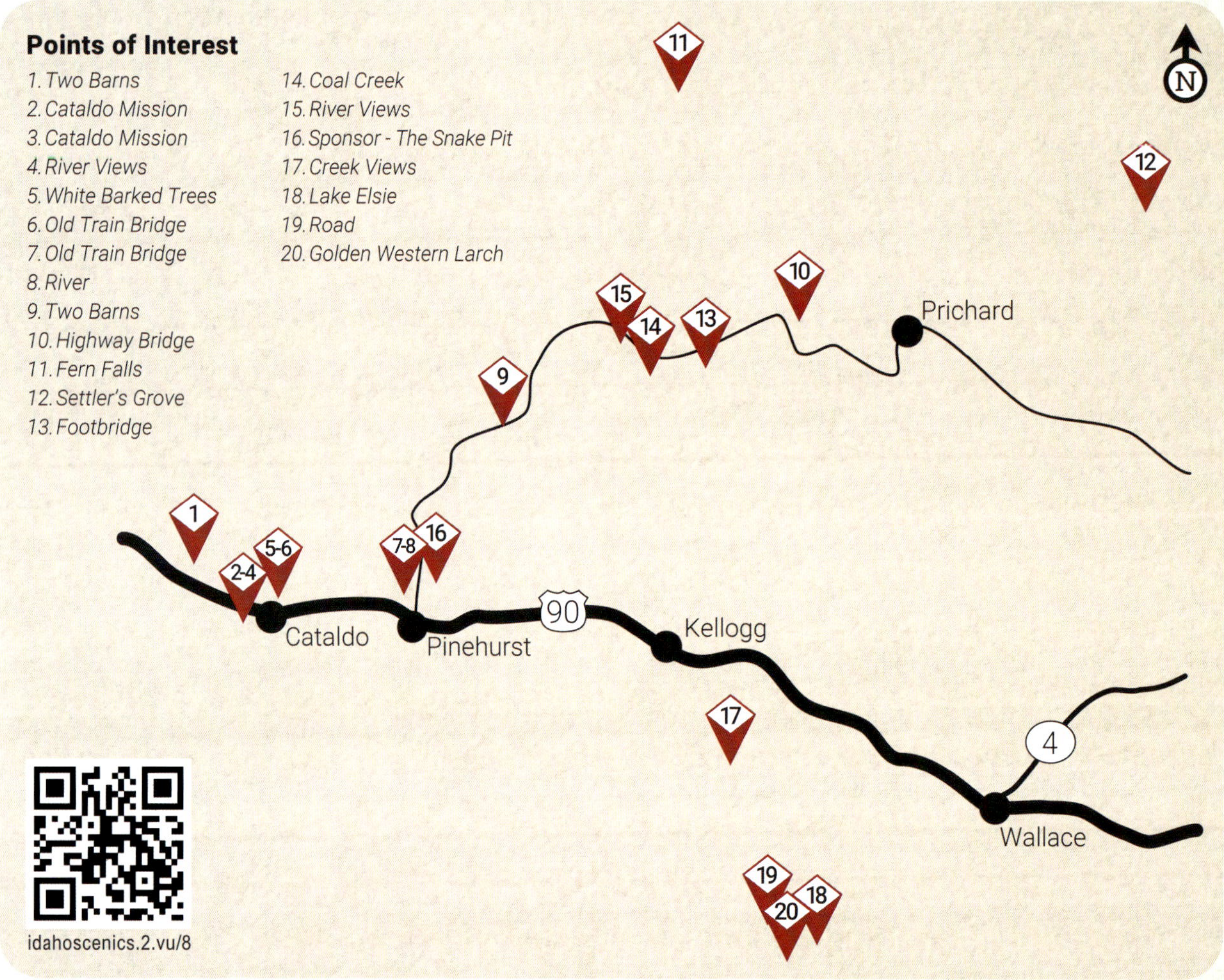

Points of Interest
1. Two Barns
2. Cataldo Mission
3. Cataldo Mission
4. River Views
5. White Barked Trees
6. Old Train Bridge
7. Old Train Bridge
8. River
9. Two Barns
10. Highway Bridge
11. Fern Falls
12. Settler's Grove
13. Footbridge
14. Coal Creek
15. River Views
16. Sponsor - The Snake Pit
17. Creek Views
18. Lake Elsie
19. Road
20. Golden Western Larch
N
Prichard
Cataldo
Pinehurst
90
Kellogg
4
Wallace
idahoscenics.2.vu/8

19

7

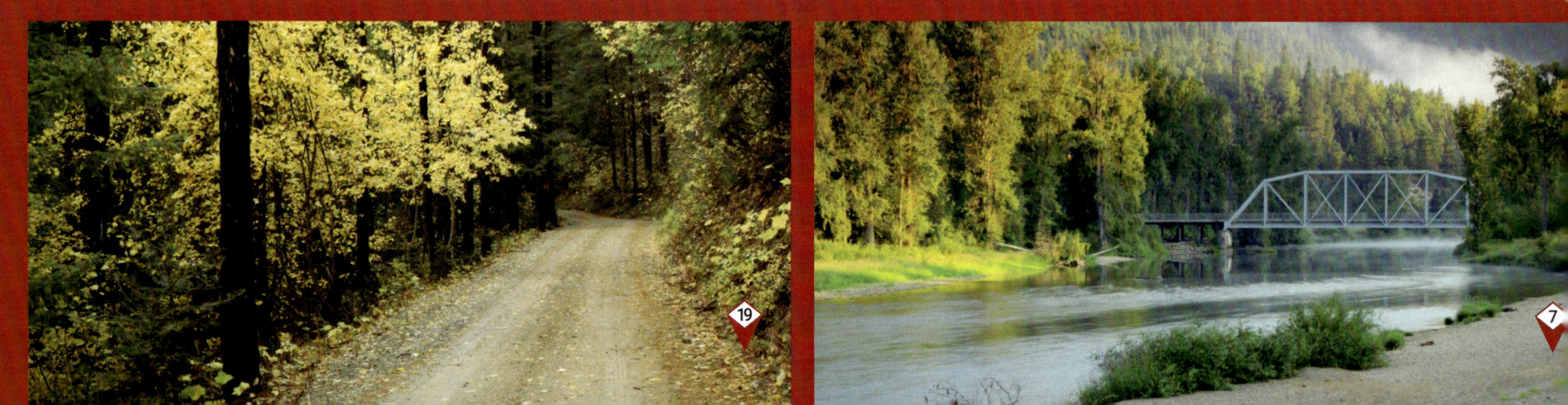

Directions Continued

right for a view of the bridge reflecting in the river. In another mile you'll have a slightly distant view of the **old train bridge (6)** (now the Trail of the Coeur d'Alene's) as it crosses the Coeur d'Alene River.

Return to Canyon Road and turn left (east). You'll reach Coeur d'Alene River Road (NF 9) and turn left (north). Watch for views of the river and another **old train bridge (7)**. There is a trailhead on the left; a ¼ mile stroll along a paved trail will give you up-close views of the **river (8)**. Continue on Coeur d'Alene River Road for 4 miles and turn left (west) on Bumblebee Road (NF 209). Turn right (north) on Old River Road just after crossing the river. In less than 2 miles you'll encounter **two barns (9)**.

For an extended river drive and the option to view Fern and Shadow Falls, follow the Old River Road for 13 miles watching for nice river views and near the end, a moderately distant view of the **highway bridge (10)** over the river. Here you can turn right on Coeur d'Alene River Road for another option to return to the Interstate, or continue on the Fern and Shadow Falls by turning left. From this junction proceed 19 miles. You'll go through the community of Prichard and past Devil's Elbow campground. Watch for a small sign to Fern and/or Shadow Falls on the left. Follow the signs. It is about 6 miles of dirt road, some of it rough. The road ends at the trailhead parking. It is about ¼ th mile walk to **Fern Falls (11)**, then the trail steepens and you will reach Shadow Falls in about .5 mile. Return to Coeur d'Alene River Road and go right.

Directions Continued

For another side trip of about 45 minutes, visit the Settlers Grove of Ancient Cedars by taking a left on Highway 9 just before entering the community of Prichard. In 2 miles turn left on NF Road 152 and follow the signs to the **Settlers Grove (12)** in about 6 miles. Return to Coeur d'Alene River Road and turn left. Follow Coeur d'Alene River Road back to Prichard. Go 3.5 miles past the turn off for Old River Road and the bridge over the Coeur d'Alene River. The parking for Trailhead 33 is on the left. The trail starts with a scenic little **footbridge (13)**. In 1.5 miles park on the left at the **Coal Creek (14)** Trailhead. Photograph this picturesque creek or hike the trail for more photo opportunities. Continue on Coeur d'Alene River Road watching for **river views (15)** and stop for a hearty meal at this route's sponsor, the historic **Snake Pit (16)** in Enaville.

The Snake Pit is the oldest restaurant in Idaho and has a unique atmosphere produced by the building's colorful history. Built in 1880, they serve house-smoked BBQ, hamburgers, steaks and the specialty of the house - Rocky Mountain Oysters. A true Idaho icon and a place you must experience.

Directions Continued

Continue the 1.5 miles back to I-90 by turning left from the Snake Pit. Conclude your route here by returning to Coeur d'Alene or continue for sunset at an alpine lake in the Bitterroot Mountains.

To continue, take a left onto I-90 and proceed to Exit 54 in 11.2 miles. Follow Big Creek (NF 264) watching for **creek views (17)** for 11.5 miles to **Lake Elsie (18)**. As the **road (19)** climbs you'll have views of slopes covered in **golden western larch (20)** in the autumn. Earlier in the year a small waterfall cascades into the lake on the distant cliffs.

Photography Tips

This is an ideal route for autumn, when mists hang in the forest valleys and the river is lined with colorful cottonwood trees. Fern and Shadow Falls as well as the cedar grove should be accessible by mid to late May depending on the winter snowpack. A drive up the river is nice anytime of year and the barn locations should be accessible even in winter, but the road may become impassable further up and require backtracking. Fern and Shadow Falls are best shot with a mid to wide-angle lens, avoiding the middle of the day unless you have cloud cover. As always a polarizing filter can be useful when photographing water.

This Route's Sponsor

The Snake Pit
1480 Coeur d'Alene River Road
Enaville, ID
208-682-3453
snakepitidaho.com

See page 266 for coupon

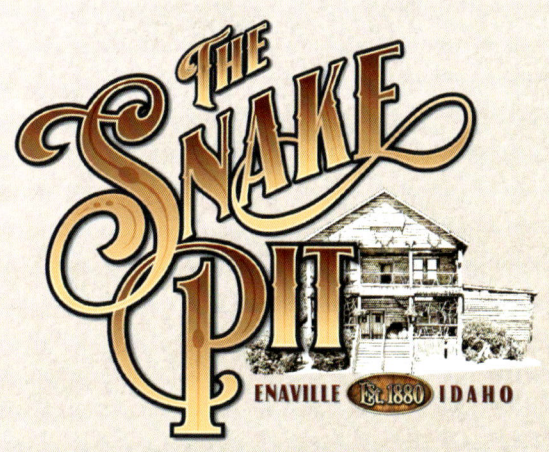

Up Next: Routes 7, 9, or 16

Route of the Hiawatha

Route 9 ◇------------------▶ Wallace to St. Maries

This Route at a Glance:

Estimated Driving Time: 4 hours

Highlights: Tunnels, Trestles, Bridges and Rivers

About This Route: Follow the Route of the Hiawatha as it descends the western slopes of the Bitterroot Mountains. En route, it passes through numerous old train tunnels. Then, follow the gorgeous St. Joe River as it leisurely winds its way to St. Maries. Don't forget your fishing gear!

Notes and Cautions: This is a great autumn color route and a nice summer tour with wildflowers on Moon Pass in mid-summer. Bring your fishing rod to cast a fly on one of Idaho's premier fishing rivers. Roads through the mountains are winding and narrow, with steep drop offs. Old rail bridges and tunnels are especially narrow. Use caution when crossing. Drive slowly through tunnels and turn on your headlamps. Use care when walking near or crossing highways. The road over Moon Pass is likely not maintained in winter. The optional side trip to Baldy Mountain is steep and narrow with deadly drop offs.

Directions

From eastbound Interstate 90, take exit 61 into Wallace. Turn right, then left onto Front Street. Turn right onto Second Street in .2 mile (Two roads split at this unsigned intersection. Take the second right). In .3 mile turn right on Cedar Street, then left on 1st Street, right on Bank Street and left on King Street. Follow for about 9 miles to the top of Moon Pass. Stay straight on Cedar Mountain Road (NF 71). Start watching for views over the **valley (1)** in about a mile. Return to Moon Pass Road and turn right.

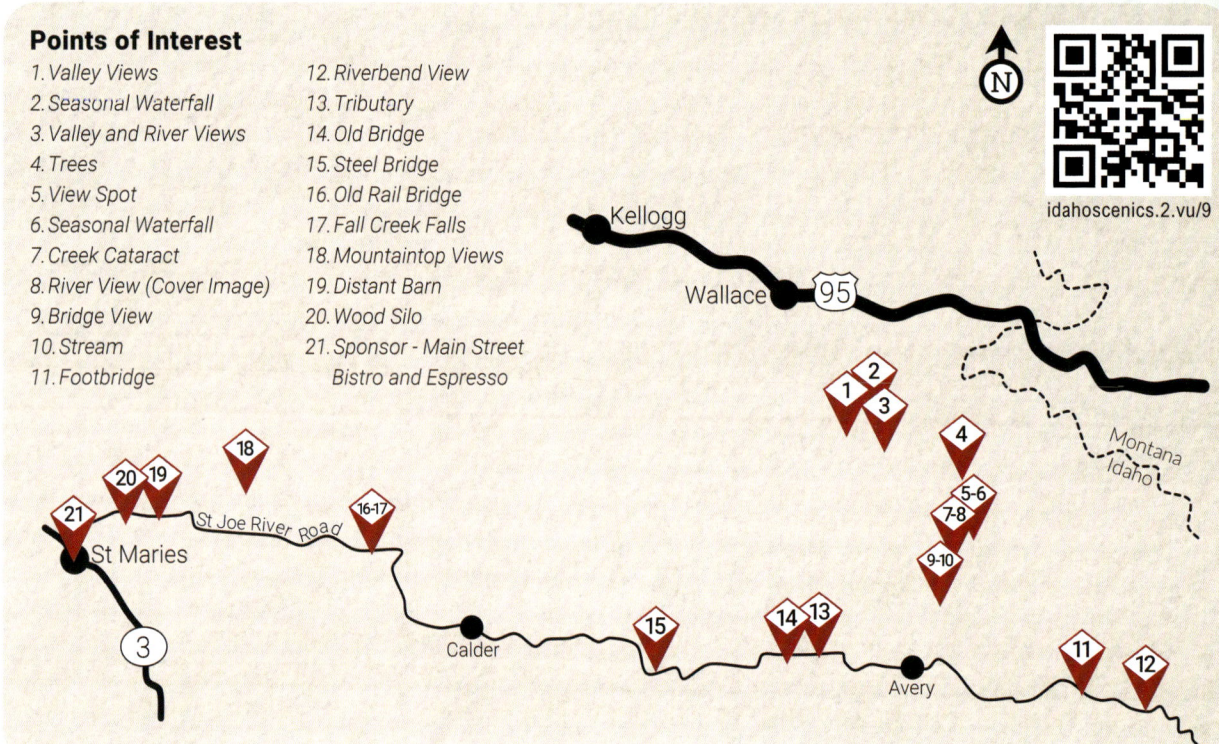

Points of Interest
1. Valley Views
2. Seasonal Waterfall
3. Valley and River Views
4. Trees
5. View Spot
6. Seasonal Waterfall
7. Creek Cataract
8. River View (Cover Image)
9. Bridge View
10. Stream
11. Footbridge
12. Riverbend View
13. Tributary
14. Old Bridge
15. Steel Bridge
16. Old Rail Bridge
17. Fall Creek Falls
18. Mountaintop Views
19. Distant Barn
20. Wood Silo
21. Sponsor - Main Street Bistro and Espresso

idahoscenics.2.vu/9

A **seasonal waterfall (2)** is on the left in 2.5 miles. You'll have **valley and river views (3)** in another 1.8 miles. In 4 miles you'll travel past a marshy section with charred remains of **trees (4)** still standing from the "Great Burn" of 1910. In another 3 miles stay straight. You'll reach the first tunnel in .8 mile. Watch for a pullout immediately after exiting the tunnel for a **view spot (5)**. You'll travel through and over a series of tunnels and trestles over the next few miles. There is a mossy green rock wall at the entrance of tunnel 33 with a **seasonal waterfall (6)**.

You'll cross another trestle in 1.6 miles. Turn right just after it, then stay left on NF 1997. There's a creek with a small photogenic **cataract (7)** on the left in .9 mile. There are up-close river views over the next few miles, including the book **cover image location (8)**. Travel as far as you'd like, then return to Moon Pass Road and turn right.

In .1 mile there's a view with brief glimpses of a **river bridge (9)** below. You'll travel through 3 more tunnels over the next few miles. Another **small stream (10)** is on the right, 4 miles from the junction.

Directions Continued

Turn left on St. Joe River Road. In 5.7 miles there's a slot canyon across the river. In 3.5 miles there's a pullout on the right for views of a **footbridge (11)**. You'll reach a **big riverbend view (12)** in 3.9 miles. Return to Moon Pass Road then continue on St. Joe River Road for .4 miles.

Turn right, then follow Siberts Old River Road across the river. In about 2 miles stay right over Fishhook Creek. A pullout on the left in 2.5 miles provides views of a **St. Joe tributary (13)**. In another mile watch for a view of a **old bridge (14)** across the river, then turn right across the bridge and rejoin St. Joe River Road. Turn left. In 2.2 miles there's a pullout on the left for river views. The Marble Creek interpretive area comes up in 4.2 miles. A pullout on the right in .5 mile allows for parking to walk back along the highway for a view of another **steel bridge (15)**. In another 4.5 miles, another pullout gives you views of a sweeping river curve. You'll find a pretty grove of trees on the right in 3.7 miles. These are exceptionally nice in autumn. In another mile there are two old signs (one for each direction) designating "Calder".

In about 8 miles a large pullout on the left gives you a beautiful view of the **old rail bridge (16)**. Walk back outside the guardrail

Directions Continued

for best views. Continue .2 mile, then park again on the left. **Fall Creek Falls (17)** is just ahead on the right and flows under the road. The best views are found by walking under the road. We do not recommend viewing from the road, as this would be extremely dangerous.

For an optional side trip with great views, turn right on Reeds Gulch Road in 4 miles. This side adventure of about 1.5 to 2 hours round trip, will take you to the summit of Baldy Mountain. It's a great place to watch the sunset. Otherwise, skip to the next paragraph. In 1.3 miles the road turns right and becomes NF 550. In 8 miles continue straight on NF 551. The last mile to the top is steep and narrow and requires absolute attention. Enjoy the **views (18)** including beargrass in mid summer then return to St. Joe River Road.

Proceed 5 miles to another pullout on the left for river views. In less than a mile there is a distant barn on the left. In another mile a **barn (19)** sits on the back side of a pond and provides reflections on a calm day. Continue almost 2 miles to a very small pullout on the left. Here you can cross the highway for a distant view of an old **square wood silo (20)** that was leaning severely at the time of this

Photography Tips

Start this route about 50 minutes before sunrise to arrive on Moon Pass for potential pre-sunrise color. While we always recommend a tripod, it is a must for photographing waterfalls and into dark tunnels on this route. A variety of focal-length lenses are recommended for this route, from zooms for photographing distant barns to wide-angles for sweeping river and valley views.

This Route's Sponsor

Main Street Bistro
806 Main Ave,
St Maries, ID 83861
(208) 245-5539

See page 266 for coupon

Directions Continued

writing. You'll arrive at the intersection of Highway 3 in 2.5 miles. Go left to St. Maries In .5 miles turn right on Highway 5. Turn right in 1 block to stay on Highway 5. In 4 blocks you'll arrive at this routes sponsor, **Main Street Bistro and Espresso (21)** on the right.

Visit Main Street Bistro and Espresso for great food and fantastic service. They have a full espresso bar, beer and wine and a great variety of sandwiches, wraps, pizzas, salads, Ice cream and fudge. They are open 7 am to 8 pm, 7 days a week. It's a great place to stop and unwind over lunch or dinner.

Staying the night in St. Maries will perfectly position you for starting route 6, or continue west on Highway 5 to Plummer. Turning right at Highway 95 will take you to Coeur d'Alene in 32 miles. Turning left will take you to Moscow in 50 miles.

Up Next: Routes 6 or 10

North Central Region

Route #
10. Barns and the Palouse
11. Palouse and the Clearwater River Canyon
12. Waterfalls and the Clearwater Mtns
13. Clearwater River
14. Camas Prairie and Winchester
15. Whitewater and the Bitterroot Mtns
16. The Clearwater River North Fork
17. White Bird and Hells Canyon
18. The Salmon River and The Seven Devils Mtns
19. Gospel Wilderness and Hells Canyon

Seven Devils Lake on route 18.

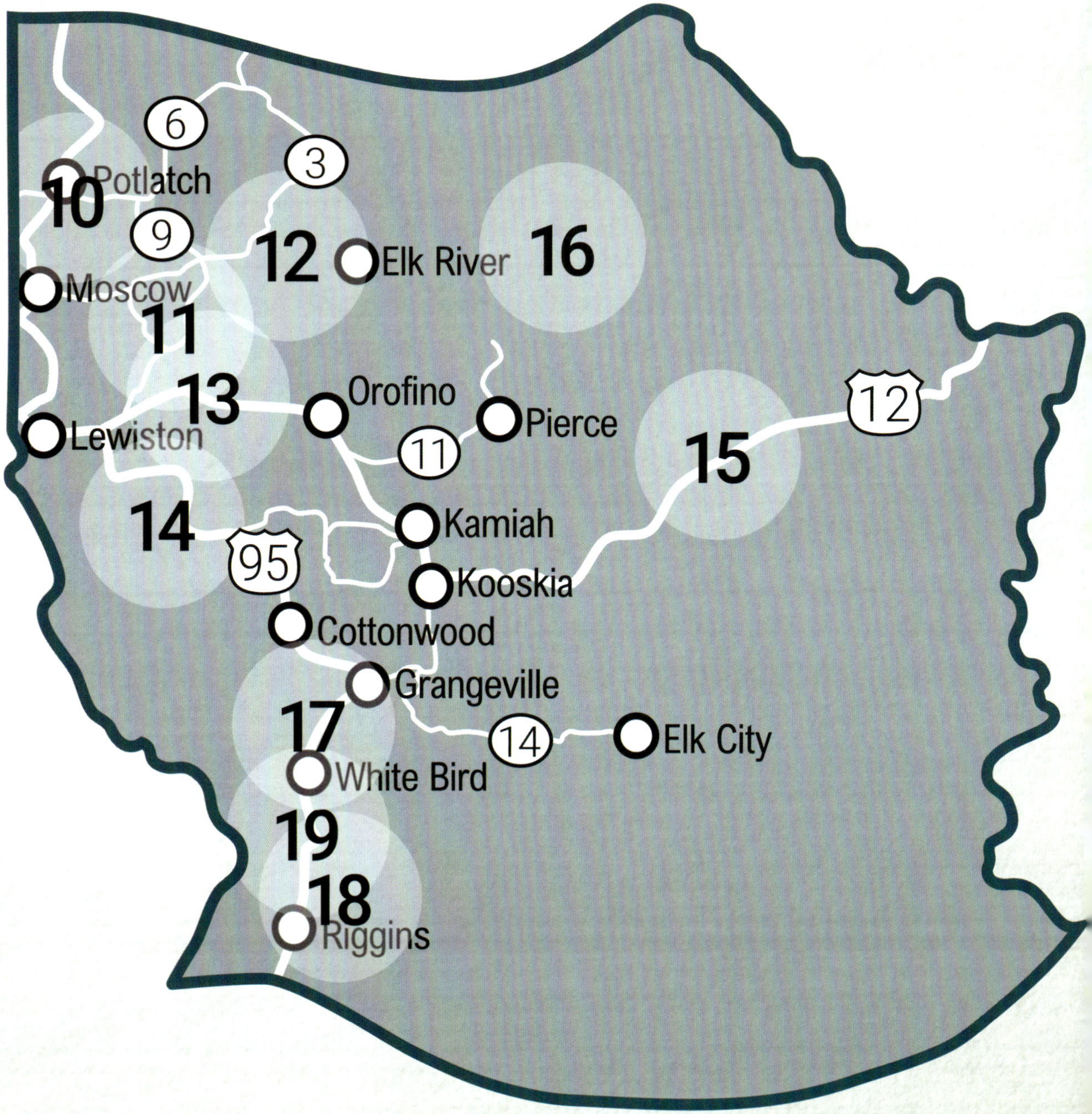

Welcome to Idaho's North Central Region

Climb from low river valleys to the peaks of the Seven Devils and Gospel Hump Wilderness areas on these routes. En route, you'll encounter many old and weathered barns, numerous railroad trestles, three camas prairies and the rolling hills of the Palouse. This is where the Salmon River emerges from the River of No Return Wilderness Area and joins Hells Canyon. Traversing this area culminates at the convergence of the powerful Clearwater, Lochsa, and Selway rivers, as they emerge from the Bitterroot Mountains and become the mighty Snake River. You'll also be exploring the region of the Nez Perce tribe. The Niimiipuu (literally, "the people"), were historically nomadic, and their lives are largely centered on fishing and their iconic salmon. This is also the region where the Lewis and Clark Expedition journeyed more than 200 years ago, in search of the Northwest Passage. You'll also visit high prairies and historic battlefields.

The Salmon River on route 18.

Dawn on the Palouse north of Potlatch, a road driven on route 10.

Barns and the Palouse
Route 10 ◇------------------------▶ North of Moscow

This Route at a Glance:

Estimated Driving Time: 5 hours

Highlights: Barns, Crops and Rolling Hills

About This Route: This 4,000 square-mile region of rolling, asymmetrical hills composed of loess features unforgettable views of the farmlands of the Palouse. We'll criss-cross into Washington finding many old barns along the route before ascending Steptoe Butte for glorious views of the rolling Palouse hills. Spring and summer are ideal times to visit this route, but we also love the barns in winter.

Notes and Cautions: This route zigzags across the state line into Washington, and makes a loop to bring you back to Moscow. Start this route early for sunrise light or plan to finish at Steptoe Butte for sunset. Most roads should be maintained for winter travel. Do not attempt any unmaintained side roads during wet weather. Steptoe Butte Road does close after deeper snow. This road is pitted and winding with steep drop-offs, so drive slowly and pay special attention.

Directions

From Moscow head north on Highway 95. In 6.8 miles turn left on Trestle Road. There is a very **old barn (1)** roadside in 1.8 miles. In 1.7 miles turn right on Estes Road. You'll see a **grain elevator (2)** on the left in 1.4 miles.

This option is for dry weather only. Do not attempt when wet. Turn left on McGreevy Road. There is a **lone tree (3)** here. In .7 mile turn right on an unmarked road. There is a barn on the left in .3 mile. Make a U-turn and go back to Estes Road and turn left.

In 1 mile turn right on Highway 27. Turn left on Palouse-Albion Road n 1.1 mile. In 1.2 miles turn right on Tate Cut-off Road. There is a **barn (4)** on the left in .8 mile. In .5 mile turn right on Parvin Road. In 1.7 miles you'll have a distant view of a fallen structure and windmill on the hill on the right. In .9 mile turn left on Highway 27. In 1.6 miles turn left on Clear Creek Road, then stay straight on Fugate Road in .4 mile. Turn left on Kamiak Butte Road in .7 mile. Enjoy this park by walking the 2.4 mile loop trail for views over the **Palouse (5)**. Wildflowers are usually abundant in spring. Return to Fugate Road and park carefully to photograph the unique barns on the right.

Back at Highway 27 turn left. Continue 3 miles into the town of Palouse and turn right on Palouse Cove Road. In 3.7 miles turn left

Points of Interest
1. Old Barn
2. Grain Elevator
3. Lone Tree
4. Barn
5. Palouse Views
6. Barn
7. Large Barn
8. Nice View
9. Nice Views
10. Tree-lined Drive
11. Steel Bridge
12. Barn
13. Old House
14. Barn
15. Nice Barn
16. Old Truck
17. Brick Silo
18. Old Tractor
19. Nice View
20. Winding Road
21. Old Barn
22. Freeze Church
23. Old Homestead
24. Distant Barn
25. Nice Barn
26. Distant Barn
27. Barn
28. Nice Barn
29. Two Nice Old Barns
30. Two Barns
31. Amazing Vista
32. Amazing Vista
33. Amazing Vista
34. Barn
35. Barn
36. Barn
37. Old Windmill
38. White Barn
39. Sponsor - Monarch Hotel

idahoscenics.2.vu/10

Directions Continued

on McKenzie Road. A **barn (6)** on the right and a large grove of trees on the left in .2 mile provide nice photo opportunities. Respect private property. Return to Palouse Cove Road and go left. In 1.8 miles turn left on Potter Road. You'll see a large **barn (7)** in .3 mile. Follow this road uphill to where it joins Highway 95. Just before the intersection, you'll have a nice **view (8)** looking back, including a couple more barns.

Turn left on Highway 95. In 1.1 miles turn left on Cove Road. There's a barn on the right in 1 mile and, in 1.3 miles there's a big barn on the left. Stay right on River Road going uphill. Over the next mile are some nice **views (9)** and a **tree-lined drive (10)**. Turn left on S. River Road. Stop at the bridge for a view upstream of an old **steel bridge (11)**. Turn right on Wellesley Road, then stay straight. Turn right on Highway 6. A **barn (12)** with two cupolas is on the right in 1 mile. Park safely. In .8 mile there's a nice river view with 2 bridges. Use caution when parking to photograph this. Turn right on Highway 95.

Turn left on Cove Road in .9 mile. In 1.4 mile at the intersection of Cove and Walker there is an **old house (13)** in the trees on the right and a **barn (14)** straight ahead. Turn left (east) on Walker Road. A nice **barn (15)** is on the right in .4 mile. You'll pass some old farm implements roadside, then turn left on Flannigan Creek Road in 1.4 miles. You'll find an old homestead with barn and a shed houses an **old truck (16)** in .7 mile.

Stay straight on McBride Road. There is a falling barn and old **brick silo (17)** on the right in .4 mile. Turn right on Cove Road and right on Highway 95. In 2 miles turn right on Highway 6.

Turn left on Onaway Road in 4.6 miles. An **old tractor (18)** sits under a tree roadside in .4 mile. In 1.1 miles stay left on Onaway Road, then turn right on Crane Creek Road in .5 mile. You'll have a nice **view (19)** in another .7 mile. In .4 mile turn right on Boller Road and stay left in .2 mile. There is a barn on the left. In .9 mile stay left, then right in .2 mile. In .6 mile you'll have a view of a barn on a hill. Turn left on Fiscus Road. Pass the barn in about .3 mile, then look back at a great **winding road (20)** shot with barn. You'll find two more barns in 1.6 miles. In .7 mile turn right on Freeze Road. In 1.4 mile turn left on Highway 95. In 1 mile turn right on Scoville Road. You'll have a nice, albeit distant view of the barns to the north in .1 mile. In one mile there's a distant view of the Freeze Church, followed by a nice **old barn (21)** on the left in 1.5 miles. Return to Highway 95 and go left (north).

Directions Continued

In 1 mile turn left on Freeze Road. You'll have views of the **Freeze Church (22)** in 1.2 miles. In summer and fall you can continue beyond the church entrance road about .3 mile for more nice views of the church. Make a U-turn. Turn left on Deep Creek Road about .5 mile from the church entrance road, then turn left on Garfield Road in .4 mile. Stay right in .2 mile. There's a barn in .9 mile. There are

two more barns at the intersection just beyond here. Stay straight. You'll pass through a grove of young Ponderosa pine trees that are very pretty when covered with snow or frost. In 1.4 miles there's an old **homestead (23)** on the right. In .7 miles turn right on Garfield Road. There's a distant **barn (24)** with a creek in the foreground in .1 mile. Turn right on Cora Road in .2 miles, then right on Cora Road again in 1.7 miles. In .5 mile turn left on Cora Road. In .5 mile a nice **barn (25)** is on the left. Make a U-turn.

Turn left on McKown Road in .6 mile and find a barn on the left in 1 mile. In 1.2 miles a somewhat distant **barn (26)** is on the right. Stay left on Deep Creek Road in .3 mile, then turn left on Deep Creek Road in .9 mile. Follow for 4 miles, staying on Deep Creek Road through all intersections. Right before rejoining Highway 95, there is a **barn (27)** on the right. Turn left on Highway 95. In 6 miles turn right on Sanders Road. A nice **barn (28)** sits on the left in .5 mile. Return to Highway 95 and turn right. In 12 miles turn left on Highway 60. In 5.7 miles stay left on Highway 60. In 1.9 miles turn right on Washington Street. Two nice old **barns (29)** sit below the road in .6 mile. Make a U-turn and watch for a view of the large old trestle on the right. Cross Poplar Street (Highway 27) in .3 mile, then stay right onto Ramsey Street in .2 mile.

In another .2 mile stay straight onto Highway 27. In 6.2 miles turn left on Fanning Road. You'll find **two barns (30)** on the left in 1.4 miles. In 1.7 miles turn right on Warner Road and, in another 1.7 miles, turn right on Highway 27. In 1.5 miles turn left on Hume Road. Turn right for a red barn in 2.6 miles, then make a U-turn back to Hume Road and turn right. In 4.8 miles turn right on Steptoe Butte Road. Follow this road to the top for **amazing vistas (31, 32, 33)** over the rolling hills of the Palouse. Wildflowers abound in the spring and June is prime time for viewing the patchwork greens. Any time of year can be amazing, but the road does close if there's much snow. Stay here to view sunset or continue to a few more barns on your way back to Moscow.

Leaving the park turn right on Hume Road. After sunset follow Hume Road 3.8 miles to Schlotz Road and go left. You'll join Highway 195 in 1.3 miles. Follow Highway 195 south for 20.5 miles then stay left onto Highway 270. Follow through Pullman and into Moscow in about 9 miles.

To continue for more barns and scenic vistas turn left on Cronk Road in 1.8 miles. There's a **barn (34)** on the right in .4 mile. In .8 mile stay right on Cronk Road. There's a **barn (35)** on the right here. In .7 mile turn right on Dry

Directions Continued

Creek Road. Then turn right on Imler Road. There is a **barn (36)** here on the left. Return to Dry Creek Road and go right. In 2 miles turn left on Glenwood Road. A seasonal road on the right will take you to an **old windmill (37)** and truck in .7 mile. Return to Glenwood Road. In 2 miles you'll cross the Palouse River. In 1.5 miles turn left on Highway 272, then immediately right on Clear Creek Road. In 5.5 miles there's a nice viewpoint if you can park safely off the road. In 1.5 miles there's a **white barn (38)** on the right. In 5 miles turn right on Highway 27. It's 11 miles to Pullman and Highway 270. Turn left on Highway 270 and follow back to Moscow. At S. Jackson Street turn right and arrive at our route sponsor **The Monarch Hotel (39)** on the left.

The Monarch Motel is a newly renovated mid-century modern boutique motel in the heart of downtown Moscow, Idaho. It boasts the only place to stay that is located next to all the restaurants, bars, art galleries and the Saturday Farmers Market right on Main Street. All guests receive 10% off all food, wine and cocktails at Nectar Restaurant & Wine Bar right across the street. Get immersed in their clean, crisp white linens, classic style and warm hospitality and discover for yourself why the Monarch Motel is Idaho's newest gem.

Photography Tips

You'll want a variety of focal length lenses for this route. Some barns are distant others are so close you'll need a wide angle. Landscapes from Steptoe Butte can be expansive or you can use a telephoto to isolate patterns, distant towns, farms, a storm, or a lone tree. Morning or evening are best here when the hills cast their shadows over the small valleys. Lupine usually peak in mid May and balsamroot a few weeks earlier. It's great if you can catch both of them in bloom in one image.

This Route's Sponsor

The Monarch Hotel
120 W 6th St, Moscow, ID 83843
(208) 882-2581
moscowmonarch.com

Up Next: Routes 11 or 12

Palouse to Dworshack

Route 11 ◇ ----------▶ Moscow to Orofino

This Route at a Glance:

Estimated Driving Time: 4 hours

Highlights: Barn, Rolling Hills, Views, Old Schools

About This Route: Highlighted by old structures including barns, abandoned houses, a country church and old schoolhouses, this route begins south of Moscow and covers the eastern edge of the Palouse before dropping into the Clearwater River Valley. Visit the Dworshak Reservoir and dam, then finish your route in Orofino.

Notes and Cautions: This route has several steep and winding roads, which may make winter travel unsafe or require chains. Get an early start for the best light for photography. Respect private property.

Directions

Start your morning with a fresh steamed bagel sandwich at this route's sponsor. Located at 310 S Main Street, **Moscow Bagel and Deli (1)** has been a staple business in the downtown community since 2006. "The Bagel Shop" (as known by the locals) offers a unique variety of roughly 100 bagel sandwiches that come steamed and customized to your liking. Steaming our sandwiches creates an unbelievable fusion of flavor among the ingredients. They offer 12 bagel varieties to choose from including gluten free. They are open 20 hours a day from 7am to 3am for breakfast, lunch, dinner and late night! They do close earlier on Sunday (7pm). Rest assured the Bagel Shop will most likely be open when you roll through town.

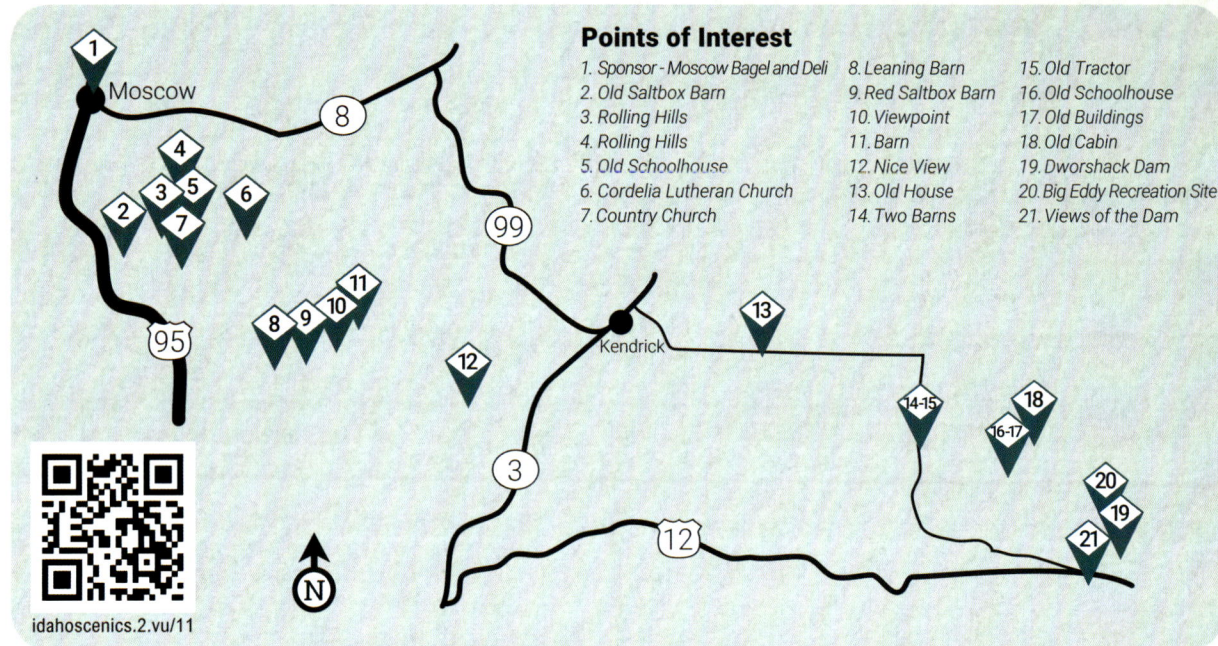

Points of Interest

1. Sponsor - Moscow Bagel and Deli
2. Old Saltbox Barn
3. Rolling Hills
4. Rolling Hills
5. Old Schoolhouse
6. Cordelia Lutheran Church
7. Country Church
8. Leaning Barn
9. Red Saltbox Barn
10. Viewpoint
11. Barn
12. Nice View
13. Old House
14. Two Barns
15. Old Tractor
16. Old Schoolhouse
17. Old Buildings
18. Old Cabin
19. Dworshack Dam
20. Big Eddy Recreation Site
21. Views of the Dam

idahoscenics.2.vu/11

Continue south on South Main Street for about 5 blocks then turn left on South Main Street (Highway 95). Turn right on Highway 95 and proceed 5.3 miles south. Turn left on Eid Road. In 1.4 miles you'll have a moderately distant view of an **old saltbox barn (2)** on the right. In 1.2 miles there is a nice view over the **rolling hills (3)** and in .5 mile turn left on Blaine Road for another nice view over the **rolling hills (4)** and a good view at dawn. Go to a large pullout up the hill in about 2 miles. Return to the intersection of Blaine Road and Eid Road. There is an **old schoolhouse (5)** on the left. Turn left on Eid Rd. Go 1.6 miles then stay left on Genesee Troy Road. In .8 mile make a sharp right on Danielson Road. **Cordelia Lutheran Church (6)** is on the right in .6 mile. Retrace your route to Blaine Road.

Turn left on Blaine Road. In 1.8 miles there is a barn on the right. In .5 mile turn right on Genesee/Troy Road. In .8 mile stay straight on Old Highway 95. In .7 mile there is a **country church (7)** on your left. In 1.6 miles turn left on Danielson Road, where there are some red barns in .5 mile. Stay straight on Berger Road in 1.4 miles. Turn right on Berger Road in 1.1 miles. In .5 mile, look back for a moderately distant view of a unique barn. There is another distant, **leaning barn (8)** uphill at 1.2 mile. In .3 mile turn left on Magee Road.

In 1.2 miles there is another **red saltbox barn (9)** on the left and, in another 1.2 miles you'll come upon an excellent **viewpoint (10)**. In 1.5 miles turn right on Jones Road. There is a **barn (11)** on the left at the junction. In 1.5 miles

Directions Continued

there is another barn on the left. In .5 mile turn left on Genesee/Troy Highway, then turn right on Genesee/Julietta Road in .3 mile. There are old buildings and vehicles on the left in .7 mile. These are on private property so view from the road. In 3.1 miles turn left on Genesee/Julietta Road, where there is a nice **view (12)** in 1.3 miles. In .3 mile stay left on Genesee/Julietta Road. Go slow on this steep, winding road. In 2.6 miles turn left on Main Street (Highway 3).

Travel 5.1 miles on Highway 3. Turn right on Cedar Ridge Road, then right on Southwick Road in .3 mile. In 3 miles there are barns on each side of the road. Park safely if you want to shoot these. Watch for an **old house (13)** on the right in about 2.5 miles. A different view is to pass the house and turn right on Hepler Road, and shoot with a telephoto lens. Do not trespass. In 2 more miles there is a barn and old house on the left and another old house 1.6 miles farther. Travel just over 4 miles to the intersection of Freeman Creek Road on the left and McIver Road on the right. Turn right. There are **two barns (14)** here, one on each side of the road. Return to the intersection and travel straight across what is now called Old Highway 7 or Cavendish Road. Park immediately at the grain elevator lot for an **old tractor (15)** across the road. In 1.6 miles from the intersection there is an old truck on the left. View from the road.

Turn right on Yenni Road in .8 mile. In one mile there is a cemetery on the right. In .2 miles turn left on Middle Road. There is an **old schoolhouse (16)** in .3 mile on the left. In .5 mile turn left on Brown Road. In .4 mile you'll encounter a variety of **old buildings (17)** on the left. Do not trespass. Turn right in .8 mile on Freeman Creek Road. In .9 mile you'll find an **old cabin (18)**. View from the road. Make a U-turn and return to Brown Road and turn left. In 1.1 miles stay straight. Turn left in another 1.6 miles on Old Ahsahka Grade Road. Go slow on this steep, winding, moderately rough gravel road. In 2.8 miles turn left on Viewpoint Road to visit the **Dworshak Dam (19)**. In .9 mile turn right for the visitor center or go left another 1.5 miles to **Big Eddy Recreation Site (20)**. Follow Viewpoint Road back down the hill all the way to the Cavendish Highway, turning left. In .7 mile turn left on North Fork Drive for river access spots and dam views from below. Return to Cavendish Highway (Old Highway 7) and turn left, crossing the bridge over the North Fork of the Clearwater River. Pull off on the left immediately across the bridge and walk back onto the bridge for one of the best **views of the dam (21)**, being very careful of traffic. In .9 mile turn right into Orofino.

Photography Tips

Lenses with a variety of focal lengths are very useful on this route. The structures vary from up-close roadside to distant views. A polarizing filter on blue-sky days will help make the clouds pop and darken blue skies.

This Route's Sponsor

Moscow Bagel
310 S Main St, Moscow, ID 83843
(208) 882-5242
moscowbagel.com

Up Next: Routes 10, 12, or 13

Waterfalls and Clearwater Mountains

Route 12 ◇------------------▶ Potlatch to Orofino

This Route at a Glance:

Estimated Driving Time: 4 hours

Highlights: Waterfalls, Rolling Hills, Barns

About This Route: Starting on the Palouse and finishing in the Clearwater River Valley, this route through the Clearwater Mountains features a hike to Elk Creek Falls, and access to Elk Creek Reservoir for camping, fishing and picnicking opportunities. Dent Bridge Road winds its way through lush evergreen forests en route to scenic vistas. Part of the Rocky Mountains, the scenic Clearwater Range is the largest mountain grouping in the state, covering most of north-central Idaho.

Notes and Cautions: The Dent Bridge Road is a shortcut through the Clearwater Mountains from Elk River to Orofino. It is winding and gravel, but well maintained from mid-spring through fall. The road to Elk Falls is usually accessible by end of May, but of course varies from year to year.

Directions

Beginning at the Junction of US Highway 95 and Highway 8 in Moscow, travel 3.3 miles east. There is a **barn (1)** on the left. In 9.2 miles stay left on Highway 8. In 1.8 miles turn left to Spring Valley Reservoir. You'll reach the reservoir in 3 miles. This scenic little lake can have some nice reflections. Return to Highway 8 and turn left. In 7.2 miles turn right on Old Highway 8. In .9 mile turn left on Watermill Road. There's a barn on the right. Do not trespass. Return to Highway 8 and turn right. In 2.4 miles you'll find this route's sponsor, **The Pie Safe (2)** on the left.

The Pie Safe Bakery is located in a newly renovated, 100-year-old Ford garage at the corner of Main Street and Highway 8. Open Tuesday-Saturday, they make delicious pastries from scratch and serve breakfast and lunch from their wood-fired brick oven. Peruse the fine craft shop stocked by local artisans and watch national award-winning cheese being made at the neighboring Brush Creek Creamery.

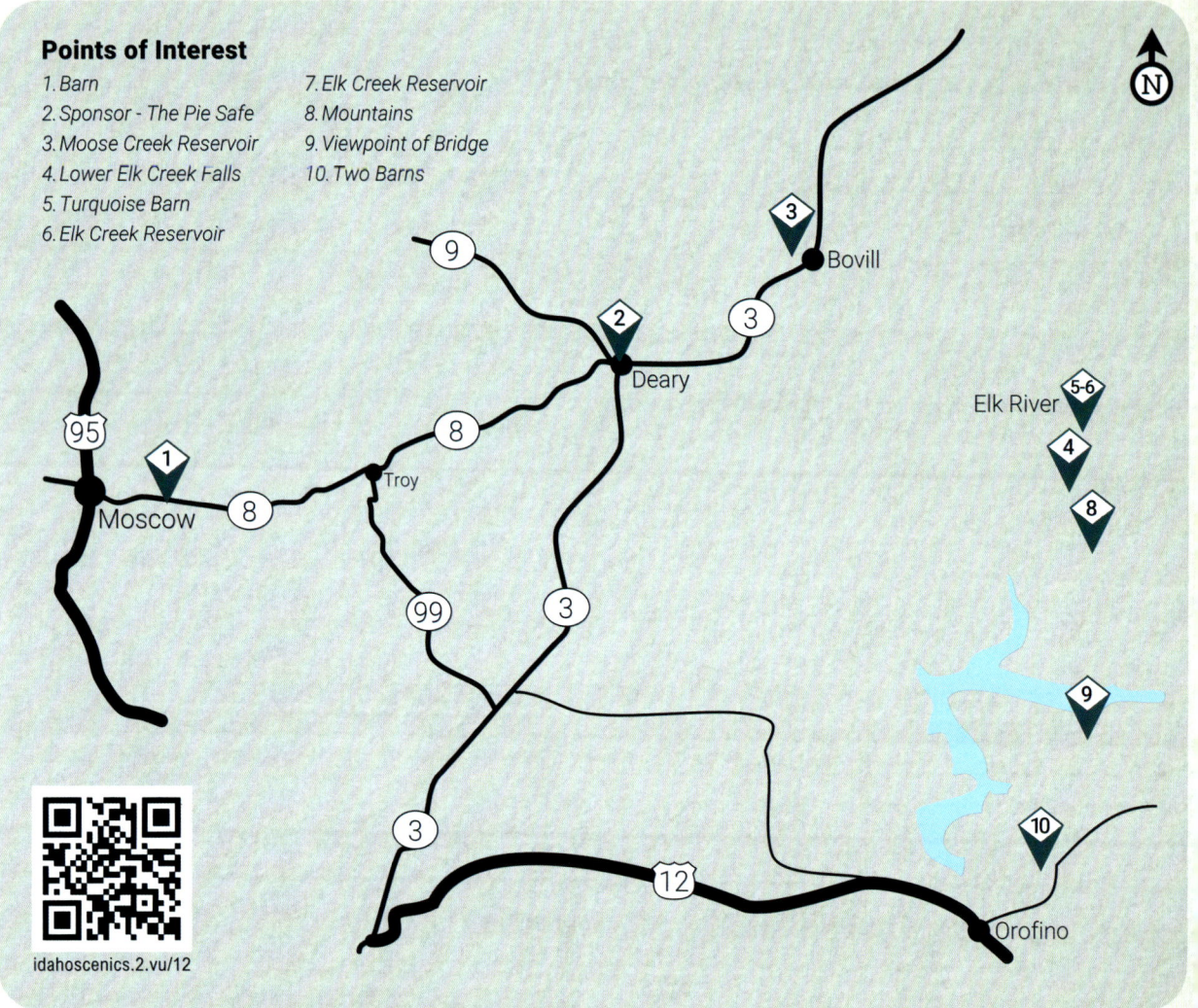

Points of Interest
1. Barn
2. Sponsor - The Pie Safe
3. Moose Creek Reservoir
4. Lower Elk Creek Falls
5. Turquoise Barn
6. Elk Creek Reservoir
7. Elk Creek Reservoir
8. Mountains
9. Viewpoint of Bridge
10. Two Barns

idahoscenics.2.vu/12

Continue east on Highway 8. In 10 miles turn left (north) and go 2.1 miles to reach **Moose Creek Reservoir (3)**. This is a pretty little lake surrounded by forest, and a great spot to fish and camp. Return to Highway 8 and turn left (east). You'll reach the town of Bovill in .5 mile. Take a little tour of the town and see all the old buildings. There's also a pretty white church on the main street. Return to the town entrance and go south on Highway 8. In 15 miles turn right (south) on Shattuck Ridge Road (Signed for Elk Falls). In .5 mile stay left, then right. Cross a gravel pit, then stay left. In 1.2 miles stay left at the sign for Elk Falls. In .6 mile you'll arrive at the trailhead for Elk Creek Falls. This 1-mile hike takes you to **Upper or Lower Elk Creek Falls (4)**. The Lower Falls are the main attraction but also require the most effort hiking out. Beautiful anytime (inaccessible in winter), but exceptionally so in late spring when the canyon walls are still green. Retrace your route to the highway, ignoring the sign for Elk River as this shortcut causes you to miss some photo opportunities.

Photography Tips

We recommend a wide angle lens for the landscapes on this route. A polarizing filter can help make your clouds pop against a blue sky. If shooting sunrise at the first location a graduated neutral density filter will be helpful. We like the waterfalls on this route in late May when the canyon walls are still green.

This Route's Sponsor

The Pie Safe
307 Main St, Deary, ID 83823
(208) 877-1200
piesafebakery.com

See page 266 for coupon

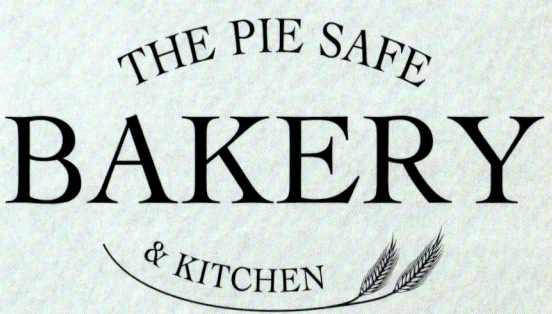

Up Next: Routes 13 or 14

Directions Continued

In 2.2 miles, as you enter town, you'll see the enormous old schoolhouse on the right. In .2 mile turn right. In .4 mile there are some old vehicles on the left followed by a big faded **turquoise barn (5)**. You'll reach **Elk Creek Reservoir (6, 7)** shortly with several access spots for camping, fishing and picnicking. The pavement ends 4.7 miles past the barn. Return to Potlatch or Moscow via Highway 8, or continue to Orofino.

To continue to Orofino, Dent Bridge Road winds through lush evergreen forests. At 8.9 miles you'll have a view of the **mountains (8)**.

In another 2.5 miles there is a partially obscured view overlooking Dworshak Reservoir. In .3 mile keep right on Dent Bridge Road. You'll find a better view of Dworshak Reservoir in .7 mile. The pavement begins in 1.8 miles. In .4 mile stay left. You'll reach Dent Bridge in 1.7 miles. In another mile there is a signed scenic **viewpoint of the bridge (9)** and reservoir. Travel 6 miles to an old barn on the right, and **two barns (10)** on the left. All are posted no trespassing, so view from the road. There is a pull-out on the right just past the second barn. Stay straight on Dent Bridge Road all the way into Orofino in about 6 miles.

Clearwater River Valley

Route 13 ◇ ----------------------------------▶ Lewiston Hill to Elk City

This Route at a Glance:

Estimated Driving Time: 5 hours

Highlights: River views, Barns, Bridges

About This Route: Start this route by making your way from the top of the Old Spiral Highway outside of Lewiston. This marvel of road engineering descends 2,000 feet into the Clearwater River Valley. Follow the river east, exploring less traveled side roads, where you'll find barns, views and small cascades. Spring is magical here, with wildflowers and raging rivers en route to Elk City, and colors abound in autumn.

Notes and Cautions: Some roads are winding with steep drop-offs and require extra attention. Respect private property. Side roads may not be accessible after fresh snow.

Directions

From Moscow, travel 23 miles south on Highway 95 or from Lewiston, travel 6 miles north. Turn onto Old Spiral Highway to the south. Stop at the Lewiston Hill Overlook in .4 mile for amazing views of the Lewis and Clark Valley and the confluence of the **Snake and Clearwater Rivers (1)**. Continue on Old Spiral Highway. In 2.2 miles there is a **lone tree (2)** on a hairpin curve. Continue downhill, watching for views and **spring wildflowers (3)** in April. You'll arrive at Highway 128 in about 5 miles; turn left. In 1 mile turn left on Highway 12. In 8 miles exit right on Highway 12. There's a view of an **old train bridge (4)** in 2 miles. In 2.7 miles cross the river on Highway 12. In 6.2 miles turn left on Cherry Lane, crossing the bridge. On the far end of the bridge you'll find a pullout for bridge views.

Continue on River Road and keep right in 1 mile toward Lenore. There is a cabin on the right in the trees in .9 mile, followed by a river view in .8 mile. You'll find a small seasonal waterfall on the left in .9 mile. Watch for an **old barn (5)** on the right in 1.5 miles. View from the road.

There's a pullout on the left for river views on the right in another .5 mile. In 1.3 miles, a shed is decorated with old signs and a quaint tire swing hangs nearby. Again, respect private property. You'll find another view in .2 mile with a narrow pullout. In .8 mile there is a barn at the intersection with Lenore Grade Road. Turn right.

Turn left on Highway 12. Proceed 18 miles to a red barn with a stone foundation on the right, and river access on the left. In 4 miles there's a pull-off on the right. Carefully cross the highway for a view of a **trestle (6)** across the river. Another trestle crosses the river in 2.7 miles. You'll find a pullout on the left in 12 miles; walk back carefully (off the highway), for views of a **train bridge (7)**. Continue into Kamiah and turn right on Main Street. Go 2 blocks to find this route's sponsor, **Hearthstone Bakery and Tea House (8),** on the right.

Steeped in Victorian-style history, the Hearthstone Bakery and Tea House in Kamiah offers freshly-baked pastries and breads, old fashioned sodas and home-baked pies. Hearthstone is open weekdays from 6 a.m.-3 p.m. serving breakfast and lunch, and until 8 p.m. on weekends for dinner. The Bakery and Tea House also caters weddings and receptions, conferences and company dinners, private parties and more. Guests and visitors love visiting this historic building, which is eligible for the National Registry of Historic Places.

From Hearthstone Restaurant and Bakery, turn right on 6th Street. Turn left on Hill Street in 2 blocks. In .5 mile turn left on Ridgewood Drive. In 2 miles you'll cross some **old tracks (9)** that look nice in spring and fall and, in

idahoscenics.2.vu/13

Points of Interest
1. Snake and Clearwater Rivers
2. Lone Tree
3. Wildflowers
4. Old Train Bridge
5. Old Barn
6. Trestle
7. Train Bridge
8. Sponsor - Hearthstone Bakery and Teahouse
9. Old Tracks
10. Viewpoint
11. Winding Road
12. Old Barn
13. Canyon Views
14. View over the River Canyon

Directions Continued

another .5 mile, watch for an old tractor on the right. There's a pullout on the left for valley and river views in 2 miles, followed by another **viewpoint (10)** in 1.7 miles. A small seasonal waterfall slides down a rock face on the right in .3 mile. Follow Ridgewood Drive to Thenon Street and turn left, then right on B Street. Turn left on Highway 13.

Turn right on Broadway Avenue in .2 mile, then stay right on Toll Road in .7 mile. In 2 miles there's an old house and barn. In .3 mile stay right on Clear Creek Road; in 1.8 miles, a small barn on the right makes a nice shot with the **winding road (11)**. There's a barn on the left in 3.7 miles. In .8 mile stay right on Clear Creek Road.

In 3 miles turn right on Jericho Road, then right on Battle Ridge Road in .1 mile. A very **old barn (12)** still stands on the right in 4.3 miles. Stay left in 1.3 miles. In 2.2 miles turn left on Highway 13. There's a barn on the right in 5.8 miles. A pullout on the right 2 miles farther provides river access. In 1 mile there's a small pullout on the left; walk back along the highway for bridge views. In 1.5 miles there's a falls on the right. Park carefully off the highway. Park in the large pullout on the right in .9 mile and walk upstream for a cabin view, then down the bank to the river for bridge views. In 2.4 miles go right to conclude the route in Grangeville. You'll reach the town in 10 miles, or extend your tour by going left on Highway 14.

Continue along the scenic South Fork of the Clearwater River at least 11 miles to see the best river and **canyon views (13)** along the route. You may wish to go farther, turning around when you desire or when it reaches the small town of Elk City. On your return, turn left on Mt. Idaho Grade Road. In 1.7 miles there's a hay shed on the right with a pullout just beyond. In .3 mile a large pullout on the left gives you a view over the **river canyon (14)** far below. There are several more viewpoints over the next two miles. Evening light should be nice here. Watch for a rusty old kiln on the right in a couple of miles. Stay on Mt. Idaho Grade Road through a series of corners, then turn left on Highway 13. Arrive in Grangeville. See routes 14 or 17 for excellent lodging options.

Photography Tips

A mid-range zoom lens will be good for most of the barns on this route. A telephoto may be desired for the distant trestles. Valley views begin and end this route and should be nice in both evening or morning light.

This Route's Sponsor

Hearthstone Bakery and Tea House
502 Main, Kamiah, ID 83536
(208) 935-1912
hearthstonebakery.com

See page 268 for coupon

Up Next: Routes 14 or 17

Camas Prairie and Winchester

Route 14 ◇ ------------------▶ Grangeville to Lewiston

This Route at a Glance:

Estimated Driving Time: 6 hours

Highlights: Trestles, Barns, and Lake

About This Route: On this route, we'll see many of the old Camas Prairie Railroad trestles, and visit scenic Winchester Lake State Park. We'll also see many old barns, and a historic schoolhouse. Known as the "railroad on stilts," the short line ran from Grangeville to Lewiston for 92 years, beginning in December 1908. Besides featuring more than a dozen trestles in one five-mile stretch, the line's second subdivision features a large steel viaduct over Lawyer's Canyon. Several other trestles can be seen from the highway, although one on the Winchester Grade burned in a wildfire in 2011.

Notes and Cautions: This route takes advantage of lodging offered by our route sponsor and is divided into two sections. The first, a loop in the Grangeville area, can be done in an afternoon. The following day you can proceed on the remainder of the route heading north. Some roads may not be accessible after snowfall. Be very careful when parking along and crossing the highway on foot. Respect private property. Winchester State Park requires a day-use fee. Bring your fishing gear and spend some time here.

Directions

From Main Street and Hwy 95 in Grangeville, head south on Hwy 95. In 1.6 miles turn right on Tolo Lake Road. In .8 mile continue straight across Johnston Road. In 1.4 miles there is a unique **old red barn (1)** on the right. You'll find a private collection of **old colorful tractors (2)** in .5 mile, which can be shot from the road. Turn right on Lake Road in 1.7 miles and, in another 1.7 miles turn left on **Canyon Road (3)**. In 1 mile turn right on Market Road. Cross Hwy 95 in .8 mile. There are 2 barns on the left in .9 mile. In .3 mile turn right on Two Mile Road. In 1 mile turn right on Lake Road, then in 1.2 miles turn right on Denver

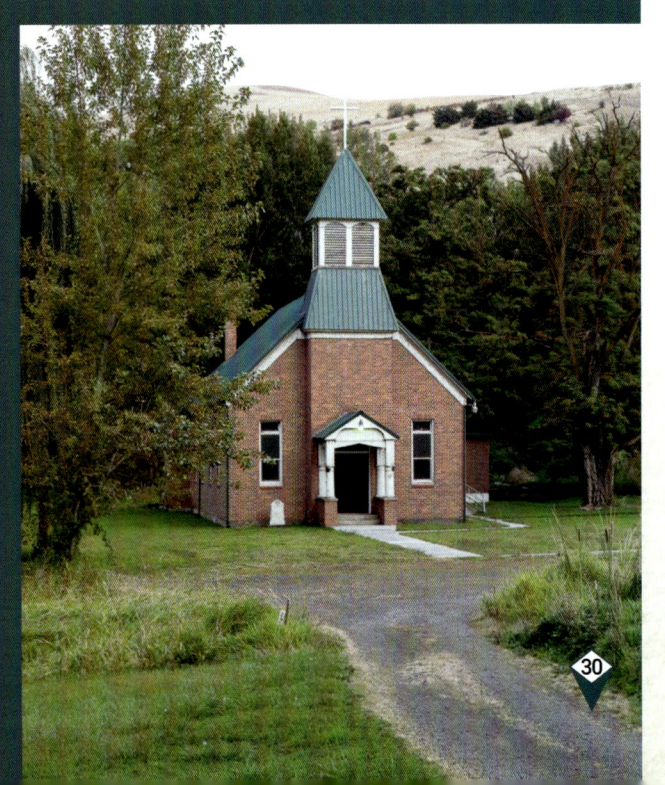

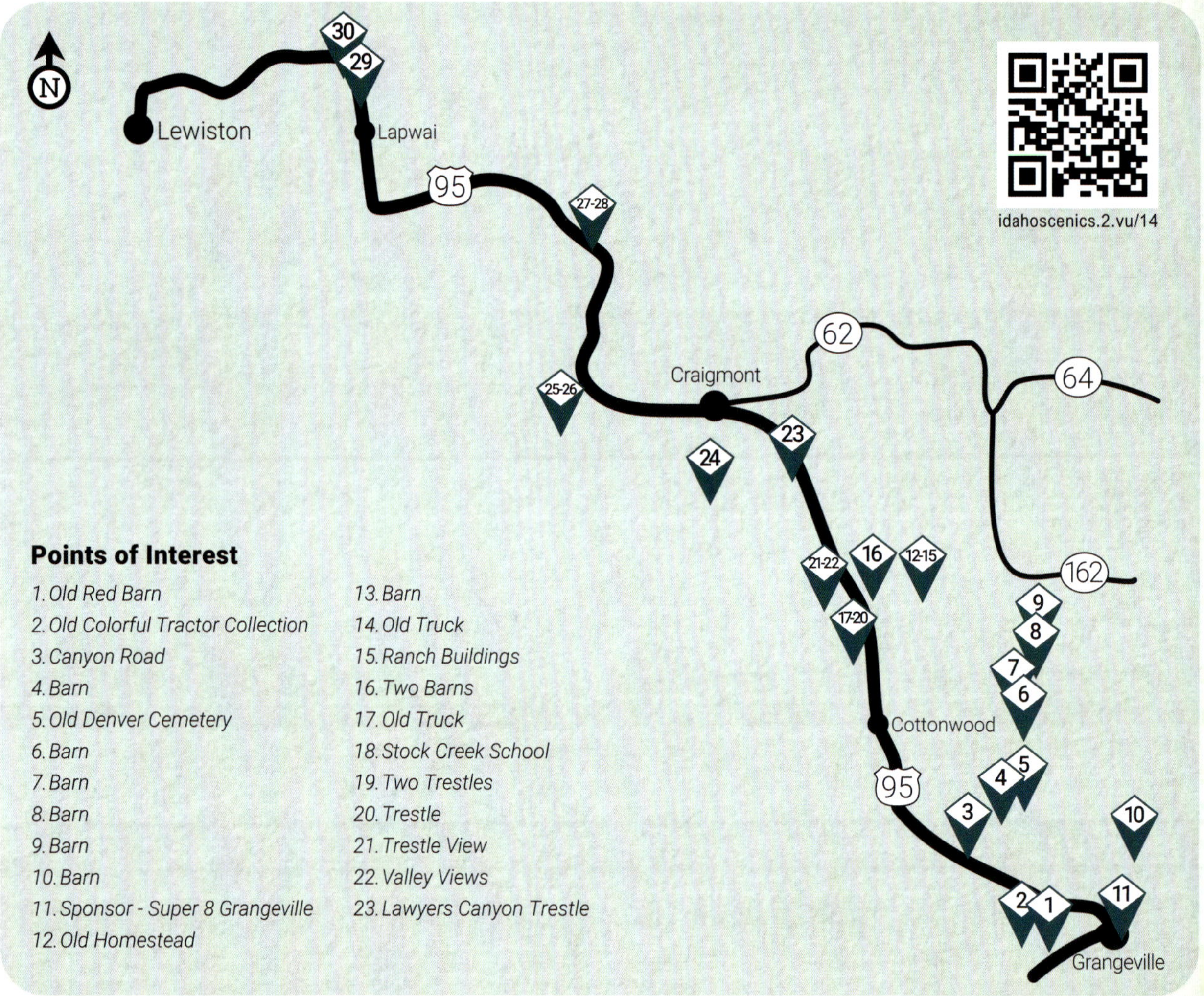

30

N
Lewiston
Lapwai
95
Craigmont
62
64
162
Cottonwood
Grangeville
idahoscenics.2.vu/14
30
29
27-28
25-26
24
23
21-22
16
12-15
17-20
9
8
7
6
5
4
3
10
2
1
11
Points of Interest
1. Old Red Barn
2. Old Colorful Tractor Collection
3. Canyon Road
4. Barn
5. Old Denver Cemetery
6. Barn
7. Barn
8. Barn
9. Barn
10. Barn
11. Sponsor - Super 8 Grangeville
12. Old Homestead
13. Barn
14. Old Truck
15. Ranch Buildings
16. Two Barns
17. Old Truck
18. Stock Creek School
19. Two Trestles
20. Trestle
21. Trestle View
22. Valley Views
23. Lawyers Canyon Trestle

Road. There is a **barn (4)** here at the intersection. In .6 mile turn left on Denver Cemetery Road. You'll reach the old **Denver Cemetery (5)** in .8 mile. In .7 mile turn right on McDonald Road. Turn left on Kube Road in 1.2 miles, then stay right on Kube Road in .5 mile. In .9 mile, look back for a view of a **barn (6)** with a quilt motif. Turn left on Old Highway 7.

In .4 mile another quilt barn is on the right. In 1.3 miles a **barn (7)** sits on the right side of the highway. Park safely to photograph this. Turn right on Bryant Road in .9 mile, then left on Crea Road in 1 mile. There's a **barn (8)** on the right in .3 mile. Another **barn (9)** in 1.1 miles sits in a valley. In 2 miles turn right on Hwy 162. In 1.2 miles turn right on Yellow Bull Road, then turn right on Red Rock Road in 3.6 miles.

Directions Continued

Turn left on Reservation Line Road in 3.7 miles. In 2 miles there's a small barn on the right. In .9 mile turn right on Long Haul Road. In almost 2 miles turn left on Day Road, then right on Long Haul Road. In 1.6 miles there's a **barn (10)** on the right. This is a good sunset location.

In .4 mile turn left on Halford Road. There's another barn on the right in .3 mile. Turn right on Stites Road in .7 mile. Follow a few miles as it bears right into Grangeville, then turn right on Main Street. Turn left on Hwy 95 in 1 mile, then turn left on W. South 1st Street and arrive at this route sponsor, **Super 8 Grangeville (11)**.

Awarded the title of #1 Super 8 hotel in North America in 2016-2017, at the Super 8 Grangeville all rooms include en suite bathrooms and flat-screen TVs with cable/satellite channels, plus mini fridges and coffeemakers. Some have skylights. Suites add living areas and/or whirlpool tubs. There's free WiFi in every room and kids 17 and under stay free with an adult. Amenities include complimentary continental breakfast, an indoor pool and a fitness center.

Continue on this route by heading right (north) on Hwy 95. In 18 miles turn right on Jentges Road, then, in 2.5 miles, turn left on Riener Road. In 1.5 miles, a valley view to the right

Directions Continued

with an **old homestead (12)** provides a great sunrise location. In .3 mile there's a **barn (13)** on the left with two cupolas. In .8 mile an **old truck (14)** sits in front of an old shed. There are other vehicles here too, but you'll need permission to photograph them. Do not trespass. There are **old ranch buildings (15)** on the right in another .2 mile. Turn left on Meadow Creek Road in .3 mile. In 1.4 miles turn left on Windy Ridge Road then turn right. In 1.3 miles **two barns (16)** are on the right. In .4 mile turn right on Windy Loop then turn left (south) on Highway 95 just ahead. In 2 miles turn left on Substation Road. There is an **old truck (17)** here beyond the fence. In .3 mile you'll arrive at the **Stock Creek School (18)**. It sits in a field behind a fence but is relatively easy to photograph or view. Respect the property. Turn right on Reservation Road in .3 mile for a view of **two trestles (19)**. Continue under the trestle for .4 mile, then make a U-turn for a great view of the **trestle (20)** you crossed beneath. Return to Highway 95 and turn left. In .2 mile turn left onto Sandspur Road and follow it for views of another trestle, until it reaches Cummins Road in about 2.4 miles. Turn left on Cummins Road.

Stay right at the 'Y'. in .6 mile, then turn right (north) on Lauer Crossing (Crossing) Road. In less than 1 mile you'll find trestle views on the left. Return to Cummings Road and turn right.

In .2 mile park and walk south on the route of the old Camas Prairie to an up-close **trestle view (21)** in about .5 mile. Continue on Cummins Road 1 mile to Ferdinand Butte Road and turn right. Starting here, you'll encounter great views over the **valley (22)** with distant trestles and barns over the next mile. In two miles from Cummins road you'll arrive in Ferdinand. Turn left on 3rd Street, then left on Main Street. There is a barn on the left. Stay right on Old Hwy 95. In 2.7 miles turn left (north) onto Highway 95. In 1.3 miles there's a large pullout on the left with interpretive signage. View the **Lawyers Canyon Trestle (23)** here. In 5.2 miles turn left on Westlake Road for another old cabin. In one mile there's a cemetery on the left. There's an **old cabin (24)** on the right in 2 more miles. Continue another mile for a small older house. Return to Highway 95 and turn left.

Photography Tips

Start the first portion of this route in the late afternoon to shoot in the evening light. For the second portion depart about 45 minutes before sunrise for potential pre-sunrise color at a great location. A telephoto lens is useful for some of the trestles and barns. A graduated neutral density filter would be useful for sunrise.

This Route's Sponsor

Grangeville Super 8
801 W South 1st St,
Grangeville, ID 83530
(208) 983-1002 | super8idaho.com

See page 268 for more information

Directions Continued

In 4.3 miles turn left on US Bus 95 (Joseph Avenue). In 2.3 miles turn left on Camas Street and follow to **Winchester Lake State Park (25)**. Explore the State Park day use areas, especially the cove with the **footbridge (26)** near the back of the park. Return to US Bus 95 (Joseph Avenue) and turn left. In .2 mile turn right on Clark Street. Follow back to Hwy 95 and turn left. In 6.3 miles a large pullout on the left of the highway gives a distant view of one of the **high trestles (27)** and a **close-up (28)** of another.

In 15.7 miles turn left on Red Duck Lane then stay left. There is a **barn (29)** in less than .3 mile on the left. Make a U-turn and follow Thunder Hill Road back to Hwy 95. Cross Highway 95. You'll find the Old Watson Store and **Spaulding church (30)** within .4 mile. Continue on Watson Store Road over Lapwai Creek to a parking area and explore this area on foot. You'll find a riverside park, historical buildings, an old bridge over tracks and Lapwai Creek. On your return, after crossing the creek and tracks, turn right to visit the Nez Perce Historical Park Visitor Center, then exit onto Hwy 95 by turning right. Arrive in Lewiston in 10 miles.

Up Next: Routes 11, 12, or 13

Whitewater and Bitterroot Mountains

Route 15 ◊ ------------------→ Kooskia to Lolo Pass

This Route at a Glance:

Estimated Driving Time: 6 hours

Highlights: Rivers, Pack bridges, and Waterfalls

About This Route: This is a dream trip for anyone who enjoys driving along scenic river corridors. Watch whitewater rafters battle with Class V rapids in May and June. In mid to late June you can visit another camas marsh near the crest of the Bitterroot Range. The route also takes you to a small cedar grove and a couple of roadside waterfalls. Or take a hike to a hot springs to stretch your legs. You can cast a line for trout, or pick your own huckleberries later in the summer, or enjoy the colors of autumn as you wind your way through this gorgeous river canyon.

Notes and Cautions: This route features primarily winding river roads. The side trips are mostly gravel and can be bumpy. Rattlesnakes are especially common along the Selway River. Wildlife is abundant and can include cougar, moose, elk, deer, black and grizzly bear. Hike with bear spray. Leave Kooskia with a full tank of gas and travel with an ax, shovel and bucket. Downed trees are common on side trips, especially in burned areas or early in the season. The start this route in the afternoon to take advantage of lodging with our route sponsor.

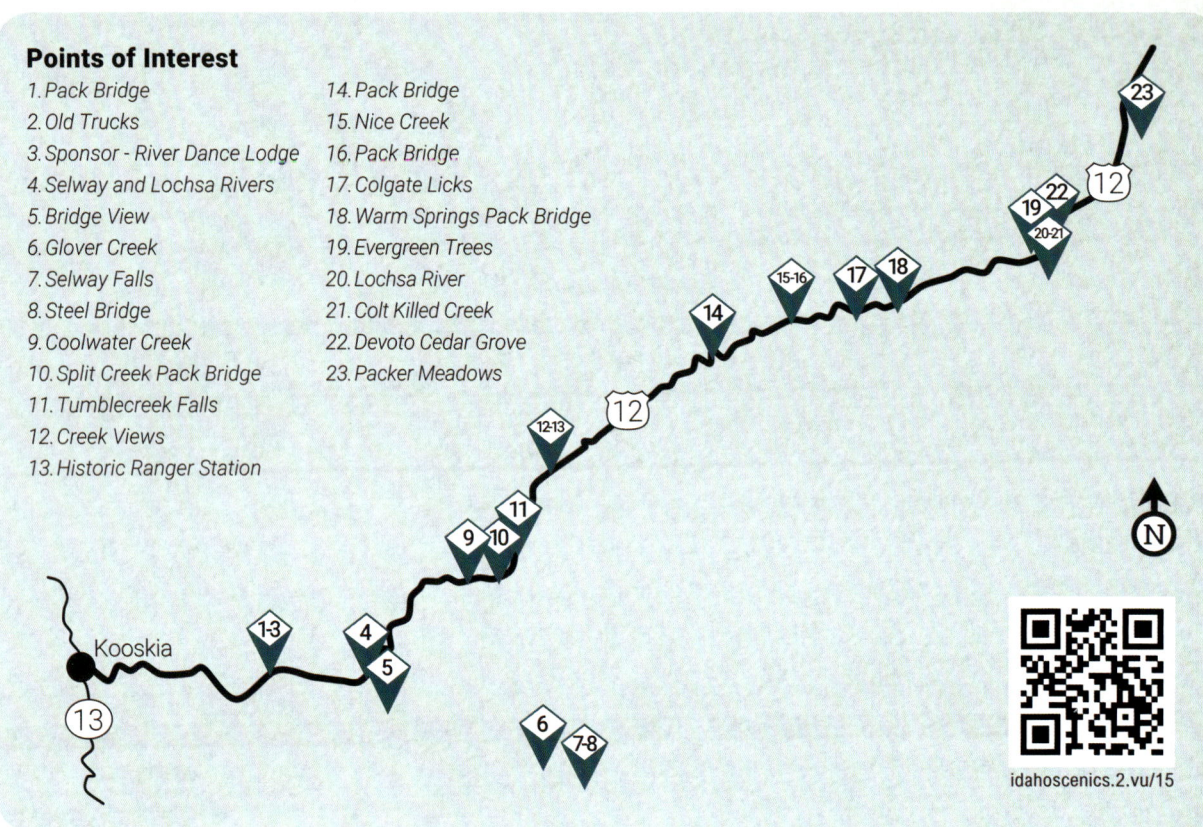

Points of Interest
1. Pack Bridge
2. Old Trucks
3. Sponsor - River Dance Lodge
4. Selway and Lochsa Rivers
5. Bridge View
6. Glover Creek
7. Selway Falls
8. Steel Bridge
9. Coolwater Creek
10. Split Creek Pack Bridge
11. Tumblecreek Falls
12. Creek Views
13. Historic Ranger Station
14. Pack Bridge
15. Nice Creek
16. Pack Bridge
17. Colgate Licks
18. Warm Springs Pack Bridge
19. Evergreen Trees
20. Lochsa River
21. Colt Killed Creek
22. Devoto Cedar Grove
23. Packer Meadows

idahoscenics.2.vu/15

Directions

Go east on Highway 12 from the junction of highways 12 and 13 at Kooskia. At 3.7 miles there are some unique rock formations in the river, accessible via a pullout on the right. In another 3.8 miles, watch for a barn on the left. Park in a small pullout on the left in another 8.5 miles for a view of the **Pack Bridge (1)** over the Middle Fork of the Clearwater. Cross the highway carefully! In another .2 mile there is a large collection of **old trucks (2)** on the left. Respect the property.

In .4 miles the **River Dance Lodge (3)** is on the left. Check in to our route's sponsor for lodging before proceeding. Idaho's finest adventure resort featuring hand-crafted custom log cabins that offer rustic luxury and are complemented by an exciting choice of outdoor adventures including whitewater rafting, biking, fly fishing, hiking and more. River Dance Lodge, an impressive lodge in the heart of Idaho, is the ultimate location for adventures on the trails, rivers and

Directions Continued

mountains of Idaho. Enjoy a unique dining experience at the Lodge's onsite restaurant, the Syringa Café, serving healthy Northwest style cuisine and featuring our famous homemade huckleberry pie. The resort is located near the banks of the Clearwater River where views are stunning and while relaxing in your own private hot tub you'll gaze upon forested mountains and the free-flowing Middle Fork of the Clearwater.

You'll find the confluence of the **Selway and Lochsa Rivers (4)** in 2.6 miles. For an extended side trip for a view of Selway Falls (about 1.5 hours and 36 miles, round trip), turn right (south) on Selway River Road. In 2.5 miles there is a **bridge view (5)**. In another 2 miles there is a fishing pond on the right. This is a nice spot for a stroll, or to dip your fishing line. In 2 miles there are 2 old cabins on the left. Watch for a nicely-formed waterfall across the river just past a mid-stream island in 5.3 miles. This could be shot with a telephoto lens. In 3.3 miles you'll cross **Glover Creek (6)**. This stream with lush vegetation can have wild roses lining its banks in mid-June. You'll pass several photogenic creeks on this side trip, some unnamed. Arrive at **Selway Falls (7)** in another 3.1 miles. These rapids rage in the spring. Be

Directions Continued

careful at this roadside view that drops steeply to the river below. From here you also have a distant view of a nice old **steel bridge (8)**. Proceed up the road until you can safely turn around. Retrace your route to Highway 12 and Riverdance Lodge, then continue this route in the morning.

From the lodge turn left (east) on Highway 12. **Coolwater Creek (9)** joins the Lochsa on the opposite side of the river in 12.6 miles. Fire Creek also emerges from the forest on the far shore 2 miles farther. Both are very pretty. In .4 mile there is a pull-out on the right where you can view the **Split Creek Pack Bridge (10)**. In another .2 mile you'll reach the official parking lot on the left. In almost 2 miles **Tumble Creek Falls (11)** cascades right next to the highway. There is a pull-out on the right just beyond the falls. You can park here and walk back for a photo opportunity.

Cross Fish Creek in 7 miles. Take the road (NF 462) immediately across the bridge to the left. In about .1 mile you'll reach a bridge on the left. Stop here and walk out on the bridge for **creek views (12)**. Find a place to turn around and return to Highway 12. Turn left. In 1.4 miles you can stop on the left to visit the **historic ranger station (13)**. In 7 more miles there is another pretty creek on the left with a pullout on the right.

Travel 7 more miles to another **pack bridge (14)**. These are great stops to walk out over the river and take in the view. In 6.8 miles there is a nice **creek (15)** with a trail alongside. It's .8 mile to the next **pack bridge (16)** and, 5 miles beyond that, you'll reach **Colgate Licks (17).** This 1 mile interpretive trail takes you on a loop through the forest and by the historic salt licks. Continue east 3.5 miles to the **Warm Springs Pack Bridge (18)** and the trail to Jerry Johnson Hot Springs. This 2.6 mile out and back trail is relatively easy, and the reward is a soak in a hot pool with a waterfall. Continue east on Highway 12 for 10.7 miles.

Option to Lolo Motorway: All-wheel drive recommended. Turn left on NF 569 (Parachute Hill Road). Travel through lush **evergreen trees (19)** as you make your way up Parachute Hill. In 4.5 miles stay left on NF 569. In .5 mile you'll reach a view over the Lochsa River Valley. In one more mile Powell Junction will be signed. Take

Directions Continued

NF 500. You'll reach another view in .4 mile. Continue .6 mile to the sign for the Lolo Motorway. This is the beginning of the 100-mile backcountry road roughly following the route of Lewis and Clark. It takes several days and should not be attempted without research, detailed maps, extra gas and a chainsaw, as well as survival supplies. Return to Highway 12 and turn left.

In 1.6 miles turn right (south) on NF 111 (Elk Summit Road). In .4 mile stay left. In .7 mile you'll reach two creek crossings; these are the headwater streams of the **Lochsa River (20)**; Crooked Fork Creek and **Colt Killed Creek (21)**. Return to Highway 12 and turn right. In 1.7 miles you'll arrive at the **Devoto Cedar Grove (22)** on both sides of the highway. Two short trails (one on each side of the highway) take you through a beautiful cedar grove. In 11 miles you'll reach Lolo Pass. Just past the visitor center at the second entrance, turn right on NF 373. Stay left on NF 373. In 1.3 miles you'll arrive at **Packer Meadows (23)**, an exceptional camas lily viewing spot in mid-June. Continue on to Missoula, then back into Idaho via Missoula and Interstate 90 to the north or Highway 93 south to Salmon, or return to Kooskia.

Photography Tips

Some cross-river creeks and falls require a telephoto lens. Packer Meadows camas bloom is usually peak in mid-June. Both sunrise and sunset should be good here, but you'll want waterproof boots for the best viewing opportunities. In spring the streams and rivers on this route run high and fast. Moderately fast shutter speeds are recommended to prevent highlight blow out. Later in the summer and fall, slower shutter speeds can be preferable. In October there's lots of autumn color to be found along this route.

This Route's Sponsor

River Dance Lodge
7743 US-12, Kooskia, ID 83539
(866) 769-8747
riverdancelodge.com

See page 268 for coupon

RIVER DANCE LODGE
IDAHO'S OUTDOOR ADVENTURE RESORT

Up Next: Routes 16 or 23

Clearwater River North Fork

Route 16 ◇----------▶ Hoodoo Pass to Kamiah

This Route at a Glance:

Estimated Driving Time: 8 hours

Highlights: Wildflowers, Rivers, Autumn Color

About This Route: Those who enjoy remote routes will be rewarded on this trek through the Bitterroot Mountains. It features showy summer wildflower displays, riverside stands of cedar trees in riparian habitats, blue ribbon trout fishing, barns, impressive pack bridges and one of the lesser known camas prairies. This roughly 160-mile route intersects with the Lewis-Clark Trail near Weippe.

Notes and Cautions: This is one of the longest and most remote routes in the book. You'll be in grizzly and black bear country, and other big game may be encountered. Roads are winding, often with sections that can be dusty and rough. Start with a full tank of gas and travel with emergency food, water and supplies including ax, shovel and bucket. This route is only accessible during summer and fall. Take camping equipment or start early.

Directions

Exit Interstate 90 at Superior Montana (Exit 47). Turn south and then left (east) on Diamond Match Road. The pavement ends in 5.9 miles. The road winds up the Bitterroot Mountains and reaches a small pullout on the left in 9.6 miles, for views over a scenic canyon. In 4.9 miles you'll pass the trailhead for Heart Lake and then Hoodoo Lake in another 1.9 miles. These alpine lakes are both accessed via hikes of fewer than 3 miles each way.

In 2.7 miles, take in the view at Hoodoo Pass. You are now entering Idaho. In .3 mile a pullout on the right affords nice views of summer **wildflowers (1)** and the view into Idaho. Enjoy the descent into the Clearwater National Forest. In 6.1 miles, stop along the creek and relish the summer **wildflowers (2)**. The road crosses Long Creek in 4.3 miles. Keep left on NF 250. In another .5 mile cross Lake Creek and stay right on NF 250. In 3.4 miles stay straight, again on NF 250, and cross the North Fork of the Clearwater River. Here you begin the journey through the Black Canyon of the North Fork of the Clearwater. This scenic section has some primitive campsites, large cedar trees and beautiful river views. In 4 miles you'll cross Hidden Creek, a very pretty little stream. There's a pullout on the right and a developed campground just after the creek. Not far beyond the campground there was a large blowout on one of the streams. For a very short section the road is rough and not recommended for low clearance vehicles. Go very slowly.

Watch for a **small waterfall (3)** on the right in about 9 miles. For an optional trip up Kelly Creek, turn left on NF 255 in 1.2 miles. **Kelly Creek (4)** is a blue ribbon trout stream. This wild trout fishery is catch and release only. Kelly Forks Campground is on the right In ¼ mile. In 1.2 miles **Junction Creek Pack Bridge (5)** crosses Kelly Creek. Explore and/or fish as far as you desire before returning to the Junction of NF 255 and NF 250. Stay straight on NF 250. In 9.9 miles you'll reach another pack bridge, this time over the North Fork of the Clearwater River.

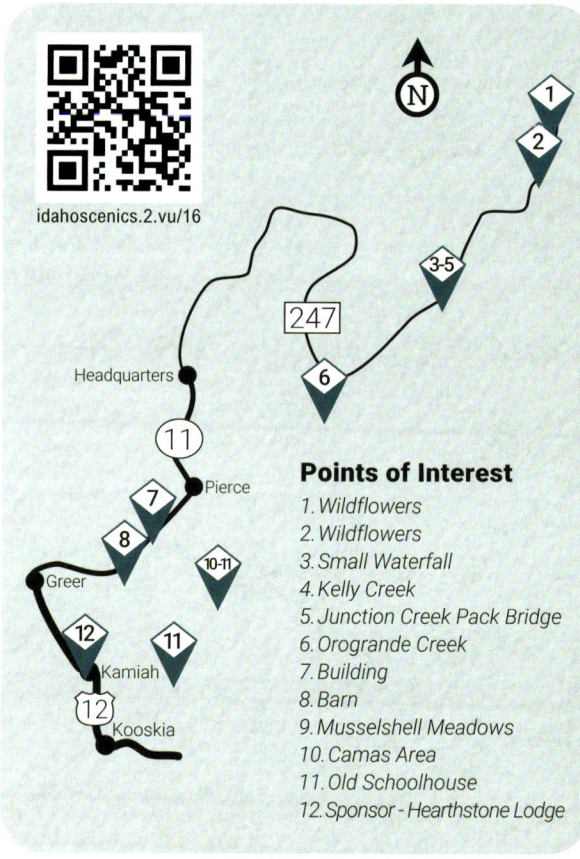

idahoscenics.2.vu/16

Points of Interest
1. Wildflowers
2. Wildflowers
3. Small Waterfall
4. Kelly Creek
5. Junction Creek Pack Bridge
6. Orogrande Creek
7. Building
8. Barn
9. Musselshell Meadows
10. Camas Area
11. Old Schoolhouse
12. Sponsor - Hearthstone Lodge

In 1 mile a small stream provides a nice photo opportunity. Weitas Creek Campground, in 3 miles, provides another camping option.

Enjoy the views as you travel along the North Fork of the Clearwater. In 4.3 miles turn left on French Mountain Road, which follows **Orogrande Creek (6)** and is moderately rough gravel. In 8.5 miles there's a small waterfall on the right. In 2.7 miles the pavement begins. Stay left on NF 250 and view the summer

Directions Continued

wildflowers and evergreen forests as you cross French Mountain Saddle. In 9.4 miles turn left on Highway 11. In .4 mile there are some vintage vehicles on private property. Shoot from the road. Another batch of old farm implements and a **building (7)** can be found in 5.6 miles on the right. In 4.9 miles there is a barn on the right. Continue into the community of Weippe, turning left on Pierce Avenue. Turn right on Cemetery Road in .3 mile. In .7 mile is a distant view of a nice **barn (8)**. In spring there can be wildflowers in the foreground. In 1.1 miles turn left on Camas Road, and the access for the Camas Prairie is in .4 mile. The camas generally bloom in late May to mid-June. There is a visitor center just ahead.

In .4 mile turn left on Larsen Road. In another .4 mile turn left on Chapman Road. There is a barn on the left in .3 mile. In .9 mile turn right on Musselshell Road and in 7.2 miles stay straight. In .2 mile there is another barn on the left. Go right toward Kamiah in 3.5 miles. In .7 mile you'll see the access point to **Musselshell Meadows (9)**. This is another **camas area (10)** and usually nicer than the first. You'll cross Lolo Creek in 1 mile. There is a pullout just past the bridge. In 4.7 miles is Lolo Creek Campground. There is a partially obscured view of the Canyon in 3.9 miles. Park very carefully.

In 7.4 miles you'll see an **old schoolhouse (11)** on the right. In 11.4 miles go left on Woodland Road and turn right on Highway 12 in .5 mile. Proceed on Highway 12 for 2.8 miles through the town of Kamiah to our route sponsor, **Hearthstone Lodge (12)** on the left.

Overlooking the peaceful Clearwater River and the historic Lewis and Clark Trail, the elegant and romantic Hearthstone Lodge is equipped with world-class amenities. Guests will find Jacuzzi tubs for two, forest and river view balconies, cathedral ceilings, canopied custom beds with antique headboards, wood burning fireplaces, embroidered robes, and delicious breakfasts in their in-town bakery to start your day. Each guest room features its own unique style and decor.

Photography Tips

A polarizing and/or neutral density filter may be useful for photographing the small streams and waterfalls on this route. You'll want a wide angle for the pack bridges, and may wish to wade into the river for the best angles, provided the water is low in mid to late summer and fall. A wide angle lens is great for expansive valley views.

This Route's Sponsor

Hearthstone Lodge
MP 64 3250, US-12,
Kamiah, ID 83536

(208) 935-1492
hearthstonelodge.com

See page 268 for coupon

Up Next: Routes 14, 17, or 23

White Bird and Hells Canyon
Route 17 ⬦------------▶ South of Grangeville

This Route at a Glance:

Estimated Driving Time: 5 hours

Highlights: Views, wildflowers, barns

About This Route: If you're crazy about views and don't mind winding mountain roads, consider taking this route, which starts on Whitebird Summit on Old Highway 95. Relish the views over the Salmon River Valley, with the Seven Devils Mountains visible on a clear day. From there, we'll cross the mountains before dropping into the heart of Hells Canyon at Pittsburg Landing. This route features frequent ascents and descents. With wildflower viewing in the spring, we recommend this route for late April or May.

Notes and Cautions: This route contains many elevation changes. Roads are winding with steep drop-offs. Drive slowly and with extreme caution. Make sure your brakes are in good working order before proceeding on this route. Rattlesnakes are very common in Hells Canyon. Do not walk through tall grass. Watch your footsteps on all trails. Not all roads may be accessible in early spring, late fall or winter.

Directions

From Grangeville go south on Highway 95 and cross Whitebird Summit. As you round the corner, you'll find an expansive view of the Salmon River Valley below. Pull off in the large turnout on the left and enjoy the immensity of this **scene (1, 2)**. On a clear day the Seven Devils Range can be seen on the horizon. This would be a good place for a sunrise shoot, especially if you have had the pleasure of staying the night at the **Whitebird Summit Lodge and Ranch (3)**. Our route sponsor is perfectly positioned for starting this journey. Located on the summit of White Bird Hill, this bed and breakfast is just what you are looking for. A place with a lot more peace, quiet and relaxation, while you can explore their wide open spaces on a hike, horse trail rides, sightseeing adventure, fishing, photography or just grab a good book and relax on the deck overlooking the Salmon River canyon. You'll rediscover the true meaning of life, at this safe haven.

Even if you didn't spend the night there, you can still make the short drive to the lodge and enjoy the **views (4)** along the way. Take Old White Bird Hill Road east from the parking pullout and proceed up the hill one mile. The lodge is on the left.

Return to Highway 95 and turn left. In one mile turn left on Old Highway 95. This old grade winds its way down many switchbacks with **views (5)** and wildflowers in spring, eventually reaching the trailhead to the site of the Battle of White Bird Canyon, where the Nez Perce fought the first battle of the Nez Perce War against the U.S. Government in 1877. At the bottom of the hill watch for Free Use Road, and turn left. There is a nice **barn (6)** on the right as you head up the hill. In 2 miles there are **twin barns (7)** on the left.

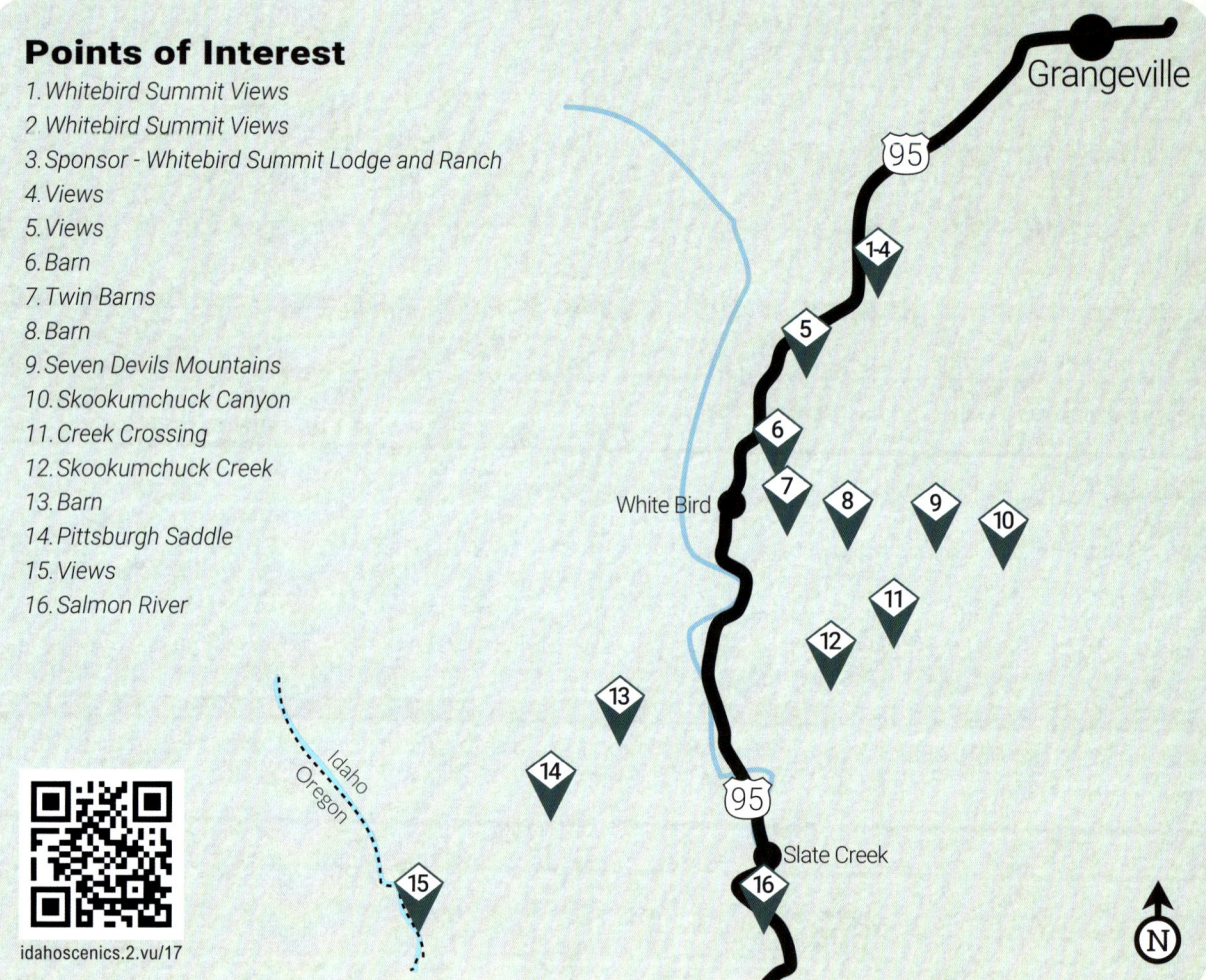

Points of Interest
1. Whitebird Summit Views
2. Whitebird Summit Views
3. Sponsor - Whitebird Summit Lodge and Ranch
4. Views
5. Views
6. Barn
7. Twin Barns
8. Barn
9. Seven Devils Mountains
10. Skookumchuck Canyon
11. Creek Crossing
12. Skookumchuck Creek
13. Barn
14. Pittsburgh Saddle
15. Views
16. Salmon River

idahoscenics.2.vu/17

Be careful parking on the hill. In another .5 mile there is a distant downhill view of another **barn (8)**. As you climb, watch for views of the **Seven Devils Mountains (9)**. In spring you can have this view with the added bonus of wildflowers in the foreground. After 5 more miles stay left on NF 243. In another mile turn right on a two track. In a short distance through the trees you'll arrive at an enormous view over the

Photography Tips

Photography notes: A wide angle lens is best for the landscapes on this route. You may want a telephoto lens to shoot distant views of the Seven Devils Mountains. A mid range zoom is good for Skookumchuck Creek as well as most of the barns.

Directions Continued

Skookumchuck Canyon (10) with the Seven Devils Range as a backdrop. This can be a great wildflower location in May and is also a good spot to car camp. Return to Banner Ridge Road and turn left. When you reach the junction in 1 mile, turn left. In 3 miles turn left on Foskett Grade Road. In 1.5 miles turn right on Skookumchuck Road. It's a little over 1 mile to a **creek crossing (11)** worth a look. For the next 5.5 miles, follow **Skookumchuck Creek (12)** with numerous photo opportunities as you make your way back to Highway 95.

Cross Highway 95 into the Skookumchuck Creek day use area. Here you'll find Salmon River access and a couple of old cabins on the far side of the picnic area. Turn left (north) on Highway 95 as you exit the day use area. In 2.7 miles turn left on Old Highway 95. In 1 mile turn left to cross the Salmon River. Just across the river turn left on Deer Creek Road. Follow Deer Creek Road for about 19 miles to Pittsburg Landing, watching for a **barn (13)** on the right and expansive views into Hells Canyon from the top of **Pittsburg Saddle (14)**. At the base of the hill in Hells Canyon turn left for the Kirkwood Ranch Trailhead and Snake River views. It is about a 2 mile hike to Kirby Creek Lodge, but a walk of any distance along the river is worth the **views (15)**. On the way out stop back at Pittsburg Saddle and watch sunset over Hells Canyon. Return to Highway 95. Turn right to go south into Riggins and enjoy the drive along the **Salmon River (16)** or left to return to Grangeville or Whitebird Summit Lodge.

This Route's Sponsor

Whitebird Summit Lodge
2141 Old White Bird Hill Road
Grangeville, ID
(208) 983-1802
whitebirdsummitlodge.com

See page 268 for coupon

Up Next: Routes 14, 18, or 19

Salmon River and the Seven Devils

Route 18 ◇----------------------------▶ Riggins East and West

This Route at a Glance:

Estimated Driving Time: 5 hours

Highlights: River, bridges, barns, mountaintop vistas

About This Route: Watch sunrise over the Salmon River as it emerges from the River of No Return Wilderness area. Then follow the river back to town seeing old barns, beautiful tributaries, bridges and Canyon vistas. Wind your way up the Seven Devils mountain road for a sunset view from Heaven's Gate fire lookout.. You'll also have a view into Hells Canyon and can visit an alpine lake.

Notes and Cautions: This route involves very winding gravel roads with extreme changes in elevation. Make sure your brakes are good and be alert at all times. Falling rocks are a hazard along the Big Salmon River Road. Rattlesnakes are common in the rocks along the river. The last section of road to the Heavens Gate Lookout tower can be very intimidating. Drive slowly. Respect private property at sites along the river. French Creek Road rises high above the river and crosses the mountains into McCall by way of Burgdorf Hot Springs. Only attempt this loop during the summer and fall.

Directions

From Riggins, head south on Hwy 95. Approximately .6 mile past town turn left on Big Salmon River Road. In 6 miles, a small pullout on the left gives you a nice spot to wait for sunrise with a view of a **bridge (1)** over the Salmon River and canyon. Continue and cross the bridge. Park on the right and walk on the two-track road on the left (west) for another angle to view the **bridge (2)**. From this parking area you can also view a creek cascading in across the river. A short distance up the road another pullout gives views of the other side of the bridge. In 2.5 miles parking on the right gives views of the private bridge to Riggins Hot Springs. Then park at the day-use for Allison Creek in .4 mile for river access. Walk across the road for views of **Allison Creek (3)**.

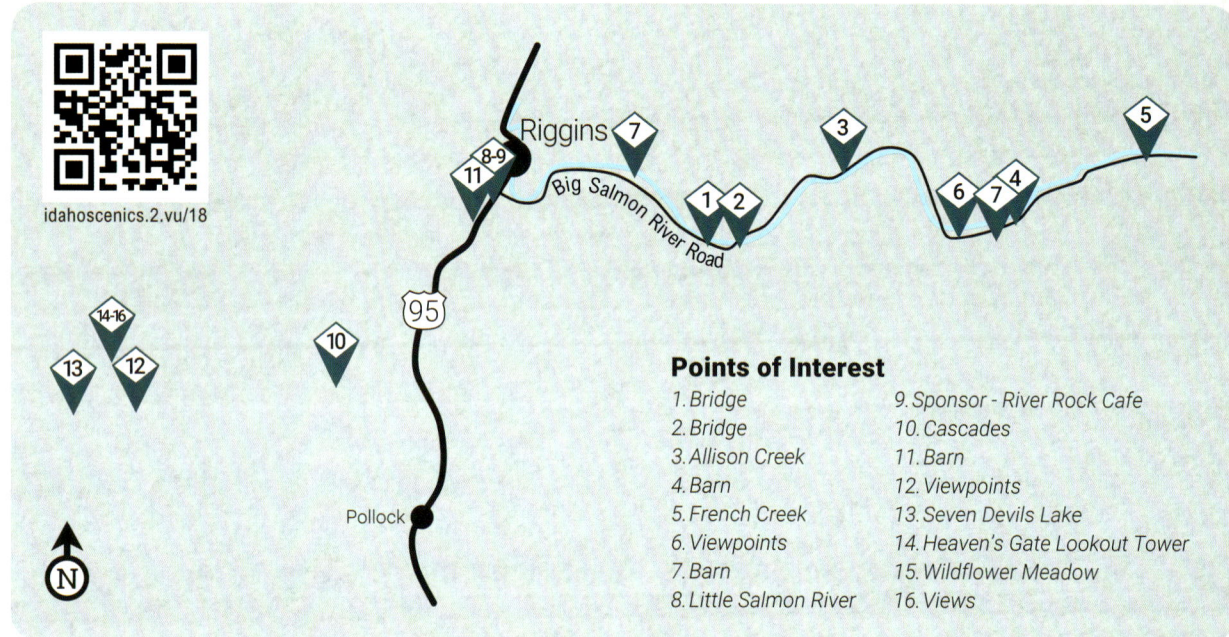

idahoscenics.2.vu/18

Points of Interest

1. Bridge
2. Bridge
3. Allison Creek
4. Barn
5. French Creek
6. Viewpoints
7. Barn
8. Little Salmon River
9. Sponsor - River Rock Cafe
10. Cascades
11. Barn
12. Viewpoints
13. Seven Devils Lake
14. Heaven's Gate Lookout Tower
15. Wildflower Meadow
16. Views

There are many great river and canyon views over the next 3 miles. The pavement ends, and in .8 mile there's a pullout on the right for another great bridge view. In 1.2 miles there's a **barn (4)** and creek view. In 4 miles you'll reach **French Creek (5)** and road. View the creek, then turn around and retrace your route 19 miles toward Hwy 95, watching for a variety of **viewpoints (6)** going the opposite direction, along with a couple of **barn (7)** viewing opportunities. Just before the last bridge before Hwy 95, park on the right and walk carefully onto the bridge to view the old walking bridge just downstream over the **Little Salmon River (8)**. It's very pretty, especially in autumn.

Grab some lunch now or dinner later at our route sponsor, **River Rock Cafe (9)**, by turning right and going back into town for .6 mile. You'll find River Rock Cafe, your celebration destination, nestled in the Salmon River Canyon on your left! Proudly serving breakfast, lunch and dinner 7 days a week, year-round. They specialize in a variety of deliciousness including, but not limited to homemade biscuits and gravy, French toast, eggs benedict, omelets, hand-pattied burgers, Reubens, French dips, stuffed sandwiches, pizza, calzones, specialty salads, steak, seafood, pasta, beer, wine and more!

Photography Tips

Start your route about 40 minutes before sunrise for potential pre-sunrise color in the sky above the Salmon River. Bring wide-angle and telephoto lenses for this route. An ultra-wide lens is necessary at Seven Devils Lake to fit the entire scene of mountain peaks and reflection in your image. You'll also want a polarizer to accentuate those reflections. A graduated neutral density filter comes in very handy for a sunset scene over Hells Canyon.

Directions Continued

In season, we recommend taking a half-day rafting trip with one of the local vendors in town. In late May visit the Rapid River Fish Hatchery and watch the Salmon work their way upstream through a series of cascades, or allow some time to hike to one of the alpine lakes in the Seven Devil Mountains by proceeding on this route.

Head south on Hwy 95 for 1.3 miles from the Big Salmon River Road. Turn right on Rapid River Road and follow the signs to the Rapid River hatchery. Ask the hatchery staff for directions for viewing the **cascades (10)**. Return to Hwy 95 and turn left. In 3.1 miles, turn left on Seven Devils Road (NF 517). There's a **barn (11)** on the left in .3 mile. Continue 16.5 miles uphill to the crest of the Seven Devils Range watching for **viewpoints (12)** along the way. At the "T" junction, park and take a high hike above Hells Canyon or turn left into the campground. Find a parking spot in the back of the campground and walk the quarter-mile trail to the **Seven Devils Lake (13)** lakeshore with towering peaks on the opposite side. Then return to the junction and continue straight. This narrow road along a sheer drop of thousands of feet takes you to the **Heavens Gate lookout tower (14)**. There is another trail from the parking lot here that wanders through a **wildflower meadow (15)** even into September. A short climb to the lookout tower will give you a 360-degree panoramic view, but the **views (16)** from the parking lot and road are nice too. Make your way back into town. You'll find an excellent lodging option on route 19.

This Route's Sponsor

River Rock Cafe
1149 Main St,
Riggins, ID 83549
(208) 628-3434

See page 268 for coupon

Up Next: Routes 17 or 19

Gospel Wilderness and Hells Canyon
Route 19 ◇ ------------------▶ Slate Creek to Cow Creek

This Route at a Glance:

Estimated Driving Time: 5 hours

Highlights: High Mountain Vistas, Bridges, Rivers

About This Route: If you're ready to climb to the next level, we're going even higher than the last route. Not for those with a fear of heights, the road into the Gospel Hump Wilderness Area climbs to almost 11,000 feet, with spectacular views to reward you. You can drive this route from either direction, and end your day at your choice of two amazing sunset locations. You'll be rewarded with views that stretch on forever.

Notes and Cautions: This is a seasonal route and will only be accessible June through September. It features very winding roads with extreme changes in elevation and steep drop offs. Make sure your brakes are good. The roads in the high country can be rough and not maintained or suitable for passenger vehicles. We recommend all wheel drive for this route. Call the Hells Canyon Recreation area for road conditions into Saw Pit Saddle before driving this section of the route. (208) 628-3916. Pack a lunch and water and begin with a full tank of gas as there are no facilities on this route. This route can be run either direction ending with a nice sunset view at the routes' high points.

Directions

From E. Main Street in Grangeville, turn right on Mt. Idaho Grade Road. In .8 miles stay straight on Grangeville-Salmon Road. In 2.7 miles there's a **view over the valley (1)** on the left. Stay on the pavement for about 21 miles then turn left. In 4.5 miles there's a **view of larch (2)** and mountains to the east. Turn left on NF 444. In 5 miles you'll enter the Gospel Hump Wilderness area. In .4 mile there's a vantage point on the left. In .8 miles you'll encounter amazing **views (3)**. In 1 mile you'll reach the **overlook for Upper Gospel Lake (4)**. Continue on this moderately rough road for several more miles for more wonderful **views (5)** then return to Grangeville-Salmon Road.

Turn left on Grangeville-Salmon Road. in .7 miles turn right on Slate Creek Road (NF 354). This is a good **gravel road (6)** that descends to Hwy 95. In 4.2 miles stay right. You'll start to encounter views of **Slate Creek (7)** over the next several miles. In 3.4 miles park at the trail bridge and walk back a little ways for river access with a **bridge view (8)**. In 4.7 miles stay straight. In 4.6 miles turn right. Turn left on Hwy 95 in .3 miles.

In 10 miles turn right on Cow Creek Road through the little community of Lucile. Cross the bridge over the Salmon River and stop for a **view of the bridge (9)**. Stay left at the next intersection in about .2 miles. In 2.4 miles stay right on Cow Creek Road (NF 242). In 2 miles stay straight then turn left in 1.3 miles. In .6 mile stay right. In 1 mile you'll arrive at Cow Creek Saddle. You can stop here for nice **views (10)** if you don't have all wheel drive. This saddle has 5 road junctures. To proceed to a great viewpoint take the 2nd road from your left which traverses the opposite side of the ridge and heads south (NF 420). In 1.2

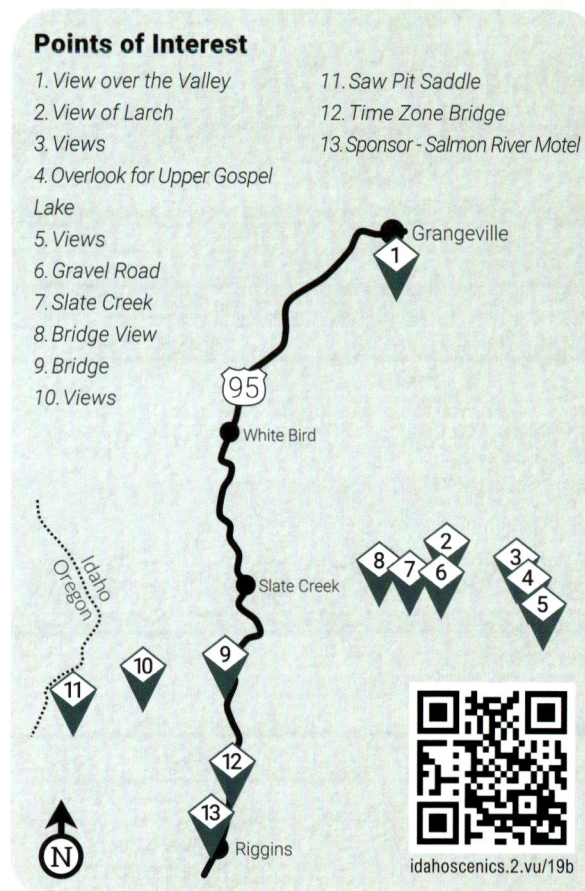

Points of Interest
1. View over the Valley
2. View of Larch
3. Views
4. Overlook for Upper Gospel Lake
5. Views
6. Gravel Road
7. Slate Creek
8. Bridge View
9. Bridge
10. Views
11. Saw Pit Saddle
12. Time Zone Bridge
13. Sponsor - Salmon River Motel

idahoscenics.2.vu/19b

Photography Tips

We love our wide angle lenses for the landscapes on this route, but you'll also want a telephoto if you happen by some whitewater rafters, or want to shoot the distant ridge lines from a high mountain vista or want to zoom in on some golden larch. A graduated neutral density filter is a good idea if you stay for sunset at Sawpit Saddle.

This Route's Sponsor

The Salmon River Motel
1203 Main St,
Riggins, ID 83549

(208) 628-3025
salmonrivermotel.com

Directions Continued

miles turn right on NF 1819. In about 2.5 miles turn right on NF 1819. In 7.2 miles turn right on NF 2060. Continue to **Sawpit Saddle (11)** in 2 miles. Retrace your route to Lucile. Turn right on Hwy 95. In 7.4 miles a pullout on the right provides views of the **"Time Zone" bridge (12)** over the Salmon River. Arrive at this route's sponsor, the **Salmon River Motel (13)** on the right in 2.5 miles.

Sit in front of your room and enjoy the view of the Salmon River Canyon. The Salmon River Motel offers one, two and three bed rooms with queen size beds. Included are Wifi, in-room satellite TV, microwave, refrigerator and coffee maker. Complimentary bags of ice and use of the freezer for ice packs or any of your frozen items. Park in front of your room for easy access, then converse around our firepit or just enjoy the shade. Military and senior discounts available. With economical rates, they are the best choice for your lodging needs.

See route 18 for a dining option next door.

Up Next: Routes 17 or 18

Central Region

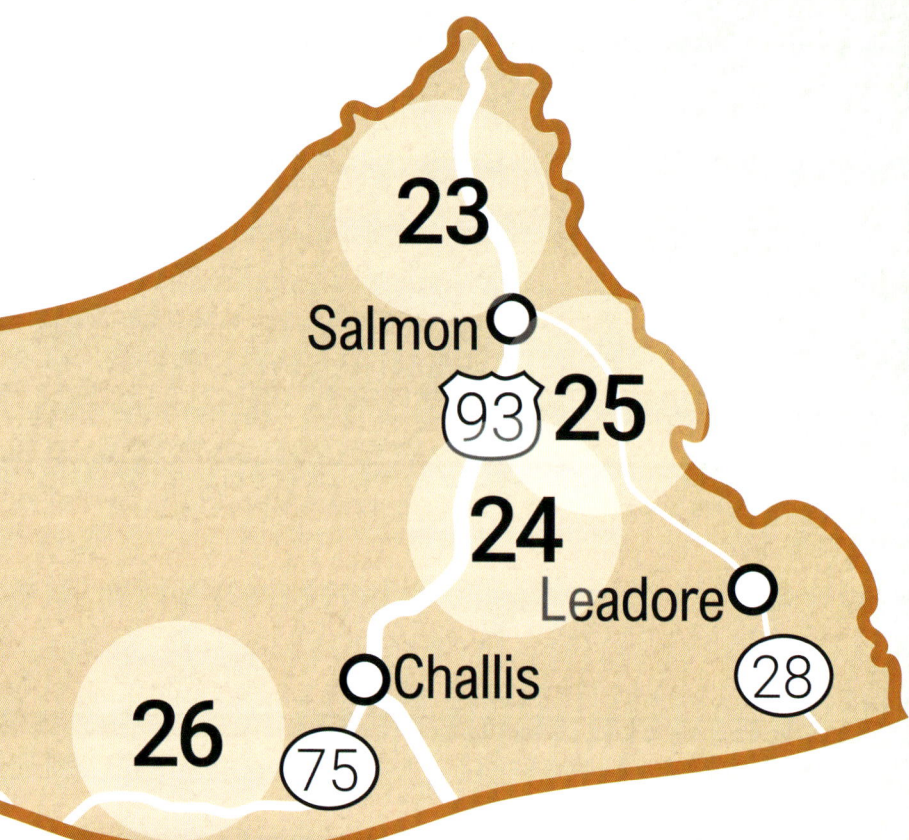

The Salmon River winds its way north along route 24.

Route #
20. Historic Roseberry and the Salmon River Mountains
21. Snowbank Mountain and Lakes
22. Dunes Rivers and Canyon Views
23. The Bitterroot and Salmon River Mountains
24. The Salmon River and Pahsimeroi
25. Beaverhead and Lemhi Mountains
26. Land of the Yankee Fork

Welcome to Idaho's Central Region

These routes surround you with majestic splendor as they lead you through some of Idaho's highest peaks. They include the Lemhi and White Cloud mountains, the Salmon River Mountains, and the Lost River Range. Idaho's Heartland features lakes, mountains, farmlands and old barns, as well as recreational hot spots like McCall and Lake Cascade. Hells Canyon is also a Mecca for river rafting trips and jet boating on the powerful Snake River. Snowbank Mountain boasts a plethora of wildflowers in summer and endless views. The South Fork of the Salmon River and Little Salmon Rivers join the Main Salmon as it meanders across the state. Mining history reveals itself here in the Land of the Yankee Fork, with its stage stops, ghost towns and scenic vistas.

Spring wildflowers near Mann Lake on route 22.

The Lost River Range in morning light of spring, route 24.

Roseberry and the Salmon River Mts.
Route 20 ◇------------------------------▶ Cascade to Riggins

This Route at a Glance:

Estimated Driving Time: 6 hours

Highlights: Barns, Lakes, Waterfalls, Rivers

About This Route: Start your morning at Cascade Lake, then tour the historic town of Roseberry before viewing Payette Lake and visiting the top of Brundage Mountain. We'll visit an alpine lake, more old barns, a roadside waterfall and follow the Little Salmon River into the town of Riggins. You can stop along the way for excellent salmon fishing on the wild Little Salmon.

Notes and Cautions: The two side trip options in this route have sections of rough roads. The last mile to the Brundage Lookout is exceptionally so and requires high clearance. This is black bear country. Hike with bear spray. All-wheel drive is required for side trips. State parks require day-use fees.

Directions

Proceed north on Highway 55 from Cascade, Idaho for 6 miles and take a left on Sugarloaf Road. Follow for 2.5 miles to the parking area at the end of the road. Unique **rock formations (1)** along the shore make for an interesting foreground as you watch the morning sun light up the West Mountains over Lake Cascade. Return to Highway 55 and turn left (north). There is a **barn (2)** on the right in 1.7 miles.

In 5.4 miles turn right (northeast) on Farm to Market Road. There is a cute old shed about .5 mile on the right. In 1.8 miles arrive at the historic town of Roseberry. Park here and explore the area around the intersection, including a church, store and other **old buildings (3)**. Continue on Farm to Market Road. On the right, in .1 mile, you'll find a great old leaning barn with **farm implements (4)**. Another barn follows shortly on the right. There's another **barn (5)** on the left In 2.2 miles. Continue 2.8 miles and find **Finn Church (6)** and cemetery on the right. There are two old structures in the field on the right in .6 mile.

In .5 mile turn left (west) on Lake Fork Road. Park before the bridge and have a look at **Lake Fork Creek (7)** in 1.4 miles. This can be exceptionally beautiful in winter. In .5 mile turn right on Highway 55. In 1 mile turn right on Rogers Lane. In .1 mile at the first junction there is an **old rusty car (8)** hiding in the trees on the corner. Turn around and return to Highway 55.

In 2.6 miles turn right on Elo Road and proceed 2.2 miles, then turn around. You will now have a nice, albeit distant, view of a **barn (9)** on a hill ahead of you. As you travel back to Highway 55 watch for more barns and **buildings (10)** on the right. These are

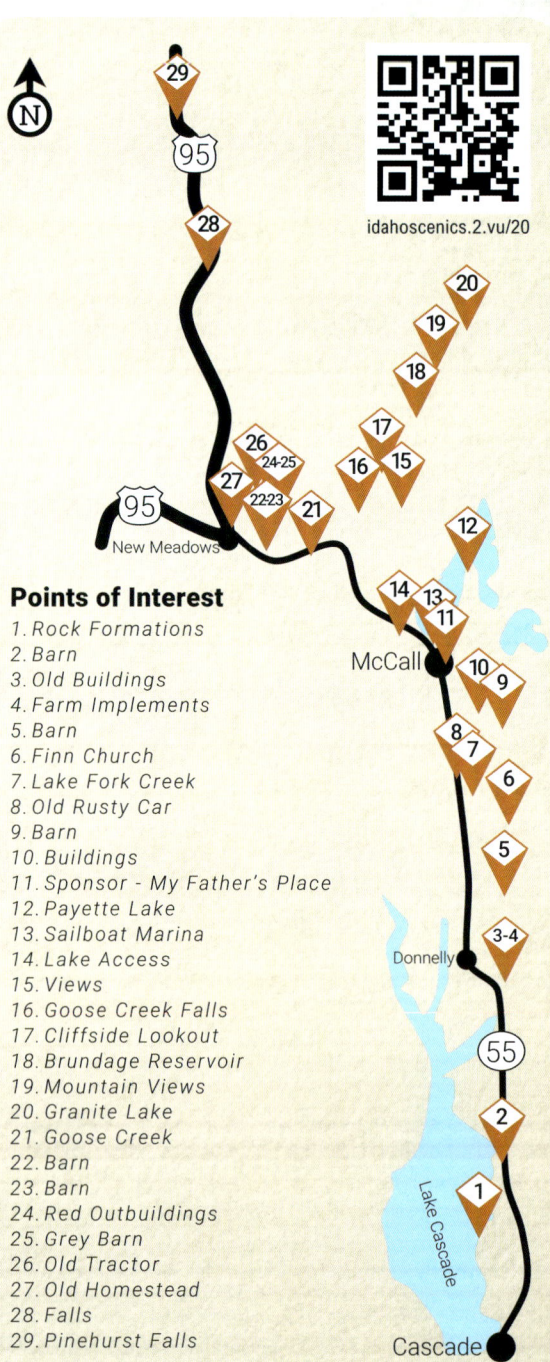

Points of Interest
1. Rock Formations
2. Barn
3. Old Buildings
4. Farm Implements
5. Barn
6. Finn Church
7. Lake Fork Creek
8. Old Rusty Car
9. Barn
10. Buildings
11. Sponsor - My Father's Place
12. Payette Lake
13. Sailboat Marina
14. Lake Access
15. Views
16. Goose Creek Falls
17. Cliffside Lookout
18. Brundage Reservoir
19. Mountain Views
20. Granite Lake
21. Goose Creek
22. Barn
23. Barn
24. Red Outbuildings
25. Grey Barn
26. Old Tractor
27. Old Homestead
28. Falls
29. Pinehurst Falls

Directions Continued

particularly photogenic with a coating of snow. Turn right on Highway 55. In 1.8 miles turn right on Park Street. You'll find our route sponsor, **My Father's Place (11)** on the left.

Forged from over 28 years of tradition, My Father's Place is a family owned and operated restaurant that blends just the right amount of vintage charm, contemporary style and unforgettable tastes to create a dining experience that transcends generations. The menu at My Father's Place boasts some of the best charbroiled burgers, fries and shakes in the great state of Idaho.

Continue east on Park Street staying straight on Thompson Avenue. In .4 mile turn left on Davis Avenue. In .9 mile you'll reach Ponderosa State Park. Pay the day use fee and follow the signs for the Scenic Loop Drive to Porcupine Point. Enjoy the views over **Payette Lake (12)**. Be very cautious at the unfenced, cliffside viewpoint. While in the park, take a hike or a swim, then exit the park by returning to Davis Avenue. In .8 miles turn right on Lenora Street (also known as Wooley Ave.) Then stay right on Pine Street. Then stay right again to keep on Pine Street. Turn left on E. Lake Street. You'll find parking here to explore legacy park and have a view of the **sailboat marina (13)**. From the corner of N. 3rd Street and E. Lake Street continue west (right) on Highway 55.

Directions Continued

In .9 mile there is another **lake access (14)** and swimming beach on the right. In 1.6 miles turn right on Old Brundage Mountain Road (Bear Basin Road) for an optional visit to Brundage Lookout. In 2 miles stay straight. In .2 mile stay right on NF 451. In 5 miles turn left. It's 1 mile to the lookout and exceptional **views (15)**. Return to Highway 55 and turn right.

Continue 3 miles to Brundage Mountain Road (Goose Lake Road). For a visit to a high alpine lake, turn right, otherwise skip the next paragraph. In 3.2 miles you'll find trailhead parking on the left for a moderate hike to **Goose Creek Falls (16)**. Stay left on Goose Lake Road as you pass the ski resort. The pavement ends here. As you climb into the Mountains you come to a pullout on the left for nice views over the valley below. Exercise caution at this dangerous, **cliffside lookout (17)**. One mile from here keep right. In 1.7 miles there is fishing and lake access to **Brundage Reservoir (18)**. In 2.2 miles you'll cross a nice meadow with **mountain views (19)** and an old fence. A creek runs through here earlier in the summer and there may be wildflowers. Stay right at the edge of the meadow. In about 1.2 miles you'll cross Fisher Creek. There is an undeveloped campsite on the left before crossing the bridge. In about 3 miles you'll turn right into the **Granite Lake (20)** access. Return to Highway 55 and turn right..

Directions Continued

In 2.6 miles there's a small parking area on the left to access an old bridge over **Goose Creek (21)**. We do not advise crossing this bridge, but view it only. In 2.2 miles turn right (north) on Cemetery Road. In .1 mile there is an old cabin on the right, followed by a **barn (22)** on the left. Travel only .6 mile to another **barn (23)** on the right. In 1.4 miles turn right (east) on Wallace Lane. You'll see a whole collection of **red outbuildings (24)** on the corner. In .3 miles there is a nice old **grey barn (25)** on the left. Return to Cemetery Road and turn right (north). In .7 mile turn left (west) on Branstetter Lane. Watch for an **old tractor (26)** parked just over the fence on the left. In .4 miles turn left (south) on Campbell Road. In 1 mile turn right (west) on Ferrel Road; in another mile there is an **old homestead (27)** on the left. In .7 mile, turn right (west) on State Shed Road. There is a final barn in .4 mile on the right. Turn right (north) on Highway 95.

Continue about 11 miles. You'll cross a bridge and, as you start to descend along the Little Salmon River, there is a pull-out on the right. Park here and walk downstream along the highway (but behind the guardrail) for views of the **falls (28)**. You'll encounter many pullouts along the scenic river section over the next few miles. In 4.6 miles turn right for river access. In 3.4 miles there is a large pull-out on the right. Park here for views of **Pinehurst Falls (29)** across the highway. It's about 13 miles to Riggins. See route 19 for a nice lodging option and route 18 for a great dinner option.

Photography Tips

Most barns on this route can be shot with a mid-range lens. A wide angle is nice for the landscapes. A polarizer filter is useful at the lakes. After driving the route you may wish to return to certain areas during more ideal lighting conditions, like morning or evening. Pinehurst Falls should be in shade by late afternoon and also looks good in early morning light.

This Route's Sponsor

My Father's Place
901 N 3rd St,
McCall, ID 83638

(208) 634-4401

Up Next: Routes 18 or 21

Snowbank Mountain and Lakes
Route 21 ◇ ----------------------------▶ The Cascade Area

This Route at a Glance:

Estimated Driving Time: 5 hours

Highlights: Wildflowers, Mountains, Lakes, Barns

About This Route: Start this route by watching sunrise from the top of Snowbank Mountain. Wildflowers bloom late here, often into August, thanks to the elevation. Hike to Blue Lake and explore the South Fork of the Salmon River, and finish your day with sunset over Cascade Reservoir.

Notes and Cautions: Snowbank Mountain Road and the Lick Creek Road will be closed once snow is on the ground. Do not attempt these routes in late fall through early summer. Snowbank Mountain road can be very dusty and has rough spots. The hike to Blue Lake is roughly 1.5 miles round trip.

Directions

Starting in Cascade, go south on Highway 55, cross the Payette River and find Cabarton Road in about 5 miles. Turn right (west). In 2.5 miles turn left (west) on Snowbank Mountain Road (also called NF 446). Follow NF 446 to the top of **Snowbank Mountain for views (1)** both east and west. This is a great sunrise location. Watch for **wildflower meadows (2)** in July and August.

Going back down the mountain take an optional one-mile, relatively easy hike to scenic Blue Lake. The trailhead (with restroom) is on the right (south) side of the road about halfway down the mountain. Return to Highway 55 and turn right. In 5.5 miles turn left (south) on Round Valley Road. There is a **barn (3)** on the left in about a mile and some pretty groves of trees. Continue a few more miles and turn left (east) on Bacon Creek Road. You'll find another **barn (4)** on the left. Take a left (north) on Spoor Road (closed in winter) for a view of an old cabin.

You can find your way back to Highway 55 by following Gray Lane left (west) back to Round Valley Road. At Highway 55 turn left and enter the Payette River Canyon. The famous **Rainbow Bridge (5)** is hard to photograph but watch for a small pull-out on the right before crossing the bridge. Be very careful of traffic as you view the bridge. Continue across the bridge and downstream until you can find an appropriate and safe place to turn around. The **North Fork of the Payette (6)** is beautiful all year but especially when lined with autumn foliage. Follow Highway 55 back to Round Valley Road and measure 10.2 miles to Gold Dust Road. Turn right and park for a view of an **old cabin (7)**. There is also an old house across the highway.

Continue on Highway 55 for .2 mile to Thunder City Road (just before the Cascade Airport) and turn right. You'll pass an old barn and several old buildings. Stay left, turn left on Warm Lake Road, and left again on Highway 55 to go into the town of Cascade.

idahoscenics.2.vu/21

Points of Interest
1. Views
2. Wildflower Meadows
3. Barn
4. Barn
5. Rainbow Bridge
6. North Fork of the Payette
7. Old Cabin
8. Sponsor - Grammys Restaurant
9. South Fork of the Salmon River
10. South Fork of the Salmon River
11. Samuels Hot Springs
12. Barn
13. Crown Point Unit
14. Spillway
15. Old Cemetery
16. Unique Rocks

In .8 mile visit our route sponsor, **Gramma's Family Restaurant (8),** for breakfast, lunch or dinner. A staple of Cascade for many years, food always tastes better at Gramma's! Homestyle cooking with breakfast served all day. Be sure to try a slice of pie.

For the afternoon, take a drive up the South Fork of the Salmon River. Just north of town, turn right on Warm Lake Road. Go about 24 miles and turn left (north) on NF 474. This route follows the **South Fork of the Salmon River (9,10)** north for over 30

Directions Continued

miles. Go as far as you want, but plan on returning the way you came. Signs will direct you to McCall by turning left (west) on Lick Creek Road, but this is a very slow and extremely rough road and goes high over a mountain pass. Only attempt with good tires and a full tank of gas in mid-summer to early fall.

Back on Warm Lake Road turn right. Stop for a soak in **Samuels Hot Springs (11)** found roadside in 4.7 miles. Continue back to Hwy 55 and turn left (south) into the town of Cascade. In .7 mile turn right (west) on Lake Cascade Parkway toward Lake Cascade State Park. Take a left (south) on Lakeshore Drive and follow around the south end of the lake, making a right (west) on West Mountain Road. There's a nice **barn (12)** roadside in less than .5 mile.

Return to Cascade and shoot sunset at the **Crown Point Unit (13)** of Lake Cascade State Park. When reaching Highway 55 turn left, then left (west) on Lake Way. You'll pass the **spillway (14)** for the reservoir, which in spring, can be quite a sight. Within 1.5 miles you'll find an **old cemetery (15)** and numerous parking spots to explore the **coves and unique rocks (16)** along the shoreline.

Photography Tips

In winter this valley often has dense fog until late morning, which can make for some nice scenes as the sun burns through. Aspen can be found interspersed throughout the valley and on the backside of Cascade Reservoir, adding nice color to an autumn scene. This route could also be run in reverse, exploring the South Fork of the Salmon in good morning light and finishing with sunset from the top of Snowbank Mountain. The South Fork of the Salmon River runs from south to north making both mid-morning and early evening light good times for photography. A few of the old buildings are best with a telephoto lens.

Up Next: Route 20 or 48

This Route's Sponsor

Gramma's Family Restaurant
224 N. Main Street
Cascade, ID 83611
(208) 382-4602

See page 270 for coupon

Dunes, Rivers and Canyon Views

Route 22 ◇┈┈┈┈┈┈┈┈┈┈┈┈┈┈► Weiser to Hells Canyon

This Route at a Glance:

Estimated Driving Time: 6 hours

Highlights: Barns, Wildflowers, Canyon and River Views

About This Route: Travel the backroads to visit old barns and an old schoolhouse, drive along the gorgeous Weiser River, then view America's deepest river canyon. Spring rules again on this route, with wildflowers flourishing in mid to late April and the canyon walls showing off verdant green.

Notes and Cautions: We recommend this route for an April visit to view the amazing wildflower displays in Hells Canyon. With the exception of the Hells Canyon high country and maybe the Weiser Sand Dunes, most of this route can be done in winter. The roads along the Snake River are winding and narrow, and Kleinschmidt Grade is exceptionally so, with deadly drop-offs.

Directions

Start your day early with a visit to the Weiser Sand Dunes or skip to the next paragraph. From Hwy 95 and Main Street in Weiser, proceed west on Main Street to West 3rd Street. Turn left and go several blocks, crossing the railroad tracks. Turn right on NF 70. Follow 4.2 miles, then stay straight on Indianhead Road. In 1.5 miles turn right on Eaton Road, then turn left on Olds Ferry Road in 1 mile. Stay on Olds Ferry Road as it travels along the **Snake River (1)** for about 10 miles, then arrive at **Weiser Sand Dunes (2)**. Arriving here after a recent wind provides fresh, untracked sand in the morning light. Continue 5 miles farther to arrive at **Steck Park (3)** for river access. Return to Weiser and Hwy 95.

From Hwy 95 in Weiser head north. Turn right on Park Street, which becomes Weiser River Road. In 1.3 miles there's a white barn with green roof and **silo (4)**. In another 1.3 miles you'll have a valley view to the south. In .6 mile turn right on Sand Road and, in another .6 mile, there's a **barn (5)** on the right. A white community hall is on the left in 1.3 miles. You'll find an old barn in 4.2 miles. In .8 mile there's a pullout on the left for Weiser River and canyon views. In another .7 mile a small pullout on the right provides more river

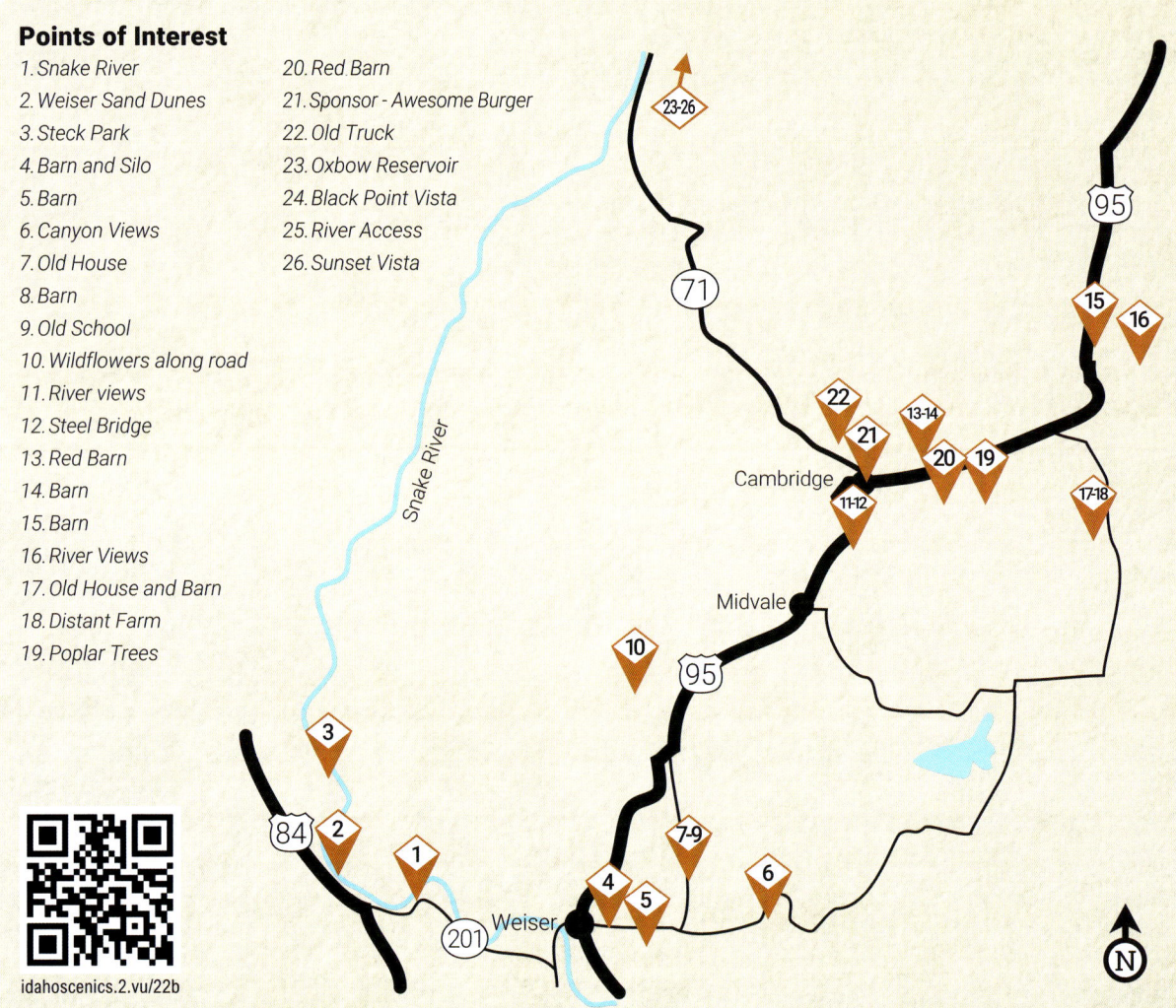

Points of Interest
1. Snake River
2. Weiser Sand Dunes
3. Steck Park
4. Barn and Silo
5. Barn
6. Canyon Views
7. Old House
8. Barn
9. Old School
10. Wildflowers along road
11. River views
12. Steel Bridge
13. Red Barn
14. Barn
15. Barn
16. River Views
17. Old House and Barn
18. Distant Farm
19. Poplar Trees
20. Red Barn
21. Sponsor - Awesome Burger
22. Old Truck
23. Oxbow Reservoir
24. Black Point Vista
25. River Access
26. Sunset Vista

idahoscenics.2.vu/22b

and **canyon views (6)**. There's Weiser River trailhead access in .3 mile. Cross the river and turn left in .4 mile. In another .4 mile stay left. You'll have mountain views over the next mile. Turn around at your leisure. Return across the bridge and watch for a better angle on the old barn on the left. In 4 miles turn right on Mann Creek Road. In 2.8 miles there's a distant view of a barn on the left. Turn left on Laird Lane in .2 mile. There's an **old house (7)** and another angle to view the **barn (8)**. Return to Mann Creek Road. In 1.3 miles there's a working white barn. Then, in .7 mile, you'll find an **old school (9)** and outhouse on the right. In .6 mile

Directions Continued

there's an old barn on the left, and a red barn on the left in 2.9 miles. In .7 mile stay left. In .4 mile turn left, then turn right (north) on Hwy 95.

In a little over a mile, turn left (west) on Upper Mann Creek Road. You'll encounter another barn shortly. Continue 3-4 miles, staying right at the beginning of the reservoir. In late April to May, yellow and purple lupine and **golden arrowleaf balsamroot line the road (10)**. Backtrack to the Monroe Creek Road and turn right (south). You'll encounter nice views over Mann Creek Reservoir with the Cuddy Mountains to the north. Return to Hwy 95 and turn left (north).

You'll find a rest stop with valley views to the north in 5.8 miles. There's a pullout along the highway for river views in another 5 miles. In 2.7 miles, turn right on Shoepeg Road. In .6 mile there are nice **Weiser River views (11)** from the bridge crossing. Return to Hwy 95 and turn right (north). In 1.3 miles there's a pullout on the right, which provides a view of the river and an **old steel bridge (12)**. There's another view and pullout in .8 mile. In .4 mile turn right for river access. Return to Hwy 95 and turn right. In 1.4 miles turn right to continue on Hwy 95.

In 1.3 miles turn left on Bain Road. In .5 mile there are outbuildings on both sides of the road. In 1 mile turn left on Mill Road, then turn right on Goodrich Road in .3 mile. In 1 mile a **red barn (13)** comes into view. Good views continue over the next .3 mile. In .3 mile there's a **whitewashed barn (14)** at the next intersection. Turn right on Cove Road. In .8 mile turn left on Schlehuber Road. In 1.2 miles turn left on Hwy 95.

In 1.6 miles there are 2 red barns on the right. Park safely if choosing to shoot any of the barns along the highway. In 3.6 miles there's an old barn on the left, and another 1.5 miles farther. There is one more barn along the highway in 1.6 miles. In 5 miles turn right on Middle Fork Road. There's an **old barn (15)** on the right in .8 mile. Continue for several miles for **river views (16)**. This is really a beautiful drive in the autumn. Return to Hwy 95 and turn left (south).

Drive south on Hwy 95 for 4 miles, then turn left on Indian Valley Road. In 1.5 miles there's a barn on the right. In .9 mile stay left and, in 1 mile you'll pass a white church. In 1.8 miles an old house and **barn (17)** are on the left. Stay straight on

Directions Continued

Swisher Road, which is a dirt road to Ben Ross Reservoir. Follow the shoreline road for a mile or two for views over the reservoir and a **distant farm (18)**. Retrace your route to Indian Valley Road. In 1.6 miles turn left on Mundy Valley Road (this road may not be passable in wet weather or winter, in which case return to Hwy 95 on Indian Valley Road. Follow Hwy 95 south for 6.6 miles and turn left on Thomason Lane, then right on Schwenkfelder Rd. to rejoin route).

Continuing on Mundy (also labeled as Monday) Valley Road, you'll cross the Little Weiser River in 1 mile. In 2.7 miles turn right on Cut Off Road, You'll have views of the Cuddy Mountains to the west. Turn left when reaching the intersection of Monday Road and Schwenkfelder Road. There's a grove of **poplar trees (19)** on the right. In 2 miles there are red barns on the left. Turn right on Gladhart Lane in .6 mile. There's a **red barn (20)** on the left in 1 mile. In 1.5 miles you'll cross the Weiser River. Turn left on Hwy 95.

Entering the town of Cambridge in 4.5 miles, stay straight on West Central Boulevard and arrive at this route's sponsor on the right. **Awesome Burger (21)** is a small cafe serving locals and travelers breakfast, lunch and dinner. It's the perfect place for a short break and a good meal before heading into the Idaho wilderness. Always friendly, clean and fresh.

Turn left on North First Street in ½ block, then right on West Hopper Avenue (Hwy 71). In .6 mile there's a barn on the right. In .3 mile turn right on Rush Creek Road. There is a big old barn in 1.4 miles. Turn left on Edwards Lane for a better view of the **barn and an old truck (22)**. There is also an old gravestone. Please respect private property and view from the road. Return to Hwy 71 and turn right. In .5 mile turn right on Hansen Lane. In .4 mile there is another barn on the right. Return to Hwy 71 and turn right.

Follow Hwy 71 for about 27 miles, passing a couple more barns and old farm equipment along the first 10 miles. Watch for views of Brownlee Reservoir. Cross the Snake River below the dam and continue following the river on the Oregon side for roughly 10 miles along **Oxbow Reservoir (23)**, until you reach the community of

Photography Tips

A variety of focal length lenses are useful on this route. You may even want a macro lens for photographing wildflowers. We planned this route to culminate with a view over the Snake River Canyon at sunset. Try to arrive a little early to enjoy the wildflowers and explore compositions. If there are no clouds, try timing your sunset shots to make a sun star by shooting at f/16 or f/18 just as the sun starts to disappear over the horizon.

This Route's Sponsor

Awesome Burger
10 W Central Blvd,
Cambridge, ID 83610
(208) 257-3636

See page 270 for coupon

Directions Continued

Copperfield. Turn right (northeast) onto NF 454 and cross the river back into Idaho. Follow Hells Canyon Road (NF 454) 22 miles to Hells Canyon Dam, watching for river, canyon and wildflower views in spring. Follow the road across the dam and continue to the end, arriving at the visitor center and canyon views in less than a mile.

Stop at **Black Point Vista (24)** on the return in 8 miles. In 3 more miles a rough two-track side trip, signed as Rock Bar #4, provides nice **views of the river (25)**. Continue 8 miles to Kleinschmidt Grade Road on the left. Not for those with a fear of heights, this winding narrow grade climbs high above the valley with deadly drops of thousands of feet. It also provides some of the best vantage points of this section of the canyon, the spring wildflowers and a **sunset vista (26)**. You'll find a wide spot to park and turn around at 4.5 miles.

Return to Cambridge by descending the grade road and turning left on Hells Canyon Road. In about 7 miles, and after crossing the Snake River back into Oregon, turn left on Brownlee Oxbow Hwy. Continue on to Cambridge.

Up Next: Routes 18, 21, or 46

Bitterroot and Salmon River Mountains

Route 23 ◇------▶ Lost Trail Pass to Salmon

This Route at a Glance:

Estimated Driving Time: 8-9 hours or overnight camp

Highlights: Rugged River Canyons, High Alpine Lake

About This Route: We begin this route at the crest of the Bitterroot Range at Lost Trail Pass and descend into Idaho by following the North Fork of the Salmon River. At the confluence with the Main Salmon we dive west and follow the mighty Salmon as it starts its journey through the roadless area of the state. From here we head into the Salmon River Mountains to the edge of the Frank Church "River of No Return" Wilderness Area.

Notes and Cautions: Get an early start or plan on camping at Yellowjacket Lake. The trip into the Salmon River Mountains to visit the Bighorn Crags and Yellowjacket Lake can be a rough road and you should not attempt without all-wheel drive and a higher clearance vehicle. Make sure you have a full tank of gas and supplies and obtain a hiking map for Bighorn Crags before starting on this portion of the trip. If you choose to do any hiking you will definitely need to plan for an overnight camp. This route will not be accessible in spring or winter.

Directions

From the Idaho-Montana state line at Lost Trail Pass, head south on Highway 93. As you begin the descent into Idaho there are a few pullouts on the right with views over the mountains and valleys. Pull off for beautiful **aspen groves (1)** on both sides of the highway in 5.1 miles. In 3.3 miles a small loop road on the left (NF007) give views of the **North Fork of the Salmon River (2)**.

In 4.3 miles, at the community of Gibbonsville, there is an old truck on the right, followed immediately by an old house and leaning **barn (3)** on the left. The turnoff for Granite Mountain is on the right in another .8 mile. This road is mildly rough, rutted and rocky. Follow .3 mile and turn left to the **Gibbonsville Cemetery (4)**. You'll find old wooden grave markers here. Return to Granite Mountain Road and turn left. In .5 mile stay straight. In .3 mile stay right on Granite Mountain Road (NF 92). In 3 miles stay left. In .2 miles stay right. Arrive at **Granite Mountain Lookout (5)** in .3 mile. Return to Highway 93 and turn right.

Watch for an **old car and truck (6)** on the left in 2.3 miles. These are on private property but can be photographed with a medium telephoto lens. Arrive at this route's sponsor, **The Village at North Fork (7)**, in 7.9 miles.

The Village is located halfway between Yellowstone and Glacier National Parks along the scenic Sacajawea Byway (Highway 93) and at the confluence of the North Fork and the Main Salmon rivers. This location is the ideal base camp to enjoy area activities including fishing, mountain biking, rafting, kayaking, ATV riding, hiking, hunting and wildlife viewing. Whether your last stop as you enter the Frank Church Wilderness Area or as your base camp for exploring this beautiful area, the Village has what you need for an excursion or for a little creature comfort in the wilderness. Their facilities include an outdoor store, a general store, lodge rooms, full hookup RV spaces, and fuel dispensers with 24-hour pay-at-the-pump access. "While we offer everything from a post office to a boat ramp to the state liquor store, our guests tell us it is our friendly hospitality that keeps them coming back. We like that."

From the parking lot turn left (west) onto NF 30 and proceed 26.9 miles. Turn left on

Points of Interest
1. Aspen Groves
2. North Fork of the Salmon River
3. Barn
4. Gibbonsville Cemetery
5. Granite Mountain Lookout
6. Old Vehicles
7. Sponsor - The Village at North Fork
8. Shoup Store
9. Pack Bridge
10. Frank Church Wilderness Area
11. Yellowjacket Lake
12. Napias Creek
13. Aspen Grove
14. Canyon Views
15. Beaverhead Mountains

idahoscenics.2.vu/23

Photography Tips

You'll want a telephoto lens if you happen across a herd of bighorn sheep on this route, which is very common along the Salmon River after leaving North Fork. A wide-angle lens and polarizing filter can be useful at Yellowjacket Lake. Both sunset and sunrise can be nice here. The shore is marshy in most spots, so a pair of boots or waders can come in handy.

Directions Continued

Panther Creek Road (NF 055), watching for river views and bighorn sheep, old cabins and the historic **Shoup store (8)**. In 19.2 miles stay straight and in .7 mile, stay straight again. In 5 miles turn left. In 2.7 miles there is a **pack bridge (9)** over the creek. In 4.1 miles turn right on Yellowjacket Road (NF 112), then stay left on NF 112. In 5.9 miles stay left. In 1.3 miles make a sharp right on Yellowjacket Lake Road. In about 5 miles there's a view over the **Frank Church Wilderness area (10)**. In another 2.7 miles stay left. In 1 mile you'll reach the junction for **Yellowjacket Lake (11)** to the left in 5 miles, or Bighorn Crags trailhead to the right in 2 miles, on Cathedral Rock Road. Retrace your route to Yellowjacket Road then Panther Creek Road. Turn left on Panther Creek Road.

In 12.5 miles turn right on Napias Creek Road. The next 3 miles are rough, winding and steep but it improves shortly. In 1.3 miles from Panther Creek Road you'll reach a beautiful cascade along **Napias Creek (12)** with more great spots over the next half mile, especially in autumn. In 1.6 miles turn right on Moccasin Creek Road. There is a beautiful **aspen grove (13)** in .6 mile. In 2.8 miles turn right and, in .8 mile turn left on NF 101 becoming NF 021. In 3 miles stay straight. In 5.7 miles there's a small pullout on the right for **canyon views (14)**. In 7.9 miles there is a nice view of the **Beaverhead Mountains (15)** and a barn. Cross the river and turn left on Highway 93. It is 5 miles into Salmon. See the beginning of route 25 for directions to Discovery Point for a beautiful sunset location and route 24 for an excellent lodging option.

This Route's Sponsor

The Village at North Fork
2046 Highway 93 N,
North Fork, ID 83466
208.865.7001
northforkidaho.com

See page 270 for coupon

Up Next: Routes 15 or 25

The Salmon River and Pahsimeroi

Route 24 ◇ ---------------------------→ Challis to Salmon

This Route at a Glance:

Estimated Driving Time: 5 hours

Highlights: Rivers, Alpine lake, Mountains and Meadows

About This Route: We'll drive downstream along the mighty Salmon River-the longest, free-flowing river within one state of the lower 48, exploring side roads for autumn color and old cabins. A side trip into the Pahsimeroi Mountains offer numerous recreational opportunities including hiking camping, and wildflower and mountain viewing.

Notes and Cautions: The majority of this route is an excursion into the Pahsimeroi highlands. Start this route with a full gas tank. All-wheel drive is recommended. The road can be rough, with small creek crossings. Avoid this route after a rain, in the winter or too early in the spring.

Directions

Directions: From Hwy 93 and Main Street in Challis turn west on Main Street. Proceed through town and turn left on Garden Creek Road in 5.2 miles. Follow for 1.9 miles to a pretty little **creek crossing (1)**. There's an undeveloped camp spot to park and turn around here. If you'd rather watch sunrise over the mountains, skip the previous location and continue right on Custer Motorway (NF 70). You'll reach a saddle in less than 1 mile. A short spur road to the right provides great views over the **Mountains (2)** to the east. Continuing on Custer Motorway, in 8 miles turn right on NF 80. In 1.5 miles continue straight through an intersection to remain on NF 80. In about 1.5 miles start watching for views to the left overlooking the **valley (3)** and Mosquito Reservoir. In another .5 mile turn left on Challis Creek Road to access the reservoir. In .8 miles, bear right past an unofficial campsite and into the meadow. Here you will find the remains of several **old buildings (4)**.

Return to the intersection of NF 80 and Challis Creek Road, this time going straight on Challis Creek Road, now also NF 80. In 6.3 miles, stay right on Challis Creek Road. In 5.2 miles you'll cross Challis Creek. The **cottonwood trees (5)** here can be splendid, backlit by the morning sun. In 1.8 miles turn left on Stephens Road. There's a **barn (6)** on the left in .5 mile. In 1.6 miles turn left (north) on Highway 93.

There is a cabin on the left in .5 mile. In .9 mile, find a pullout on the right with river, **bridge and cliff views (7)**. Proceed north 8.1 miles. There is a distant view of an old cabin on the left in the trees. In 3.1 miles turn right (east) on Custer Road. There is a **barn (8)** in .9 mile. In 6 miles turn right to stay on Custer Road. In 15 miles continue straight on Doublespring Road. Continue for a little over 6 miles to a Y- intersection, then turn right.

In 5.6 miles turn left towards Horse Haven Pass. Follow this road into the Upper Pahsimeroi for at least 10 miles or as far as you are comfortable with for **wildflower displays (9)** in spring, high mountain meadows and mountain vistas.

Retrace your route to Doublespring Road then Custer Road for 26 miles then turn right (north) on Burstedt Lane and, in .5 mile, you will reach a crossing of the **Pahsimeroi River (10)**. In another .5 mile, turn left (west) on Farm to Market Road. You will rejoin Highway 93 in 2.5 miles and turn right (north). In 4.4 miles you will enter the river canyon called **Royal Gorge (11)**. Here the Salmon River has carved a deep cut through rock as it winds its way north.

There are some old structures on the right in 2 miles. In .8 mile, pull into the Colston River access. There is a distant view of an **old cabin (12)** across the river. Continue

Points of Interest
1. Creek Crossing
2. Mountains
3. Valley Views
4. Old Buildings
5. Cottonwood Trees
6. Barn
7. Cliff Views
8. Barn
9. Wildflowers
10. Pahsimeroi River
11. Royal Gorge
12. Old Cabin
13. Rock Arch
14. Goldbug Hot Springs
15. Steel Bridge
16. Mountain View
17. Sponsor - The Stagecoach Inn

idahoscenics.2.vu/24b

Photography Tips

You'll want your polarizing filter at the first stop of the day to help slow your shutter speed while photographing Garden Creek. A mid range zoom is best here. A wide angle is well suited for the wide open vistas of the Pahsimeroi Highlands and again for Discovery Hill at sunset. Using a mid range lens practice shooting a panoramic vista of the Bitterroot Range at this location. A couple of the structures are best suited for a telephoto lens.

Directions Continued

north on Highway 93 for .5 mile to a **rock arch (13)** on the right. A seasonal waterfall may be flowing through it in the spring.

There is a pull off on the left for more river and mountain views in 1.4 miles. Be on the lookout in 1.3 miles for an old truck cab on the left. In another .7 mile there is an old cabin and cellar across the river. In 8 miles, turn right on Warm Springs Road for a 3.5-mile round-trip hike to **Goldbug Hot Springs (14)**. Fed by waterfalls, these springs have a beautiful view over the valley at sunset.

Return to Highway 93. Travel 4 more miles for a view of an old **steel bridge (15)** spanning the Salmon River. The Eightmile River access is on the left in 11.5 miles. Continue north on Highway 93 for another .1 mile to a small riverside pull-off on the left for another river and **mountain view (16)**. Arrive in Salmon in 7 miles. Turn left at the stop light and proceed through town reaching this route's sponsor in .7 mile on the right.

The Stagecoach Inn (17) is nestled in the Bitterroot Mountains along the beautiful Salmon River. They have 101 newly refurbished, clean and spacious rooms, most with private balconies. A nutritional complimentary breakfast is offered as well as a seasonal outdoor pool and hot tub. They have on site laundry services, a large conference center and a beautiful riverside grassy park with picnic tables and chairs. Complimentary parking and airport transportation are available. Pets are welcomed for a nominal fee. Complimentary wireless internet and many cozy comfortable sitting areas to relax and enjoy the peaceful view and sounds of the Salmon river.

See the beginning of route 25 for directions to Discovery Hill for a great sunset location.

This Route's Sponsor

The Stagecoach Inn
201 Riverfront Drive,
Salmon, ID 83467

(208) 756-2919
stagecoachinnmotel.com

Up Next: Routes 23 or 25

Beaverhead and Lemhi Mountains
Route 25 ◇------▶ Salmon to Birch Creek Valley

This Route at a Glance:

Estimated Driving Time: 5 hours

Highlights: Old Cabins, Mountain views, High mountain lake

About This Route: Explore your way through the back roads of the Leadore and Birch Creek valleys. You'll find cabins, beautiful wildflower settings, mountain views and historic charcoal kilns. The highlight is a side trip high into the Lemhi Mountains for an up close-view of Meadow Lake and Gilmore Peak.

Notes and Cautions: There is some rough road on this route, and all-wheel drive is recommended for side trips. Some portions of this route are more photogenic in early summer or autumn, as specified in the route text.

Directions

From Main Street in Salmon turn north on N. St. Charles Street. Follow to Discovery Point parking area in about 2 miles. Walk to many great vistas of the **Beaverhead Mountains (1)** or the **Salmon River (2)** and mountains or drive some of the two-track roads in the area. Be very careful when doing so. The road straight ahead ends as it goes over the bluff. Retrace your route down the hill to Salmon but turn left 2 blocks before Main Street on Shoup St. In .3 miles arrive at this route's sponsor, **Rise & Shine Espresso (3)** on the left.

Rise & Shine Espresso is a small family owned and operated coffee shop located in the heart of downtown Salmon, Idaho. Featuring specialty coffees, blended drinks, a variety of teas, breakfast burritos and delicious daily fresh baked muffins and pastries. Through their mission "community through coffee" we strive to create a warm and inviting environment that fosters comradery and joy.

Follow N. Daisy Street one block back to Main Street and turn left. At the intersection of Highways 93 and 28 proceed straight on Highway 28. Turn left in .5 mile on Lemhi Street. In 1.7 miles there are two **tree-lined drives (4)**, great for an autumn shoot. In 2 miles watch for a **bridge (5)** over the Lemhi River. In another 1.6 miles there is an **old homestead with a barn (6)**. In 1 mile stay straight, then find an old underground shed just beyond the junction. In .6 mile turn left on Barracks Lane. In .9 mile stay right. In .3 mile there is old machinery on the left. In 2.2 miles take the second left.

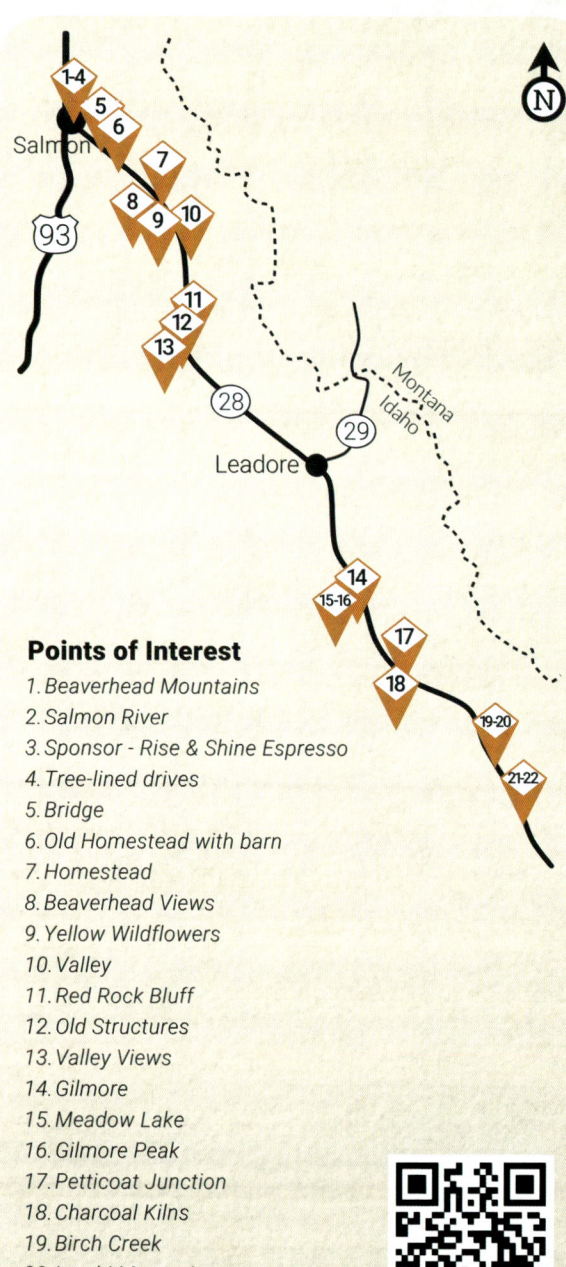

Points of Interest
1. Beaverhead Mountains
2. Salmon River
3. Sponsor - Rise & Shine Espresso
4. Tree-lined drives
5. Bridge
6. Old Homestead with barn
7. Homestead
8. Beaverhead Views
9. Yellow Wildflowers
10. Valley
11. Red Rock Bluff
12. Old Structures
13. Valley Views
14. Gilmore
15. Meadow Lake
16. Gilmore Peak
17. Petticoat Junction
18. Charcoal Kilns
19. Birch Creek
20. Lemhi Mountains
21. Two Old Structures
22. Rock Formations

idahoscenics.2.vu/25b

Directions Continued

In 1.5 miles there is a moderately distant **homestead (7)** on the right with a Lemhi Mountain backdrop. In .7 mile stay right. In .5 mile find a view over the valley. In 1.3 miles stay right and in another 2.2 miles turn right at the junction with 17 Mile Lane.

Cross Highway 28 to Haynes Creek Road. Turn right on Price Creek Road in .5 mile. In ¼ mile you'll have an unobstructed view of the Beaverhead Mountains of the Bitterroot Range. Return to Haynes Creek Road and turn right. Haynes Creek Road becomes NF 350. Turn right at the sign for Baldy Basin in 3.5 miles. In .2 mile turn right on NF 427. The road gets rougher as it climbs higher. In 1.6 miles there is a meadow on the left, abundant with wildflowers in the late spring and early summer. In .9 mile you'll catch a nice glimpse of the Beaverhead Mountains. In .4 mile turn around at the crest of the hill with more **Beaverhead views (8)**. There are lupine and alpine lilies among the sage in mid-July.

Return to Highway 28, watching for thick **yellow wildflowers (9)** along Haynes Creek in the summer. Proceed straight across Highway 28 on 17 Mile Lane. In .5 mile turn right on Lemhi Road. In 2.1 miles turn left on Warm Springs Road and, In .7 mile,

Directions Continued

arrive at a kiosk and restroom facilities. In 1.3 miles arrive at Sharkey Hot Springs on the right. This free BLM facility has nice views. Make your way back to Lemhi Road watching for views over the **valley (10)**. Turn left on Lemhi Road. In 4.8 miles stay straight on Lemhi Road, then turn left on Highway 28 in 2.2 miles. In 3.1 miles there's a **red rock bluff (11)** on the right that looks great in the right light. Park safely off the highway.

In 1.3 miles turn right on Hayden Creek Road. In 1.2 miles there is an old cabin on the right, followed shortly by several other **old structures (12)** on both sides of the road. In 1.5 miles there is another old cabin on the right. You'll find some creek access in another 1.5 miles. The pavement ends in .2 mile. You can turn around here and return to Highway 28 or continue for **valley views (13)** best seen in autumn.

To continue, stay left on Hayden Creek Road and bear left in 2.7 miles on NF 008. In .4 mile stay right. In 1 mile arrive at a small pullout on the left with views up and down the valley. Find a place to safely turn around and return to Highway 28.

At Highway 28 turn right. In 1.2 miles turn left on Old Highway 28. Follow this road for about 19 miles, watching for old structures and Lemhi Mountain views. When the road intersects with Road 29 turn right and arrive at Leadore in .3 mile. Turn left on Highway 28.

In 17 miles, turn right on Gilmore Road (NF 002). This is the road to Meadow Lake, a highlight of this route. You'll travel through the old town site of **Gilmore (14)**. Most of the structures are now private, but there is one old site on the left that warrants a look. Follow the road about 7 miles to **Meadow Lake (15)**. There is a campground and day use area here. This is a great spot to be if you can ever return for a sunrise. Take a short walk around the lakeshore to the left where the outlet emerges for up close, cross-lake views of **Gilmore Peak (16)**. Return to Highway 28. Turn right.

In 7.7 miles you'll see the iconic Idaho landmark of **Petticoat Junction (17)**. In 4.6

Photography Tips

Discovery Hill is an excellent sunrise or sunset location and a good place to shoot a panorama of the mountains. Begin your day early for the best light. A few of the cabins may require a telephoto lens. You'll want a wide angle lens and polarizing filter at Meadow Lake. Meadow Lake is beautiful at any time but best photographed in early morning light, so driving this route backwards by starting at Meadow Lake may be an option, or return another time.

This Route's Sponsor

Rise & Shine Espresso
900 Shoup St,
Salmon, ID 83467

(208) 303-1001
facebook.com/risenshine1001

See page 272 for coupon

Directions Continued

miles turn right onto NF 188, signed for the Charcoal Kilns interpretive site. This 5-mile road takes you to the remains of several historical **charcoal kilns (18)**. Return to Highway 28 and turn right.

In 3.4 miles there is an old cabin on the right. In 6 more miles you can take a break at the O'brien access to **Birch Creek (19)** on the left. Continue southeast on Highway 28 by turning left from the parking area. In about .5 mile watch for an unmarked two track road on the right. This short loop road will take you by several old buildings and views of Birch Creek and the **Lemhi Mountains (20)**, a good spot to watch the sunset. In another 5.1 miles there are **two old structures (21)** on the right. Proceed directly across the road to Skull Canyon Road (NF 298). Follow for about 3 miles to view some interesting **rock formations (22)**. Return to Highway 28 and turn left. Continue to Mud Lake, Rexburg or Idaho Falls.

Up Next: Routes 27 or 28

Land of the Yankee Fork

Route 26 ⬦┄┄┄┄┄┄┄┄┄┄┄┄┄┄┄┄┄┄┄▶ Challis to Stanley

This Route at a Glance:

Estimated Driving Time: 5 hours

Highlights: Historic Mining Towns, Hot Springs, The Salmon River

About This Route: Follow the Salmon River upstream to your Sawtooth Mountain destination. Along the way, we'll visit the historic mining towns of Bayhorse (on the National Register of Historic Places), Custer and Bonanza. Try this route in autumn for great colors or visit in June, when snow still caps the peaks and meadows fill with wildflowers.

Notes and Cautions: Roads off the main highway may not be accessible in winter or wet weather. All wheel drive recommended. Bug spray is a must for the camas areas in the spring. Bayhorse is a state park and has day-use fees.

Directions

From Challis travel south on Hwy 93 for 1.6 miles and turn right on Hwy 75. In 8.1 miles turn right to visit the historic mining town of **Bayhorse (1)**. You'll reach it in 3.2 miles by staying right then left after crossing the river. Continue past Bayhorse 5.2 miles on NF 051, watching for **kilns (2)**, old **mining structures (3)** and **creek views (4)** until you reach **Bayhorse Lake (5)**. Return to Hwy 75 and turn right. In 9.3 miles turn left on East Fork Road and begin watching for wild horses on the left. There's a **collapsing barn (6)** on the left in 4 miles. In .3 miles turn left on Spar Canyon Road. Follow this through **Spar Canyon (7)** continuing to watch for wild horses. Return to East Fork Road and turn left. In 1.4 miles there's a pullout for a view over the river. In 2.7 miles there's another **river view (8)**. In 5.4

Points of Interest
1. Bayhorse
2. Kilns
3. Old Mining Structures
4. Creek
5. Bayhorse Lake
6. Collapsing Barn
7. Spar Canyon
8. River View
9. Old Cabin
10. Steel Bridge
11. Old Barn
12. White Cloud Mountains
13. Yankee Fork Dredge
14. Custer
15. Riverbend
16. Old Bath House
17. Sawtooth Mountains
18. Sponsor - The Lower Stanley Country Store and Motel
19. Sawtooth Mountain Views
20. Old Cabin
21. Old Log Fence
22. Mt. McGown

idahoscenics.2.vu/26

miles there's an **old cabin (9)** on the left. Return to Hwy 75. Turn left.

In 3.3 miles you'll see an old **steel bridge (10)**. An **old barn (11)** is on the right in 8 miles. In 2.3 miles, turn left on Slate Creek Road. Stay left after crossing the creek. The valley opens up with views of the **White Cloud Mountains (12)** in 3.5 miles. You'll also pass a log fence, creek views, and aspen. Return to Hwy 75 and turn left.

In 11.3 miles, turn right on Yankee Fork Road. Follow for 8 miles to the ghost town of Bonanza. There are several old structures here. Stay right to continue to the ghost town of Custer. You'll pass the **Yankee Fork Dredge (13)** en route. Stay right. You'll reach the historic town of **Custer (14)** in 2 miles. Return to Hwy 75, watching for river views, especially in autumn.

Turn right onto Hwy 75 and pull into the parking area on the left. From here you have a view of the old earthen dam across the Salmon River and a sweeping **river bend (15)**. Continue left (west) from the parking lot. You'll arrive at Sunbeam Hot Springs and an **old bath house (16)** built by the CCC in .9 mile. Stop for a soak in the riverside pools. In about 10 miles you'll have the iconic views of Lower Stanley, the **Sawtooth Mountains (17)** and the Salmon River. **The Lower Stanley Country Store and Motel (18)**, this route's sponsor, is on the left just ahead.

Photography Tips

We recommend this route for early to mid-June or late September for wildflowers or autumn color, but of course mountains are beautiful any time of year. We like our wide angle lenses for mountain views and wildflower meadows, but you could easily find uses for varying focal lengths.

Directions Continued

The Lower Stanley Country Store, along the banks of the Salmon River, offers a full line of groceries, drinks, and non-food items including camping equipment, hardware and some souvenirs. They are dealers for Melissa and Doug and Camp Chef. Known as "The Biggest Little Grocery Store" in the nation, along with a gas station, they have 9 motel rooms and 15 log cabins. Eight of the cabins are on the river with decks and porches to enjoy the view of the majestic Sawtooth Mountains. Your stay includes the peaceful, quiet serenity you would expect from this unique and beautiful setting.

Retrace your route on Hwy 75 for .2 mile and turn left onto Nip and Tuck Road (NF 633). In less than 3 miles watch for **Sawtooth Mountain views (19)**. In about 2 more miles turn left onto NF 653. There's a distant **old cabin (20)** on the right in .7 mile. There are two good choices for sunset: If it's late May to mid June, retrace your route on NF 653 but stay left onto NF 432 for a great camas meadow with an **old log fence (21)**. Park at the gate. Alternately, continue on NF 653 for .5 mile to Hwy 21. Go directly across Hwy 21 and follow NF 455 for 3.1 miles to the campground entrance. Turn left into the campground, then make a right toward the day-use area. Here you'll have a great view of Stanley Lake and **Mt. McGown (22)**. Return to Hwy 21 and turn right. Follow into Stanley in 4.5 miles. Turn left on Hwy 75 and arrive back at Lower Stanley Country Store and Motel in 1.2 miles.

This Route's Sponsor

Lower Stanley Country Store and Motel
55 Lower Stanley,
Stanley, ID 83278
(208) 774-3566

Up Next: Route 37

Eastern Region

Route #

27. Dunes to Caldera
28. Teton Valley and Mountain Views
29. South Fork of the Snake River
30. Palisades and Caribou Mountains
31. Chesterfield and Oneida Narrows
32. Cub River and Bear Lake
33. Bannock Range and the Arbon Valley

Palisades Reservoir as viewed from along route 30.

Welcome to Idaho's Eastern Region

With views of the majestic Teton Range to the east, 25 miles of sand dunes, and one of Earth's largest calderas, these northeastern routes serve up a geological smorgasbord. You'll explore the Caribou Mountains to the south, along with a wildlife refuge, farmlands, rivers and historic Chesterfield. The Caribou-Targhee National Forest, which extends more than 2.6 million acres, borders Yellowstone and Grand Teton national parks and the Bridger-Teton National Forest. Mormon settlers founded the now ghost town of Chesterfield, along a route of the Oregon Trail, in 1881. It features several historical buildings, including the LDS Meetinghouse and the Denmark Jensen cabin. You'll travel through Immigration Canyon and the Oneida Narrows and visit Bear Lake, also known as the "Caribbean of the Rockies" because of its emerald blue-green waters.

An old barn near St. Anthony can be viewed on route 27.

Teton mountain views abound along route 28.

Dunes to Caldera

Route 27 ◇------▶ St. Anthony to Island Park

This Route at a Glance:

Estimated Driving Time: 5 hours

Highlights: Sand dunes, Waterfalls, Wildflowers, Mountaintop Vistas

About This Route: We'll start this route by watching the morning sun light up the quartz sands of St. Anthony Sand Dunes. This area features more than 10,000 acres of white sand dunes, reaching up to 400 feet, and is a huge draw to off-road vehicle enthusiasts. From there we'll visit old barns, three roaring waterfalls, and Island Park, in the heart of an ancient caldera. Wrap up your day by viewing wildflowers (in July) along the road to Sawtell Peak, and watch sunset over the Centennial Mountains.

Notes and Cautions: Not all road options are accessible in winter. You can find wildflowers on this route anytime from late spring to late summer depending on elevation. Watch for wildlife. Moose are common on this route; this is also black bear and grizzly bear territory. The wind can blow very hard on Sawtell Peak and you'll want a jacket even in summer.

Directions

From Hwy 20 south of Sugar City take exit 337. Turn North on N. Salem Road then turn left (west) at the first intersection on Ball Road. Follow Ball Road for 3 miles. Turn right (north) on N. Slough Road (N. 4000 W.) and follow for 5.4 miles. Turn left (west) on E. 400 N. (Egin-Hammer Road) and follow for about 5 miles to views of the **sand dunes (1)**.

Turn around and follow E. 400 N. east until you reach N. 1900 E. Turn left (north) and follow until it becomes Red Road in about 4 miles. Continue a couple miles farther for more **sand dune views (2)**. Return south on Red Road to E. 600 N. (Parker Road). Turn left and follow for 5.3 miles through the town of St. Anthony as it curves to the left and joins Business 20. Turn right on Business 20 and follow for .9 mile, then turn left on Sand Creek Road.

Follow Sand Creek Road for 1.4 miles, then turn right on E. 700 N. Turn right in .6 mile and cross the Henry's Fork of the Snake River. Turn left on S. River Road, and pull into the river access area for views of the **Fun Farm Bridge (3)** and river. Go left when leaving the access area, then left again in .6 mile to stay on S. River Road. In 1.6 miles there's a barn on the left. In .1 mile turn left on 2830 E and follow to the end for views of the **Chester Dam (4)**. Return to S. River road and turn left. In .5 mile there's a small **old barn (5)** on the left. Turn left on N 2900 E. In 1.6 miles park before the bridge on the right. Here you can view this **old steel bridge and a barn (6)**. Continue across the bridge for three miles watching for Teton views to the east. Turn right on 1100 N. In 2.6 miles **there's a barn (7)** on the left. Turn left onto Hwy 20. Proceed past the town on Ashton and across the Henry's Fork of the Snake River. Turn right on Fisherman's Drive. In about 1 mile you will reach an overlook of the **Snake River winding through aspen (8)** with a backdrop of the Teton Range on a clear day.

Return south to Ashton and turn left onto Main Street (Hwy 47). Turn right in 6 miles onto Cave Falls Road (E. 1400 N.). This 19-mile (one way) drive to visit Cave Falls includes a mildly bumpy stretch of gravel for the last half of the route. The road ends at the parking area for the falls. A short .1 mile walk will get you to views of the **falls (9)**. Return to Hwy 47 and continue north. In 8.8 miles you'll reach the parking area for a distant view of **Lower Mesa Falls (10)**. Turn left in .7 mile and follow the road to the parking for **Upper Mesa**

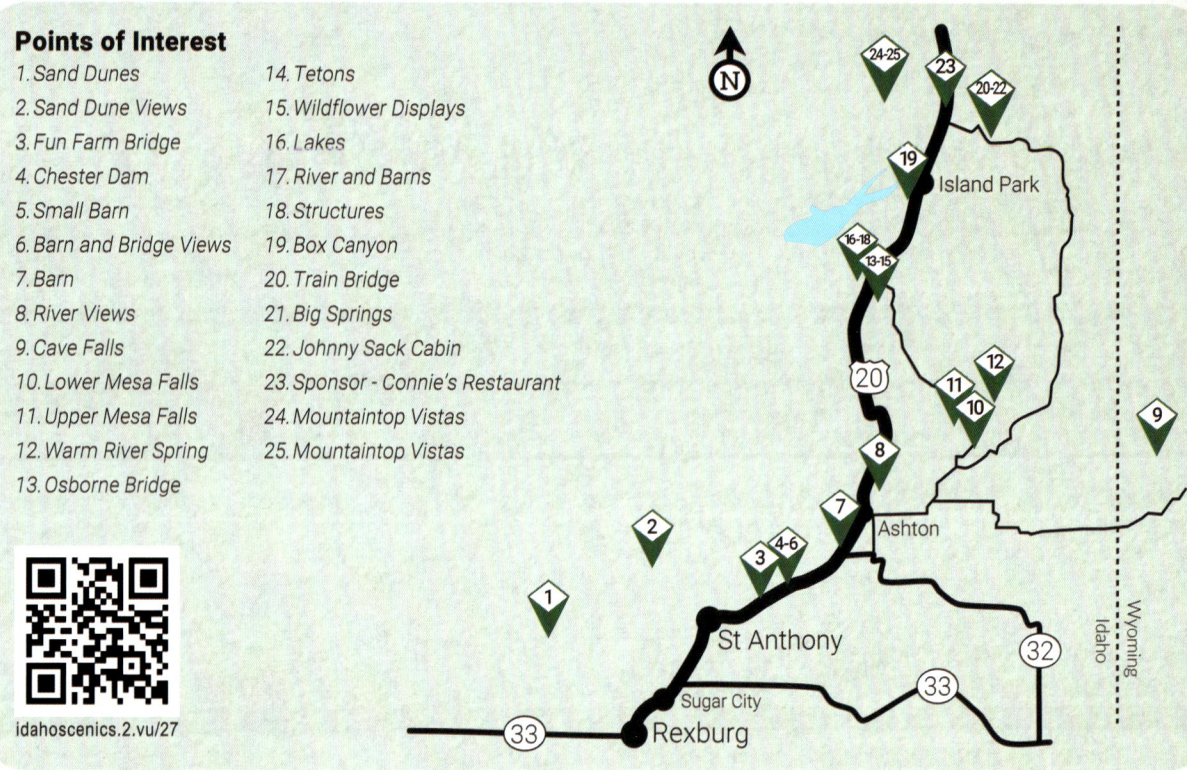

Points of Interest
1. Sand Dunes
2. Sand Dune Views
3. Fun Farm Bridge
4. Chester Dam
5. Small Barn
6. Barn and Bridge Views
7. Barn
8. River Views
9. Cave Falls
10. Lower Mesa Falls
11. Upper Mesa Falls
12. Warm River Spring
13. Osborne Bridge
14. Tetons
15. Wildflower Displays
16. Lakes
17. River and Barns
18. Structures
19. Box Canyon
20. Train Bridge
21. Big Springs
22. Johnny Sack Cabin
23. Sponsor - Connie's Restaurant
24. Mountaintop Vistas
25. Mountaintop Vistas

idahoscenics.2.vu/27

Directions Continued

Falls (11). For up-close views of this impressive falls you'll need to descend a series of steps and walkways.

Return to Hwy 47 and turn left. In .7 miles turn right on FS 150. This moderately bumpy, 5-mile side trip takes you to Warm River Springs. In 2.7 miles keep right on FS 154. In .8 mile keep left on FS 154. You'll pass a meadow, which could be filled with wildflowers in late spring. In 1.5 miles you'll arrive at **Warm River Springs (12)**. Return to Hwy 47 and turn right.

In 12.2 miles turn left on Hwy 20. Turn left in .9 mile onto the **Osborne Bridge (13)** access to Harriman State Park. This can be a beautiful sunrise location, with views of the **Tetons (14)** as well as offering plentiful **wildflower displays (15)** in a good year. Cross the highway and explore Harriman State Park for **lakes (16)**, **river and barns (17)** as well as other **historic structures (18)**. Return to Hwy 20 and turn left (north). There is a popular fishing access on the left in 3.4 miles. This is a great spot to watch fly fisherman or cast a line. In 5.2 miles turn right into the Buffalo River Campground. Follow the road .9 mile to the end for river access. Return to Hwy 20 and proceed straight across the highway on FS 139. In 1.5 miles, just before the dam, turn left and follow the road downhill for .2 mile to the boat ramp and parking area. This is a great spot to watch drift boats launch on their way through **Box Canyon**

(19), or dip your toes in the water. Return to Highway 20 and turn left.

In 5.3 miles turn right on S. Big Springs Loop Road. In 4 miles turn left on FS 144. In .5 mile arrive at an abandoned rail, re-purposed **trail bridge (20)** over the Henry's Fork. Continue on S. Big Springs Road. In .9 mile you'll find parking to explore **Big Springs (21)** and the **Johnny Sack Cabin (22)**. Continue on N. Big Springs Road 4.2 miles back to Hwy 20.

Cross Hwy 20 onto Sawtell Peak Road. In .1 mile turn right onto Quakie Lane. In .1 mile you'll find this route's sponsor, **Connie's Restaurant (23)**, on the left. For a truly enjoyable dining experience, visit Connie's. We have a variety of delicious entrees and offer a full-service saloon. Home of the original Sawtell Hamburger, homemade chili & soups, our signature cornbread with honey butter, BBQ Baby Back Ribs and a variety of steaks cooked to perfection. We take great pride in the quality of each menu item, as well as the service provided. Make sure to leave enough time in your journey to visit our Daisy's Angels' Unique Boutique. Located inside Connie's Restaurant.

Return to Sawtell Peak Road and turn right. The pavement ends in 2 miles. This bumpy narrow and winding gravel road is worth the drive for amazing **mountaintop vistas (24,25)**. Drive carefully and watch for views and wildflowers in summer. Arrive at Sawtell Peak in 9.5 miles.

Photography Tips

Plan to arrive for first light on the sand dunes for best photography. You'll want a telephoto lens for the sand dune location and Lower Mesa Falls. A polarizer and/or neutral density filters are useful for the river and barn on the Henry's Fork and Upper Mesa Falls. Sawtell Peak is an excellent place to view the sunset.

This Route's Sponsor

Connie's Restaurant & Saloon
4130 Quakie Lane, Island Park, Idaho
(208)558-6987
www.conniesrestaurant.org

See page 272 for coupon

Up Next: Route 28

Teton Valley and Mountain Views

Route 28 ◇------------------------▶ Driggs to Ashton

This Route at a Glance:

Estimated Driving Time: 4 hours

Highlights: Mountain Vistas, Seasonal Waterfall, Barns, Old Structures

About This Route: Nestled beneath the morning shadow of the Teton Range, the Teton Valley route is replete with awe-inspiring views from almost anywhere. We'll visit old barns and cabins and find favorite access points to the Teton River. We'll also head into Wyoming for a seasonal waterfall and an up-close view of the Grand Tetons before heading to Ashton. This is one of our favorite routes for autumn color!

Notes and Cautions: Teton Canyon Road can be very bumpy and dusty. This is bear and moose country, be aware and carry bear spray. This route starts with an excellent sunrise location. Allow at least 15 minutes to get there from Driggs. The Tetons can be seen from almost anywhere in the northern parts of the valley. These route directions do not pinpoint every available view. Please respect private property.

Directions

From the stoplight in Driggs, proceed west on Bates Road, about 4.4 miles. Stay straight as the road curves to the left. In .8 mile turn right (north) on 6000W. In 2 miles turn right (east) on W 2000N. In .8 mile arrive in the parking area for Rainey Bridge access. Walk along the bluff above the **river bend (1)** for excellent sunrise views.

Return to 6000 W and then Bates Road, then turn left on Bates. There is an **old cabin (2)** on the right n 2.3 miles. Continue east on Bates Road. In 3.3 miles turn right (south) on Hwy 33. In 2 miles turn left (east) on E 2000 S. Proceed 3.2 miles to Stateline Road, watching for an old tractor at around 2 miles.

Turn right (south) on Stateline Road. This short (1 mile), but rough section is not maintained but worth the effort in the autumn and in dry weather. Watch for nice aspen and an **old house (3)** on the left in one mile. Return to the intersection of Stateline Road and E 2000 S but continue on Stateline Road. There is an **old structure (4)** immediately past the intersection on the right. Continue 3.9 miles and turn right (east) on Ski Hill Road. You are now in Wyoming.

In 2.1 miles there is a small pullout on the right with views of the Tetons. In ½ mile turn right onto Teton Canyon Road This 4.5 mile dead-end road offers views of the **Tetons (5)** and ends at a trailhead into the Jedediah Smith Wilderness. Walk ¼ mile on the trailhead that leaves the parking area to the south and find a seasonal, tall but delicate **waterfall (6)** on the left.

Return to Ski Hill Road and turn right (east). In 1.7 miles you'll reach a scenic overlook parking on the right. This is an excellent spot for up close mountain views, a moonrise or to watch the last light kiss the **peaks (7)**. Follow Ski Hill Road back to Driggs and turn right (north).

You'll find this route's sponsor, **Big Hole Bagel and Bistro (8)**, at 285 N. Main, on the right in .2 mile. They make bagels the old fashioned way by boiling and baking them fresh everyday in at least 10 different varieties. Their breakfast and lunch bistro serves all day until closing, and most entrees come with a

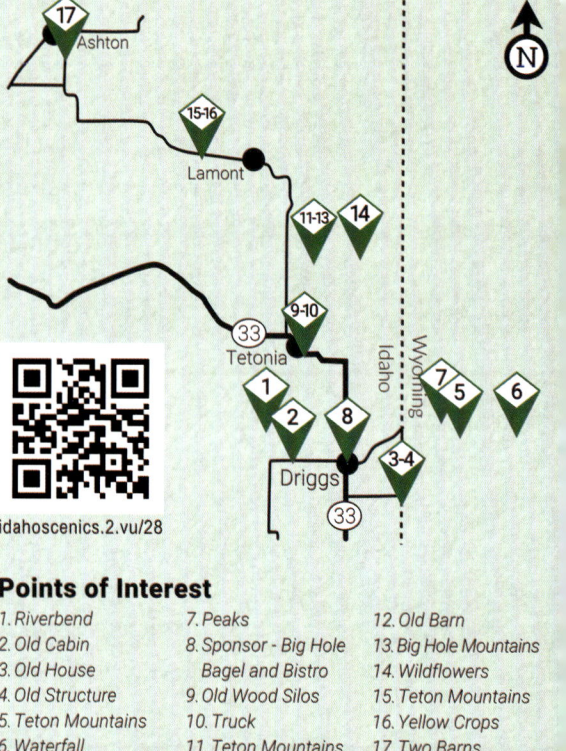

idahoscenics.2.vu/28

Points of Interest

1. Riverbend
2. Old Cabin
3. Old House
4. Old Structure
5. Teton Mountains
6. Waterfall
7. Peaks
8. Sponsor - Big Hole Bagel and Bistro
9. Old Wood Silos
10. Truck
11. Teton Mountains
12. Old Barn
13. Big Hole Mountains
14. Wildflowers
15. Teton Mountains
16. Yellow Crops
17. Two Barns

Directions Continued

fresh bagel. From eggs benedict to 5 egg omelets. Biscuits and gravy, and a huge selection of bagel breakfast and lunch sandwiches . They are very popular with locals and travelers from around the globe. "Our cinnamon rolls are world famous!"

Continue north on Hwy 33. In 5.1 miles there is a cute old house on the right. Park safely if you choose to photograph this. In three miles, just as you enter the town of Tetonia, turn left on N 3000 W then make an immediate right on Letham. You'll see some unique, **old wood silos (9)** just ahead. Return to Hwy 33 and turn left (north). There's an **old truck (10)** on the right in 1.1 mile. In .7 miles turn right (north) on Hwy 32.

In 3.3 miles turn right on Wells. There is a cute vine-covered cabin on the corner. Proceed north on Hwy 32. In 1.9 miles turn right (east) on 12000 N. This road has great views of the **Tetons (11)**. In 1.2 miles turn right (south) on Reece Road then turn left in .1 mile on 12000 N. In .5 mile there's a beautiful **old barn (12)** in the valley on the right . In another .5 mile there's another great view of the Tetons as a backdrop to some crops. Wind your way up the hill alongside aspen and lupine in mid-July, reaching a great view over the farmlands with the **Big Hole Mountains (13)** to the southwest in .7 mile. In .5 mile there are some

cabins on the right on private property. Shoot with a telephoto lens or ask permission. Continue a few more miles into the Targhee National Forest for summer **wildflowers (14)** among a mix of aspen and evergreen trees. Return to Hwy 32.

Continuing north on Hwy 32, you'll find a large pullout on the left in 2.8 miles for a view of the Teton River. Continue on Hwy 32 for 7.2 miles, watching for another old structure on the left. Turn right on N 4400 E just past the old grain elevator. In .1 mile you'll get a nice view of the elevator with the **Tetons (15)**. Continue just over the hill for possible fields of **yellow crops (16)** in late June and July. Return to Hwy 32, and turn right (west). In 11.8 miles there are **two barns (17)** on the left. In 1.9 miles turn left on E 1300 N. Arrive in the town of Ashton in .5 mile.

Photography Tips

You'll want a wide angle lens to fit the sunrise and mountains in the same shot and include the river. A telephoto can be useful throughout the valley at many locations for the mountains. The cabins can mostly be shot with a mid-range zoom. The waterfall should remain in shade for the morning. On a clear day the Tetons can be seen jutting up behind the 12000 N barn.

This Route's Sponsor

Big Hole Bagel and Bistro
285 N Main, Driggs, ID
(208) 354-2245
bigholebagel.com

See page 272 for coupon

Up Next: Route 27 or 29

South Fork of the Snake River

Route 29 ◇------------------▶ Swan Valley Loop

This Route at a Glance:

Estimated Driving Time: 3 hours

Highlights: Waterfall, River Views, Creek

About This Route: One of Idaho's best waterfalls is found on this route, as we loop the South Fork of the Snake River from Swan Valley to Palisades Reservoir. This is one of the most magnificent fall color routes in the state! The cottonwood trees lining the river can turn a vibrant gold in early to mid October. There's also a gorgeous hike along Palisades Creek and some unique rock formations to visit.

Notes and Cautions: This is one of the shorter and milder routes in the book but with no shortage of scenic beauty. We like this route best in autumn for the glorious color in the cottonwood trees. With the exception of the Sheep Creek side trip, all roads should be passable in winter after snow plows have had a chance to work. Be careful when approaching Fall Creek Falls, as it is viewed from a steep bluff above the river.

Directions

From Swan Valley go northwest on Hwy 26 for 3.3 miles, crossing the highway bridge over the South Fork of the Snake River. Take an immediate left on NF 058 (Snake River Road). Proceed 1.3 miles until crossing Fall Creek. Park at the second small, unmarked pullout on the left. Make your way through the bushes on foot to the ledge for up-close views of **Fall Creek Falls (1)** and the **South Fork of the Snake River (2)**. Continue on Snake River Road (which becomes NF 076) for 1.9 miles, watching for river views. In autumn, turn onto a two-track spur at the top of a switchback grade, park and walk .1 mile to the north for views of **aspen trees (3)** above the switchback. A large pullout on the left in another mile affords gorgeous

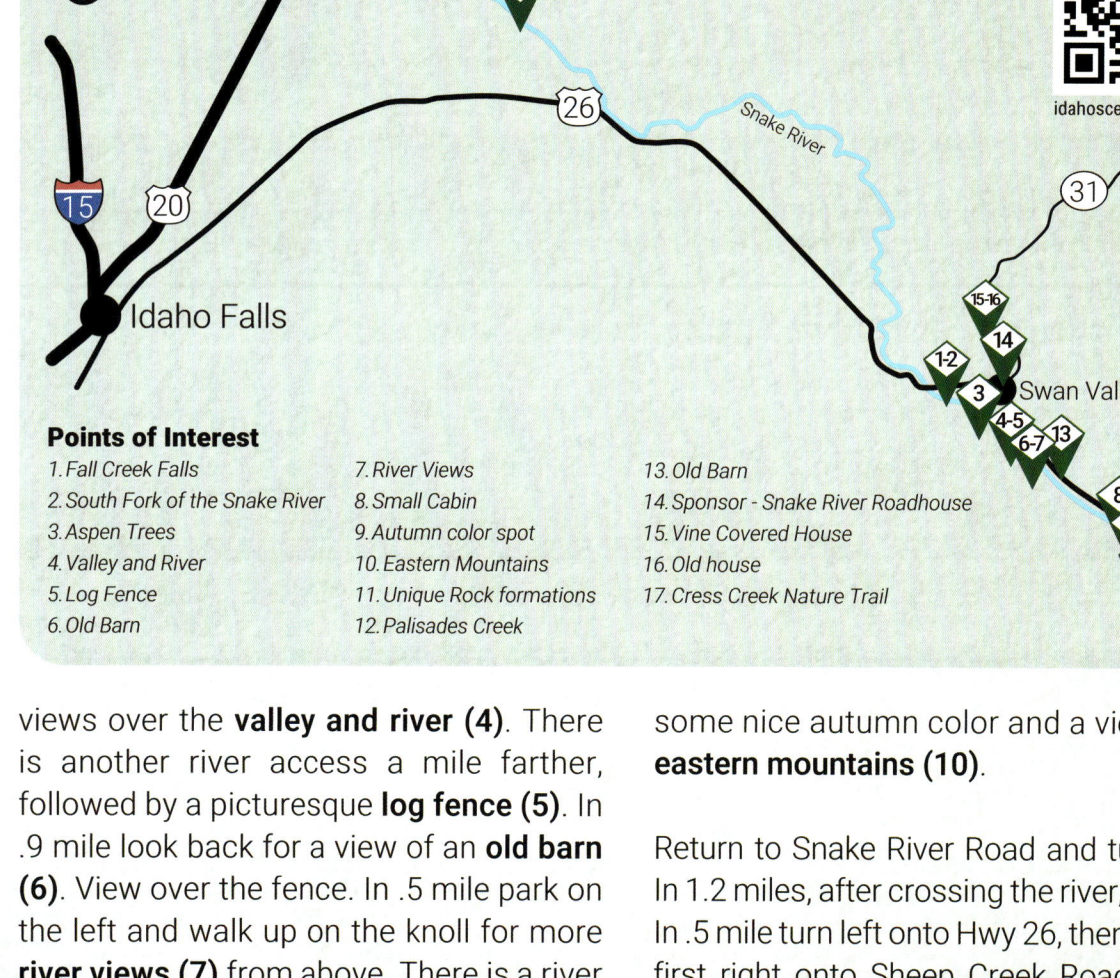

idahoscenics.2.vu/29

Points of Interest
1. Fall Creek Falls
2. South Fork of the Snake River
3. Aspen Trees
4. Valley and River
5. Log Fence
6. Old Barn
7. River Views
8. Small Cabin
9. Autumn color spot
10. Eastern Mountains
11. Unique Rock formations
12. Palisades Creek
13. Old Barn
14. Sponsor - Snake River Roadhouse
15. Vine Covered House
16. Old house
17. Cress Creek Nature Trail

views over the **valley and river (4)**. There is another river access a mile farther, followed by a picturesque **log fence (5)**. In .9 mile look back for a view of an **old barn (6)**. View over the fence. In .5 mile park on the left and walk up on the knoll for more **river views (7)** from above. There is a river access on the left in 1 mile. In 3.3 miles a **small cabin (8)** on private property can be shot with a mid-telephoto lens. You'll find a nice **autumn color spot (9)** in 1 mile. Stay straight in .3 mile and, in .6 mile, a two-track road on the right takes you about .5 mile to some nice autumn color and a view of the **eastern mountains (10)**.

Return to Snake River Road and turn right. In 1.2 miles, after crossing the river, turn left. In .5 mile turn left onto Hwy 26, then take the first right onto Sheep Creek Road. Follow until you have views of the **unique rock formations (11)** on the hillsides on the left. In mid-late September these are accentuated with red mountain maples. Return to Hwy 26 and turn right. In a little over 2.5 miles turn right on Palisades Creek

Directions Continued

Road and stay left in 2 miles. In another .3 mile park at the trailhead for Palisades Creek. Take a walk of any length along **Palisades Creek (12)**. It is exceptionally photogenic from the bridges in early to mid October. Back at Hwy 26 turn right. In 3 miles turn left on Barrus Street. There is a unique **old barn (13)** ahead on the left. Return to Hwy 26 and continue 3 miles into Swan Valley. You'll find this route's sponsor, the **Snake River Roadhouse (14)** on the left.

Located in scenic Swan Valley, Idaho, Snake River Roadhouse serves classic American cuisine: handcrafted burgers, steaks, gourmet pizza, seafood, dinner specials and homemade pie. Almost everything is made from scratch! Come dine with us in our beautiful, newly remodeled facility with a cozy, comfortable dining area and new bar, complete with shuffleboard table and multiple TV's for viewing sports. Our brand new outdoor covered dining and bar patio area, fire pit and two regulation horseshoe pits are great for the summer months! Along with our dining and bar facilities, we also have recently renovated hotel rooms and full service RV spots.

Turn right (east) on Hwy 31. A **vine-covered house (15)** is on the left in 2.8 miles. Be

careful parking and crossing the highway. In .1 mile turn left on Campbell Road for another **old house (16)**. Return to Hwy 31. From here you can return to Swan Valley, then Idaho Falls or continue to Victor and Driggs. If going to Victor, turn left. Watch for another old house on the left in 5.5 miles. Arrive in Victor in about 13 miles.

If going to Idaho Falls, return to Hwy 26 and go right. In 23.7 miles turn right on N 160 E. for a sunset vista and hike. Go 2 miles then turn right on 4949 E 100 N. In .8 mile turn left on N 5050 E. In .4 miles turn left on E. Heise Road. In 1.2 miles arrive at the trailhead for **Cress Creek Nature Trail (17)**. A hike up the hillside here will be an excellent spot to watch the sunset. Return to Hwy 26 and go right. Idaho Falls is ahead in about 18 miles.

Photography Tips

Fall Creek Falls is a great sunrise location. You'll want a wide-angle lens to shoot the sunrise and the falls together as a wide landscape. A neutral density filter can be useful here to get that velvety water effect. You may want a telephoto lens for photographing the rock formations up Sheep Creek Road and the first barn. Cress Creek Nature Trail provides exceptional views over the Snake River Plain for sunset. A graduated neutral density filter is recommended for balancing the bright sky against the landscape.

This Route's Sponsor

Snake River Roadhouse
2998 Swan Valley Hwy, Swan Valley, ID
(208) 483-2000 | srroadhouse.com

See page 272 for coupon

Up Next: Routes 28 or 30

Palisades and the Caribou Mountains
Route 30 ◇----------------------▶ Alpine to Soda Springs

This Route at a Glance:

Estimated Driving Time: 4 hours

Highlights: Autumn color, Mountain Views, Wildflowers

About This Route: Another fantastic fall tour, this route begins in the aspen-covered hills surrounding Palisades Reservoir. Aspens show off their fall colors of yellow and orange, with occasional reds punctuating the view. Take a mid-September drive through the Caribou Mountains to witness the stunning reds of mountain maple. Starting mid-May, the Gray's Lake Wildlife Refuge takes on golden hues from the multiple clumps of arrowleaf balsamroot that proliferate here. In mid June, feast your eyes on the wildflowers in the mountains.

Notes and Cautions: The majority of this route will not be accessible in winter. Park safely along Palisades Reservoir; this can be a very busy highway. The road over Bear Creek Summit is not recommended for passenger vehicles. The road is a little rough, but not as bad as the sign would have you believe. We recommend all-wheel drive.

Directions

Go north on Hwy 26 from Alpine, Wyoming. You'll cross into Idaho within a few miles of town. For the next 18 miles, enjoy the changing colors in the **aspen trees (1)** on the hillsides above the reservoir, and the reds of mountain maples across the reservoir in the Caribou Mountains. You'll find several pullouts for viewing. Turn left on Dam Road at the base of the dam in 18 miles. In .4 mile turn right and cross the river. In 1.8 miles turn left. You'll have a view of the mountains with an aspen foreground in 1 mile. Trail 266 takes off on the right just .2 mile farther. Walk a short distance up this trail for close-up **aspen views (2)**.

In 1.5 miles turn right on NF 058. In 2.3 miles, there's a nice view over the **reservoir (3)** with a pullout on the left. In 3.4 miles stay left, and in 1.7 miles stay left again. After crossing Bear Creek Summit, watch for multiple **mountain and valley views (4, 5)** while descending into the valley. In about 10 miles you'll reach the intersection with McCoy Creek Rd (NF 087). Watch for creek views. A pullout on the right in 6 miles offers a nice vista of the creek and **Caribou Mountain (6)**.

In 1.5 miles stay straight and in 1.4 miles keep straight again. In another 1.4 miles keep left on NF 087. In almost 6 miles a distant old homestead can be seen on the right. Turn left on Grays Lake Road in .5 mile. Spring wildflowers proliferate along the **fence line (7)** and into the wildlife refuge in about 1.4 miles. In 5.5 miles you'll find an **old house (8)** on the right and a **small barn (9)** on the left, with a backdrop of aspen. In .9 mile there's an old **stone cellar (10)** on the left.

In 1.3 miles turn left on Bridge Creek Road This 8.7-mile detour takes you through some beautiful **aspen groves (11)**. Turn right on Hwy 34 and, in .8 mile, turn left on Lanes Creek Cutoff. Turn left on Lanes Creek Road in 5 miles. In 6.9 miles turn right on Blackfoot River Road. In 1 mile there's a sportsman's access for river views. Stay left in .1 mile, then stay straight onto pavement in 4.4 miles. There is a nice assortment of view here, including valley, river and **railroad tracks (12)**. Stay right in .6 mile and, in 1.5 miles, stay right on

Points of Interest
1. Aspen Trees
2. Aspen Views
3. Reservoir
4. Mountain and Valley Views
5. Mountain and Valley Views
6. Caribou Mountain
7. Fenceline
8. Old House
9. Small Barn
10. Stone Cellar
11. Aspen Groves
12. Railroad Tracks
13. Valley View
14. Henry Store
15. Sponsor - Cedar Bay Marina, RV Park and Cafe
16. Blackfoot Reservoir

idahoscenics.2.vu/30

Photography Tips

You'll want a telephoto lens for the aspen trees above Palisades Reservoir. A wide-angle lens is useful for the reservoirs, mountains and fields of wildflowers. Wildflowers peak around mid June here. Fall color is great from mid September to early October, beginning with the red mountain maples followed by the yellow and oranges of the aspen trees.

Directions Continued

Blackfoot River Road. You'll find an expansive **valley view (13)** in 2.4 miles.

Cross Haul Road in about 4 miles. You'll get a view of Blackfoot Reservoir across some wheat fields in about 2 miles. For up-close views of the reservoir and a visit to the historic Henry store, turn right on Hwy 34. In 6.8 miles you'll find the historic **Henry Store (14)**. After stopping here, turn left to visit this route's sponsor **Cedar Bay Marina, RV Park and Cafe (15)**.

Nestled in a small cove on the east side of the Blackfoot Reservoir, Cedar Bay Marina, RV Park & Café is midway between Soda Springs and Wayan, ID, off Hwy 34, 18 miles north of Soda Springs. This family-oriented, private campground welcomes seasonal campers, long-term visitors and overnight travelers. Amenities include full hookups, laundry and shower facilities and an onsite cafe and general store. The café specializes in the best hand-scooped Farr's Ice Cream in many flavors, specialty shakes, biscuits and gravy and homemade Idaho potato fries. Activities include fishing, camping, hiking and water sports, with paddleboards, kayaks, and paddle boats for rent with life jackets provided. End your route here with excellent sunset views over the **Blackfoot Reservoir (16)**. Proceed south on Hwy 34 to the town of Soda Springs.

This Route's Sponsor

Cedar Bay Marina and Cafe
3429 ID-34, Soda Springs, ID 83276
(435) 730-6140
cedarbayrvmarina.com

See page 272 for coupon

Up Next: Routes 31 or 32

Chesterfield and the Oneida Narrows

Route 31 ◇------------▶ Bancroft to Preston

This Route at a Glance:

Estimated Driving Time: 5 hours

Highlights: Bear River, Oneida Narrows, Historic Town

About This Route: Start with a visit to the famous Soda Springs Geyser, then tour the historic Chesterfield ghost town site. In the morning we'll continue south following the Bear River as it makes it way through farmlands, past old homesteads and the Black Canyon and scenic Oneida Narrows. The Gem Valley, once home to the Shoshone tribe of Native Americans, features several pioneer landmarks along the Oregon Trail, which passed through the northern part of the valley.

Notes and Cautions: Oneida Narrows Road is not recommended in deep snow or wet weather. It is moderately bumpy, rocky and all-wheel drive is required in winter. There are two options for beginning this route: Either coming from the southwest at Lava Hot Springs or the east at Soda Springs. Begin this route in early afternoon to take advantage of our sponsor's special offers.

Directions

From Lava Hot Springs- Head east on Hwy 30 and turn left at the end of town on Blaser Hwy (Old US Hwy 30). In 6.8 miles a river access on the left provides nice spring or autumn views over the **Portneuf River (1)**. Continue on Blaser Hwy for 2.6 miles. **The old Pebble Store (2)** is on the right. In .8 mile there are some mildly distant older structures on the left. In 1 mile turn left on Kelly Toponce Road (or continue to this route's sponsor, the Caribou Gem in Bancroft in 6.4 miles).

From Soda Springs: Visit the famous **Soda Springs geyser (3)** at the west end of E 1st Street South and South Main Street. Continue south 2 blocks on South Main Street, then turn right on Hwy 30. Continue west on Hwy 30 for 5.8 miles, then turn left on a dirt road. This moderately rough sagebrush lined dirt road will take you to the **canyon edge (4)** for nice views of the Bear River. Walk the ¼ mile or so, if you don't wish to scratch your vehicle. Back on Highway turn left then turn right in .8 mile on Old Hwy 30. In 9.5 miles arrive at this route's sponsor, the Caribou Gem in Bancroft.

Caribou Gem (5) is a newly remodeled motel in the beautiful Gem Valley of Southeast Idaho. Located in Bancroft, Idaho, a small rural town with much history and natural beauty. The property offers a small town stay and all the luxuries of home with each of the rooms being furnished with full kitchens. The motel is a short drive from Lava Hot Springs famous hot pools as well as the historic Chesterfield townsites.

From Bancroft go west on Old Hwy 30. In 6.4 miles turn right on Kelly Toponce Rd. There's a barn on the left in 1 mile. In .5 mile you'll cross the Portneuf River. Turn

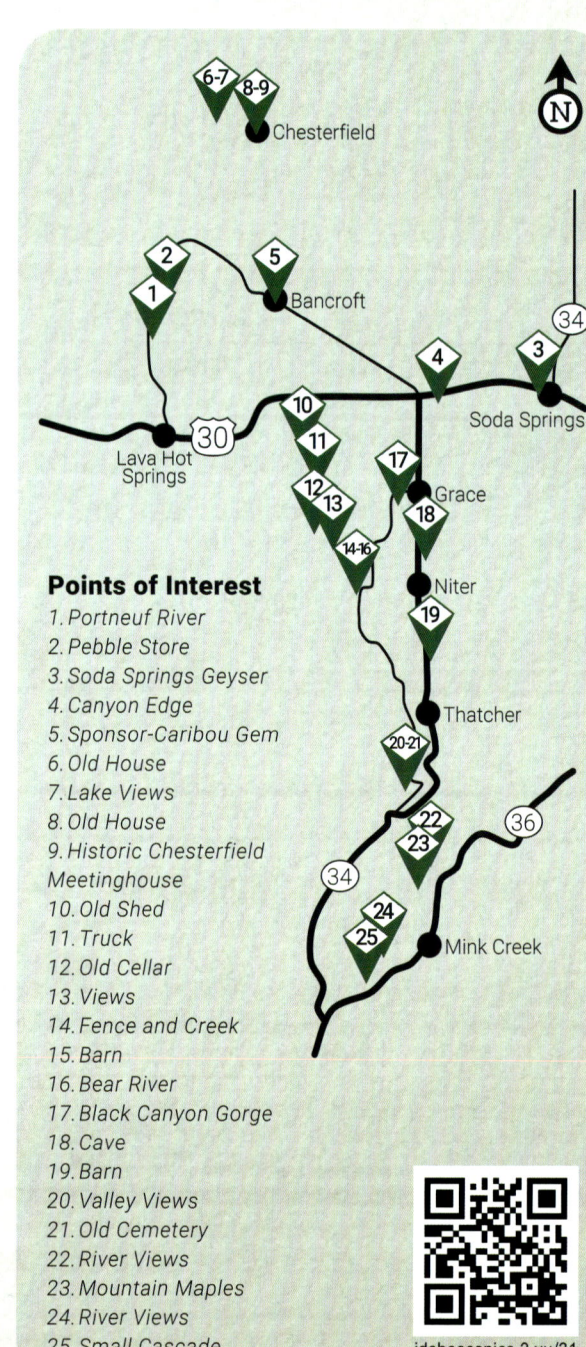

Points of Interest
1. Portneuf River
2. Pebble Store
3. Soda Springs Geyser
4. Canyon Edge
5. Sponsor-Caribou Gem
6. Old House
7. Lake Views
8. Old House
9. Historic Chesterfield Meetinghouse
10. Old Shed
11. Truck
12. Old Cellar
13. Views
14. Fence and Creek
15. Barn
16. Bear River
17. Black Canyon Gorge
18. Cave
19. Barn
20. Valley Views
21. Old Cemetery
22. River Views
23. Mountain Maples
24. River Views
25. Small Cascade

idahoscenics.2.vu/31

Directions Continued

left on Nipper Road in 8 miles. There's an **old house (6)** on the left in .5 mile. Continue on either side of Chesterfield Reservoir for **lake views (7)**.

Return to Kelly Toponce Road and turn left, then turn left on Chesterfield Road in .9 mile.. In .8 mile, turn right on Hansen Road, then left on Campground Road in .3 mile. You'll find an **old house (8)** on the left and a wagon on the right. Turn right in .1 mile, followed by another right in .2 mile on Meetinghouse Road. You'll find the **Historic Chesterfield meetinghouse (9)** here. Continue straight on Chesterfield Cemetery Road to find the old cemetery. Return to Chesterfield Road (pavement) and turn right. In .4 mile turn left for more of the historic town site. Explore this area of approximately 6 square city blocks for all kinds of finds. From the intersection of Chesterfield Road and 24 Mile Road, proceed east .5 mile and turn right on Chesterfield Road. There is another old house on the corner. Follow this road 10 miles back to Bancroft.

We recommend the following section for the morning: Head southeast on Old Hwy 30 for 1.1 miles. Turn right on Blauer Road, which becomes Bancroft Substation Road. Cross Hwy 30 in 5 miles, and in .5 mile turn left on Central Road. In .5 mile turn right on Central Road. In another .5 mile stay straight onto Mountain Road. In 1.3 miles there's an **old shed (10)** on the left, followed by an old homestead with an **old truck (11)** on the left in 1.7 miles. In .5 mile another old house is on the left. In 1.2 miles stay straight. You'll find a shack and **old cellar (12)** on the right in 1.4 miles. In .5 mile turn right on Gentile Valley Road. Stay left on Gentile Valley Road in .2 mile. You'll encounter beautiful **views (13)** over the valley. In 3 miles there's a **fence and creek (14)** on the left, followed by a neat **barn (15)** and maybe an old tractor on the

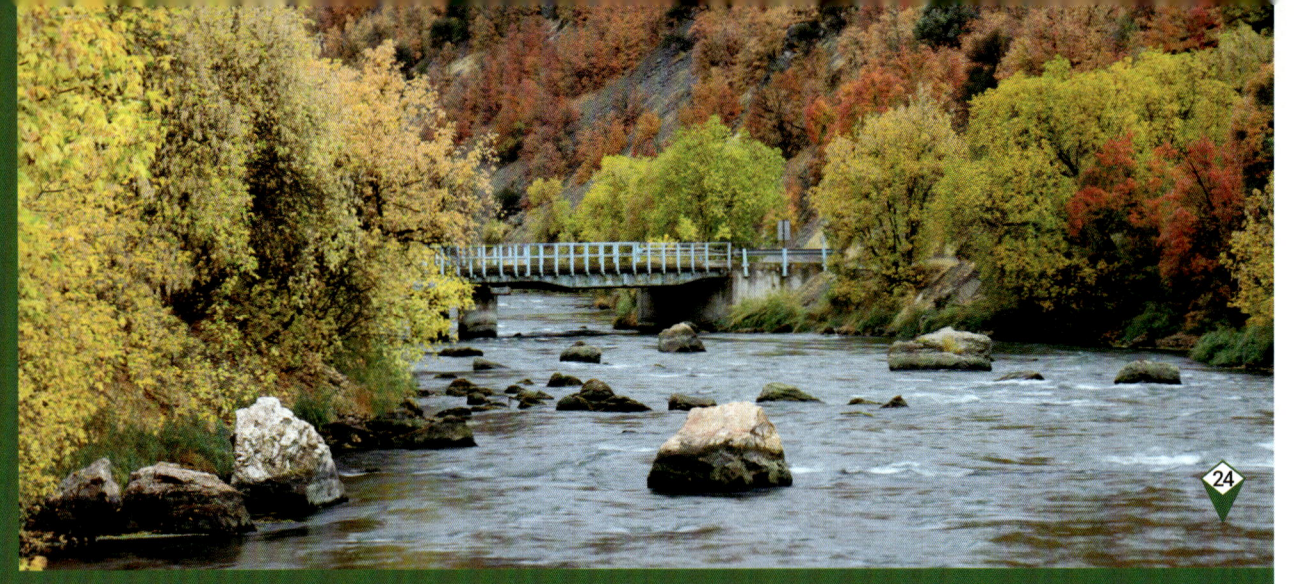

Directions Continued

right. In 1.8 miles stay straight. Cross the bridge to a pullout on the left and walk back for views of the **Bear River (16)**.

Continue for 7 miles, staying straight through 3 junctions. Just before Turner Road, park on the left for views along the rim of **Black Canyon Gorge (17)**. Be very careful. There is also an old house across the road. Turn right on Turner Road and arrive in Grace in 1 mile. Turn right on Main Street (Hwy 34). In 3.2 miles turn left on Niter Ice Cave Road. The **cave (18)** is on the left in .2 mile. Return to Hwy 34 and turn left. A large **barn (19)** at Whiskey Creek is on the left in 5.7 miles. In 1.4 miles, turn right on Thatcher Road. In .5 mile a pull-off is on the right for views of the Bear River.

Turn left on N. Cleveland Road in .8 mile. There is a barn at the junction here. Enjoy the exceptional **river and valley views (20)** over the next 4 miles, then turn left on Cleveland Cemetery Road. It is a short distance to this **old cemetery (21)** on a hilltop. Back on N. Cleveland Road, proceed 2 miles then turn left on 13400 N. Road. In .8 mile turn left on Hwy 34.

Turn right on 13800 N. Road in 1 mile, then right again on N. Maple Grove Road. This moderately bumpy gravel road travels through the Oneida Narrows section of the

Photography Tips

We recommend this route any time of year, but you'll want to see the Oneida Narrows section of the Bear River in mid-late September. Most of the historic structures on this route can be shot with a mid-range zoom. A wide angle is nice for the valley overlooks. To show water movement in your images, choose a slow your shutter speed and use a polarizing filter and/or a neutral density filter while shooting on a tripod.

This Route's Sponsor

Caribou Gem Motel
20 S 1st West St, Bancroft, ID 83217
(208) 425-6883
www.cariboulodgesoda.com

Directions Continued

Bear River. We recommend all-wheel drive in wet weather or in snow, but don't attempt in more than a few inches of snow. In 1.5 miles there is a nice river and canyon entrance view. In 1.6 miles, stay right on Oneida Narrows Road. You will pass through private property. Drive very slowly and obey all signs. Once past the hot springs area you may stop at your leisure for **river views (22)**. Maple Grove Campground is in 2.4 miles. You'll find thick groves of **mountain maples (23)** that turn a blazing red in mid-late September. Continue past the dam to the bridge crossing the Bear River, about 5 miles past the campground. The bridge provides excellent **river views (24)**. Park on the left in 1.8 miles for a **small cascade (25)** along the river. In 1.5 miles turn right onto Hwy 36. In 3 miles turn left onto Hwy 34. Arrive in Preston in 5.4 miles.

Up Next: Routes 32 or 33

Cub River and Bear Lake
Route 32 ⟶ Preston to Montpelier

This Route at a Glance:

Estimated Driving Time: 5 hours

Highlights: Autumn Foliage, Pioneer Cabins, and Lakes

Best Seasons: Spring, Summer, and Fall

Road Surface: Paved, Gravel, and Dirt

About This Route: Take a drive up the Cub River, one of Idaho's best fall color spots. Continue on to Montpelier via Emigration Canyon, with stops at a few old cabins. See the intense aqua-blue color of Bear Lake, which earns it the nickname "The Caribbean of the Rockies." Finish your day with a visit to the amazing Minnetonka Cave and its nine rooms, and a hike to a scenic mountain lake.

Notes and Cautions: The road to Bloomington Lake can be rough and will not be accessible in winter. The aqua-blue waters of Bear Lake are best viewed on a calm day. Emigration Canyon's best views are found where there is virtually no parking. Be very careful on this stretch of highway. Minnetonka Cave has a large series of steps into and back out of the cavern. Know your fitness limitations. Be respectful of private property. Minnetonka Cave and Bear Lake State Park are fee areas.

Directions

From Preston, travel south on Hwy 91 about 5 miles, then turn left on Cub River Road (NF 407). In 9 miles you'll find access to the river with amazing reds of **mountain maples (1)** in autumn. Take a small loop road to the right in .5 mile and find a **footbridge (2)** over Cub River. Continue on NF 407. There is another access spot with some **cascades (3)** on the river in another .5 mile. Stop at the junction in 2 miles to view a beautiful grove of **aspen (4)**.

Make a U-turn and retrace your route a little over 8 miles. Watch for E. Glendale Road on the right. Turn right, and in 2.7 miles stay straight. There is a moderately distant **cabin (5)** on the left in 3.7 miles. There is a **reservoir access (6)** on the right in another mile. In .4 mile turn right onto Hwy 34. In 3.7 miles turn right on Hwy 36. In approximately 14 miles you'll enter Emigration Canyon. This is an enjoyable drive and view, but very difficult to photograph due to lack of pullouts. As you descend the other side of the pass the forest changes to a unique mixture of **aspen and evergreens (7)**. Here you will find some parking areas off the highway. In 18 miles there's a small barn on the right. Turn left on Ovid Road in 13 miles, at the junction with Hwy 89.

In 3.7 miles there's an **old house (8)** out in a field on the left. Turn left up Cemetery Road for a different perspective. Back on Ovid Road, go .7 mile then turn right on Bern Road. In .4 mile stay straight, then turn left on Lower Bern Road. There is a view of Bear River in 2.4 miles. In 2.3 miles, turn right on Pescadero Lane for a **river access and view (9)**. In 1.5 miles turn right on Hwy 30. In .5 mile there is an old cabin on the right. In 1 mile there's an old homestead on the right. Continue through town and turn right on Dingle Road in 5.3 miles. Watch for a cabin on the left with **two old wagons (10)** in 5 miles. Shoot over the fence and respect private property. Watch for an **old cabin (11)** on the right in 2.6 miles. Dingle Road has become Merkley Lake Road. Stay straight on Eastshore Road in about 5 miles, and follow for a few miles more for views over **Bear Lake (12)**. If time allows, you can make the entire loop

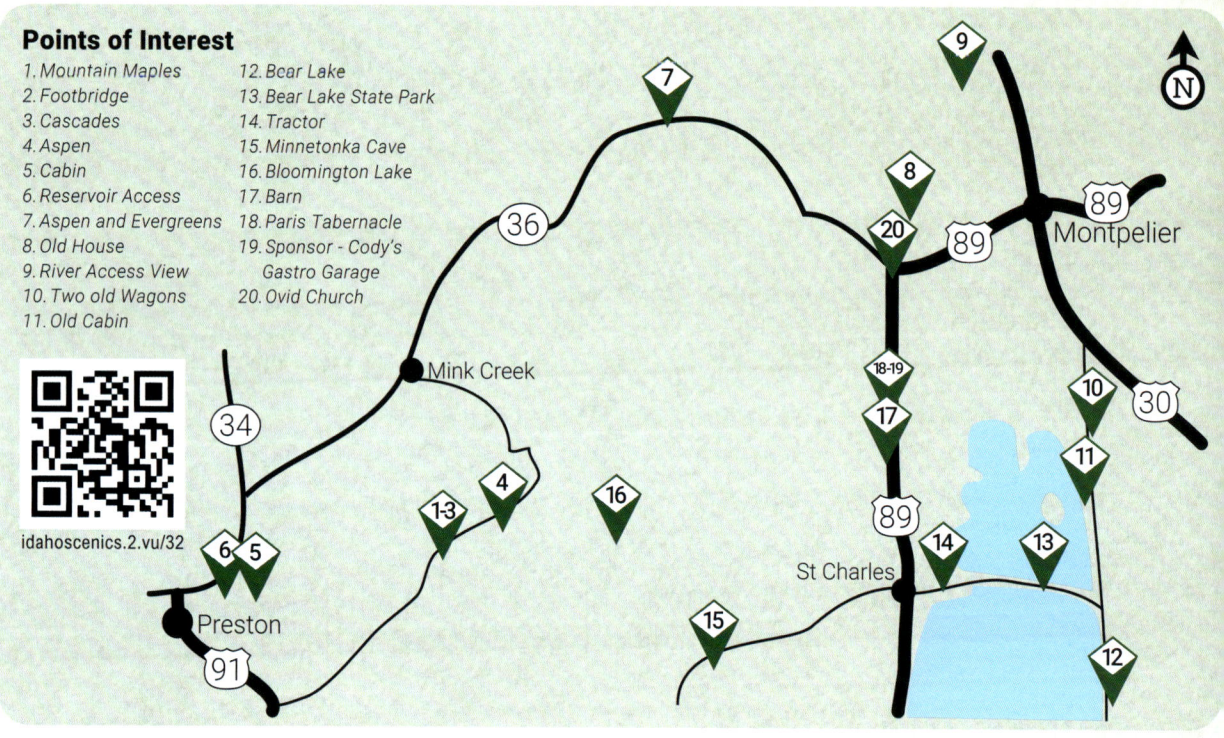

Points of Interest
1. Mountain Maples
2. Footbridge
3. Cascades
4. Aspen
5. Cabin
6. Reservoir Access
7. Aspen and Evergreens
8. Old House
9. River Access View
10. Two old Wagons
11. Old Cabin
12. Bear Lake
13. Bear Lake State Park
14. Tractor
15. Minnetonka Cave
16. Bloomington Lake
17. Barn
18. Paris Tabernacle
19. Sponsor - Cody's Gastro Garage
20. Ovid Church

idahoscenics.2.vu/32

Photography Tips

A mid-range zoom is adequate for most locations on this route. You may want a wide angle at Bloomington Lake and a telephoto for a couple of the structures. A polarizing filter is almost always useful when photographing water. We like the Cub River section of this route best in autumn, but the rest of it is great in summer.

Directions Continued

around Bear Lake's 20-mile length, covering about 70 miles. Otherwise, return at your leisure and turn left on N. Beach Road. In 2 miles you'll reach **Bear Lake State Park (13)** on the left with numerous access points. Continue 3.5 miles. There is a **tractor (14)** on the right. In 1.5 miles turn right onto Hwy 89.

Turn left onto Minnetonka Cave Road in .2 mile and proceed 10 miles to **Minnetonka Cave (15)**. This enormous limestone cave features a half-mile of fascinating stalactites, stalagmites, and banded travertine within nine rooms. Return to Hwy 89 and go left. In 4.4 miles turn left onto Bloomington Canyon Road. Continue for 8 miles, then stay left onto NF 409. In 3 miles arrive at the trailhead to **Bloomington Lake (16)**. This relatively easy trail is 1.4 miles round trip to a beautiful mountain lake. Return to Hwy 89 and turn left. In .5 mile turn left on W 4th Street and, in .1 mile, turn left onto W 1st Street. There is a view of a **barn (17)** here. Turn left onto W. 3rd Street N. Arrive back at Hwy 89 and turn left. In two miles you'll see the impressive **Paris Tabernacle (18)** on the right.

Across the street is **Cody's Gastro Garage (19)**, this route's sponsor. Founded in 2017 as part of Water's Edge Resort, Cody's Gastro Garage has become the favorite restaurant for local and visitors to Bear Lake! These family friendly restaurants are the perfect spot for a quick meal between outdoor activities. Stop in for an enjoyable breakfast or healthy dinner. They have two locations; in Garden City, Utah and Paris, Idaho.

Continue north on Hwy 89. In 4 miles there's an old house on the left, followed by the historic **Ovid Church (20)** in .4 mile, also on the left. Stay right on Hwy 89 and arrive back in Montpelier in 5 miles.

This Route's Sponsor

Cody's Gastro Garage
(208)540-0273
48 S. Main, Paris, ID
www.codysgastrogarage.com

See page 274 for coupon

Up Next: Routes 31 or 33

Bannock Range and the Arbon Valley
Route 33 ◇ ------▶ Preston to American Falls

This Route at a Glance:

Estimated Driving Time: 5 hours

Highlights: Old structures, Autumn color

About This Route: Travel from Preston to American Falls via the back roads. A smorgasbord of old structures awaits you on this route, as well as Bannock Mountain vistas and autumn color featuring mountain maples and aspen. Finish with a view of American Falls and the old powerhouse.

Notes and Cautions: Be sure to start this route with a full tank of gas. Do not attempt Sublett Canyon road in wet weather. This road is rocky and moderately rough. Good tires are highly advised as well as all wheel drive and higher clearance. Sublett Canyon will not be accessible in winter. Start this route about 45 minutes before sunrise for potential pre-sunrise color at the first location.

Directions

From Preston, follow Highway 91 west and then northwest for almost 21 miles and turn left on the Oxford Highway. In about 3 miles park safely off the highway for an expansive sunrise view to the east over **crop fields (1)**. In 8.8 miles turn left onto W. 5600 N. (N. 6th Street). In 1.8 miles turn right, then left. You'll be driving south along the western edge of Twin Lake Reservoir shortly. Over the next .6 mile, look for spots to view the **reservoir (2)** while the sun is still low in the sky. Stay left before crossing the end of the second reservoir, then left again onto W. 4800 N. (E. 2nd Street). Follow 1.5 miles back to the highway (now called Westside Highway) and turn right, then make an immediate left on 1st South Street. In .2 mile turn left on Cemetery Road. This becomes Clifton Creek Road. Follow for about 3 miles, with views of the **Bannock Range (3)** and a **distant barn (4)**, then drive through a beautiful **grove of mountain maples (5)**. Return to Westside Highway and turn right.

In 5.4 miles stay right on Highway 36, then right on Highway 36 in another 5 miles. In 1.3 miles turn left on S. 5600 W. Continue 1.2 miles to an **old structure (6)** on the right. Return to Highway 36 and go left. In .7 mile turn left on Black Canyon Road and, in 1.3 miles, you'll find an old homestead on the right. Return to Highway 36 and turn left. In 5.8 miles there's a pullout for Pass of the Standing Rock. In 1.8 mile you'll reach **Weston Reservoir (7)** and, in 3.7 miles, you'll see an old cabin on the left. There are more pioneer remnants visible on the right in 1.4 miles. Travel 6 more miles to another batch of old structures.

In one mile follow Deep Creek Road (Highway 36) across I-15 onto N Deep Creek Road. In .7 mile turn right on 3000 N. There is a **barn (8)** on the corner. In 1 mile turn right on 500 W. In .5 mile turn left on 3700 N. There are nice views of the **Bannock Range (9)** and valley. There is an **old cabin (10)** on the right in 1.6 miles. In .1 mile turn left on 2100 W. In .8 mile there is an old house on the right. In .5 mile turn right on 2800 N. There is another old house on the corner. In .5 mile stay straight. In another .5 mile there is an old cabin on the left, followed by a barn and old truck. Please respect private property and shoot from the road. In .9 mile stay straight. There are three old buildings on the right. Turn left on Daniels Road.

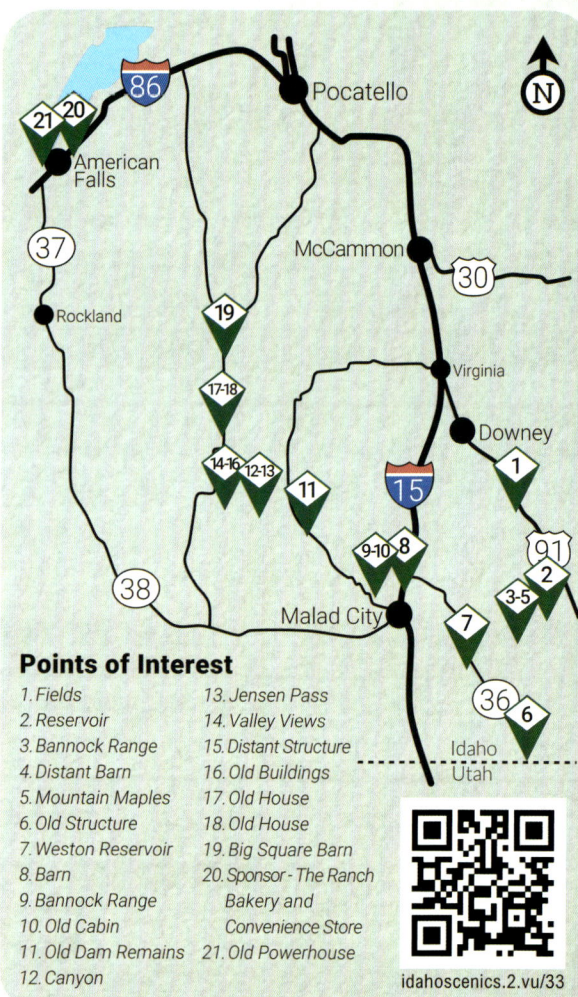

Points of Interest

1. Fields
2. Reservoir
3. Bannock Range
4. Distant Barn
5. Mountain Maples
6. Old Structure
7. Weston Reservoir
8. Barn
9. Bannock Range
10. Old Cabin
11. Old Dam Remains
12. Canyon
13. Jensen Pass
14. Valley Views
15. Distant Structure
16. Old Buildings
17. Old House
18. Old House
19. Big Square Barn
20. Sponsor - The Ranch Bakery and Convenience Store
21. Old Powerhouse

idahoscenics.2.vu/33

Directions Continued

There is a red barn in .7 mile. Continue 4.3 miles to more old structures. In another .5 mile you'll reach the remains of an **old dam (11)**. Stay left on Daniels Road in .1 mile. In 2 miles turn left on Sublette Canyon Road. Stay right on NF 608 in 2.3 miles. You'll wind your way through sagebrush hills with pockets of aspen. Turn right in 2.2 miles. There is a nice view over the **canyon (12)** here. You reach the summit in .8 mile, with great views on both sides of **Jensen Pass (13)**. Stay straight on Jenson Pass Road (NF 608). As you make your way down the western slope there's nice **valley views (14)** to be found. In 2.5 miles there is a **distant structure (15)** on the left. Turn right in .1 mile and, in .5 mile, turn left on 12000 N. There are **old buildings (16)** here. In 1.1 mile turn right onto Arbon Valley Road.

There is an **old house (17)** on the left in 8.8 miles, followed by another **old house (18)**, leaning severely, on the right in .3 mile. In 1.3 miles turn right on Lindley Lane. There is an old homestead in 1 mile. Return to Arbon Valley Highway and turn right. In 5 miles a **big square barn (19)** has an old wagon in front of it on the north side. In 2.2 miles stay left toward American Falls on Arbon Valley Highway.

In 24 miles turn left onto I-86 and go 12.5 miles. Take Exit 40. Turn right onto Pocatello Avenue. Go .9 mile to **The Ranch**

Bakery and Convenience Store (20), our route sponsor, on the right.

At The Ranch Bakery and Convenience Store "It's our business to make your day a little sweeter!" Their signature creations, The Ranch cinnamon roll and The Ranch raspberry twist, are made fresh daily along with other delicious bakery items such as, gourmet cupcakes, homemade Oreo cookies, chocolates, and much, much more. Try their deep-fried bacon on a stick, slathered with homemade bbq sauce. They also serve the best ice cream around from Reed's Dairy. While you're there, stock up on groceries and other needs from their C-Store.

Continue on Pocatello Avenue for .3 mile, then turn left onto Bannock Avenue. In .4 mile turn right onto Taylor Street. In one block turn left onto Falls Avenue. Follow to the end in 1 mile. Walk west for views of the falls, river and **the old powerhouse (21)**.

Photography Tips

We like this route best in early autumn for the mountain maples that turn the hillsides a blazing red. You'll want a wide-angle lens for the landscapes on this route, as well as a mid range lens for some of the barns and cabins. A graduated neutral density filter is useful at sunrise for balancing the bright sky against a darker foreground. At the last stop of the day you'll want your polarizing filter handy.

This Route's Sponsor

The Ranch Bakery
855 Pocatello Ave, Idaho
(208) 226-7812

Up Next: Routes 36 or 39

South Central Region

Route #
34. Craters of the Moon and Picabo Valley
35. Black Magic Canyon and Big Wood River
36. Lost River, White Knob and Pioneer Mtns
37. Sawtooth and Boulder Mountains
38. Little City and the Camas Marsh
39. City of Rocks and the California Trail
40. Waterfalls and Snake River Canyon
41. Rock Creek Canyon and the South Hills
42. Salmon Falls Dam and Three Creek Road
43. Thousand Springs and the Snake River

City of Rocks on route 39.

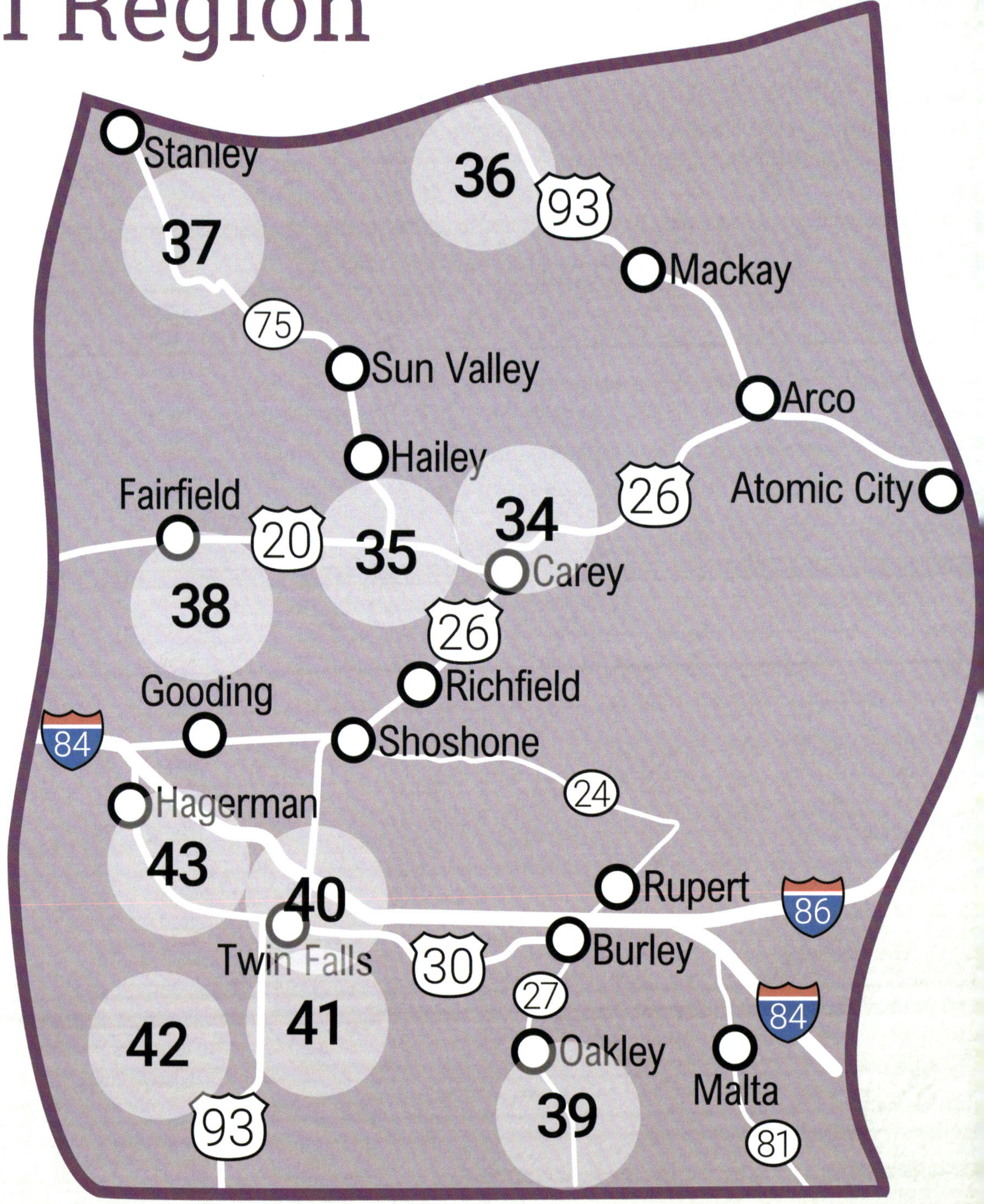

Welcome to Idaho's South Central Region

From rich mining history to the tourist towns of Sun Valley and Stanley, south-central Idaho is a land of contrasts. Along these routes you'll find barns, lakes, rivers, old cabins and historic mining areas. The Lost River Range, which features Borah Peak—the state's highest at 12,662 feet—runs about 75 miles in this region, with the Salmon and the Big and Little Lost Rivers for neighbors. The Sawtooths are unparalleled in their striking majesty and outdoor activity opportunities, and the hills surrounding the Big Wood River Valley virtually glow in evening light. In late May, a seemingly endless sea of blue coats Idaho's largest camas prairie. The Snake River traverses this region, offering raging waterfalls and bringing life to a desert landscape.

Flowers on the Snake River canyon floor, route 43.

Silver Creek Preserve along route 35 in early fall.

Craters of the Moon and Picabo Valley

Route 34 ◇----------------------▶ Richfield to Picabo

This Route at a Glance:

Estimated Driving Time: 5 hours

Highlights: Lava fields, hot springs, historic dams, and canyons

About This Route: Jump on this seven-mile loop to explore an eerie moonscape of volcanic fields and cinder cones. Sloping hills tumble down into wide fields and meadows, and creeks and streams snake through the dry desert flatlands. Travel through a world-renowned trout fishing area, and meander through small towns flying American flags, where everyone waves when they pass.

Notes and Cautions: Craters of the Moon is a great place to hike in winter. In the summer of 2018, there was a wildfire that went through the Pioneer Mountains, which caused damage to some areas along this route. These include the Muldoon Canyon and High Five areas. Watch for wildlife, especially in the Silver Creek Preserve as there are frequent moose sightings. There is no winter access in some areas except via snowmobile.

Directions

Start in Richfield, located 16 miles east of Shoshone. Richfield is a tiny town, but worth the time to tour down Main Street. Hwy 93/24 intersects Main Street. On your right, heading south on Main, you'll find an early era **mechanics garage and granaries (1)**. There is an interesting water tower on the north end and the ends at an RV park with a view of a **round-topped barn (2)** on the south end.

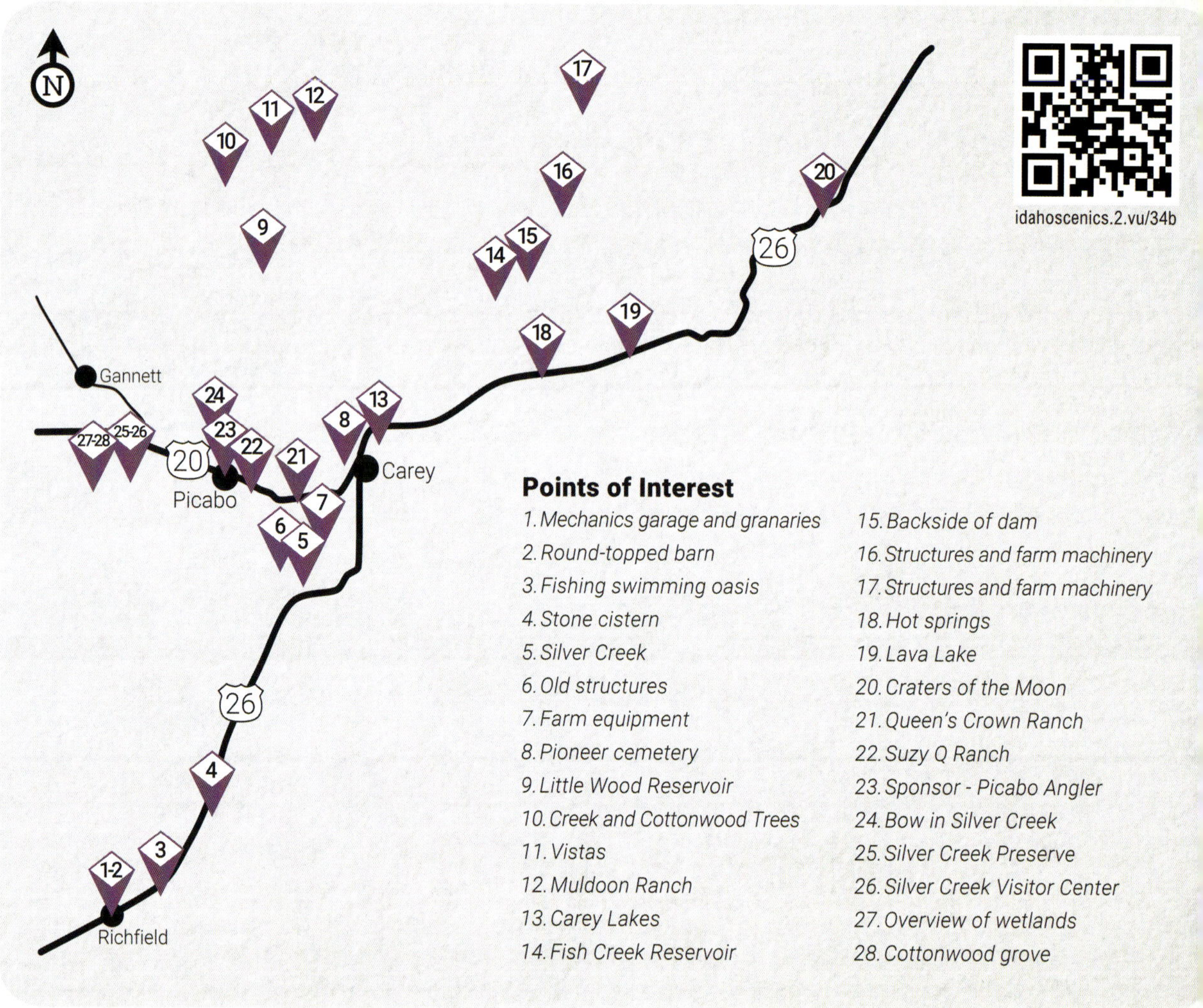

Points of Interest
1. Mechanics garage and granaries
2. Round-topped barn
3. Fishing swimming oasis
4. Stone cistern
5. Silver Creek
6. Old structures
7. Farm equipment
8. Pioneer cemetery
9. Little Wood Reservoir
10. Creek and Cottonwood Trees
11. Vistas
12. Muldoon Ranch
13. Carey Lakes
14. Fish Creek Reservoir
15. Backside of dam
16. Structures and farm machinery
17. Structures and farm machinery
18. Hot springs
19. Lava Lake
20. Craters of the Moon
21. Queen's Crown Ranch
22. Suzy Q Ranch
23. Sponsor - Picabo Angler
24. Bow in Silver Creek
25. Silver Creek Preserve
26. Silver Creek Visitor Center
27. Overview of wetlands
28. Cottonwood grove

Take Hwy 26/93 toward Carey. In 2.3 miles, just before you reach mile marker 185, turn right on an unmarked dirt road. Stay on this road for about a mile to a **wonderful oasis (3)** for swimming and fishing then return to the main highway and turn right and go another 4.5 miles.

Turn right at the Pigari Bridge sign. Just before crossing the bridge there is an interesting **stone cistern (4)** along the Little Wood River.

Return to the highway (or follow the abandoned railroad right-of-way that runs

Directions Continued

parallel to the highway) and turn right. In about 7 miles, turn left on Cutoff Road, also marked "Silver Creek Campsites". In less than 2 miles, watch for a sign "River Access" and turn right. This takes you to a small campsite with nice views of **Silver Creek (5)**. Continue on the side road as it loops back to Cutoff Road. Turn right and watch for some nice **old structures (6)** on your right. Continue on Cutoff Road until you reach the intersection with Priest Road, then turn right. In less than two miles you will pass a few well kept ranches along the banks of Silver Creek. Dropping down a small grade, you'll find another ranch and a photogenic older barn and **farm equipment (7)**. Following the curve in the road, turn right on Shed Row road heading south. You'll cross Sunset Lane. Stay right at the 'Y' in the road at the stop sign. In 2.5 miles you will reach Highways 26/93. Turn left and continue to Carey.

At the north edge of town, turn left onto Little Wood Reservoir Road. Go .5 mile to **Pioneer Cemetery (8)** on your right, then continue north on Little Wood Reservoir Road for about 11 miles. There is a well-kempt RV camp area with grass and shade with nice views of the **reservoir and hills (9)**.

Continue north a little over 4 miles to the road marked High 5 and turn left. Continue on this road down the Little Wood drainage and stay left after crossing the bridge. **Cottonwood trees (10)** line this creek and there are several campsites. This is a dead end loop, so retrace your route and stay on the High 5 road for about 1 mile past the bridge that you crossed when dropping into the drainage.

Turn right on Muldoon Canyon Road. The views coming up out of this canyon are wonderful. Stay on this road for 4 miles. You will come to Flat Top Road on your right. You'll find open **plateau and vistas (11)** as you drive the Muldoon Canyon Road. Continue on the Muldoon Canyon Road to the **Muldoon Ranch (12)**. There are some log buildings on your left that are on private property. Be respectful. Backtrack to Flat Top Road and return to the main road.

Flat Top Road will become Little Wood Reservoir Road. Continue to Hwy 26 and turn left. In 1 mile northeast of Carey, you will find **Carey Lakes (13)** on your right. Return to the main highway. Travel about .5 mile and turn left onto Austin Road. This takes you along some old ranches and farms. In about 6 miles, turn right at Fish Creek Road and follow for 5 miles to **Fish Creek Reservoir and dam (14)**. Part of the dam has been removed, so the Reservoir doesn't fill to its prior capacity. Be sure to explore the **backside of the dam (15)** while you are there.

Continue on Fish Creek Road. At 3 miles and at 7.5 miles, after leaving the Reservoir, you will find old structures and **farm machinery (16,17)**. Turn around at mile 10 and return to Highway 26. Turn left on Highway 26/93. In less than 2.5 miles, there are roadside **hot springs (18)** on the left. They are not visible from the road, but are just off the highway.

Directions Continued

In 3.6 miles, on your left, will be **Lava Lake (19)**. Park in the wide pullout area to photograph and view the Lake.

Continue traveling east for about 12 miles and turn right at the entrance to the **Craters of the Moon National Monument and Preserve (20)**. The spring flower bloom is incredible and you'll be amazed how anything could survive in such a harsh environment. There are many opportunities to photograph as you drive the scenic 7-mile loop through the park. Late spring is the perfect time to catch the bloom of spring flowers. The loop is closed to traffic in winter, but you can snowshoe or cross-country ski to experience the solitude of a completely transformed landscape when snow covered.

Return to Carey and drive less than one mile to the south end of town, at the intersection of highways 26 and 20. Turn right onto Highway 20 toward Picabo, which is in 7 miles. As you drop down the hill, you will be entering one of the most beautiful farm/ranch valleys in Blaine County. On your left is the rock formation known as the **'Queen's Crown' (21)**. The **Suz Q Ranch (22)** straddles Silver Creek. The barn and other structures are uniformly painted red. Silver Creek is famous for its world-class fly-fishing areas.

As you enter Picabo, our Route Sponsor, the **Picabo Angler, (23)** will be on your right. Picabo Angler is a favorite stop for many travelers. The store has a fly fishing outfitter, a post office, a grill, a convenience store and much more! The store is part museum and part everything else. A full and rich history is on display throughout the store. The Silver Creek Valley was one of Hemingway's playgrounds and visitors can see his unique connection with the Purdy family on display here. "Come on in for a huckleberry float or pick up the best flies for Silver Creek! We look forward to seeing you!"

Continue onto North Picabo Road, just west of the Picabo Angler. Drive 1.5 miles and park on the right where it widens. Climb a short distance up the hill for a stunning panoramic view of the

Photography Tips

You will want to have that zoom lens handy for isolating subjects in your photos, and then your wide angle for those open vistas. A circular polarizer will serve you well on most occasions as well to cut down the glare not only on the water but help saturate the colors on the rocks, plants and big sky. We recommend visiting Craters of the Moon in spring for the wildflower bloom.

Directions Continued

Picabo Valley and the bow in **Silver Creek (24)** with a backdrop of the Picabo Hills. This location is recommended for a sunrise or sunset image. Follow this road for about 2.5 miles, as it winds along the north side of Silver Creek at the base of the mountains. Turn left onto South Picabo Road and travel to Highway 20, in less than a mile. Turn right and go 1.3 miles and then turn left onto Kilpatrick Bridge Road In less than a mile to the **Silver Creek Preserve Area (25)**. Park after you cross the bridge. You can walk along the trail that follows the banks of Silver Creek, or float the creek itself.

Continue on Kilpatrick Bridge Road as it winds up the gentle slope of the Picabo Hills to the **Silver Creek Visitor Center (26)**. Shortly past the Visitor Center, watch for wide spots to park. Photograph the meandering **Silver Creek and wetlands (27)** with a backdrop of the mountain range. This is a perfect location for sunrise or sunset. Watch for wildlife, as there are often moose, deer and elk sightings as well as migratory birds and other animals. Stop after you cross another bridge at the bottom of the hill and wander through the **cottonwood grove (28)** on your right. Watch for wildlife on both sides of the road. This road will loop back to the main highway (road name changes to Stocker Creek Road). At the highway turn right and go east less than 3 miles, then turn left onto Gannett Road. In 4 miles, turn left and drive through the quaint town of Gannett. On the north side of town, just before getting back on Gannett Road, note the metal sculptures on your left. Turn left onto Gannett Road and continue 8 miles. You will be arriving at the town of Bellevue.

See route 35 for an excellent lodging option.

This Route's Sponsor

Picabo Angler
18918 Hwy 20, Box 718
Picabo, Idaho 83348

208-788-3536
www.picaboangler.com

Up Next: Routes 35, 37, or 38

Black Magic Canyon and Big Wood River
Route 35 ◇------------▶ Bellevue, Hailey, Shoshone

This Route at a Glance:

Estimated Driving Time: 6 hours or overnight

Highlights: Historic Towns, Basalt Canyon, Scenic Valleys

About This Route: In the heart of stunning Blaine County, explore the side roads that are the start of an adventure that will delight your soul and just touch on the many trailheads for further exploring. Travel to a scenic mining town, unique sculpted basalt rock canyon and end in the historic railroad town of Shoshone.

Notes and Cautions: Watch for road closures in winter weather. Do not enter Black Magic Canyon without calling the Big Wood Canal Company in Shoshone (208-886-2331) as water is released into the canyon certain times of year and access is not allowed. Rattlesnakes are also very common in the canyon. We recommend Black Magic Canyon in autumn after temperatures have dropped and snakes are dormant. Most of the route should be accessible in late spring through early winter or before deep snowfall. A fire in the summer of 2018 has affected the accessibility of some areas.

Directions

Traveling south from Ketchum, start this route at the intersection of Greenhorn Gulch Road and East Fork Big Wood River Road. Turn right (west) and travel 4 miles through a scenic canyon for seasonal wildflowers and wonderful views of the **Smoky Mountain's Mahoney Butte (1)** to the west. The road ends at the trailhead for **Greenhorn Gulch (2)**. Return to Highway 75 and proceed straight across to the East Fork Big Wood River Road. This paved road leads to the Triumph Mining area. In about 3 miles, there is a wonderful barn with a backdrop of **Hyndman Peak (3)**. In another 2 miles turn left up **Triumph Gulch (4)** and follow for a few miles. There are nice views when coming back down. Turn left and travel a little over a mile to **Triumph (5)**. You'll find interesting older buildings, mining equipment and structures. Continue past Triumph for as far as you want. The road changes to gravel.

Return to the Highway 75, turn left and travel 3.5 miles to Deer Creek Road on your right. This road leads you through a pleasant valley with **meadows, ranch settings and barns (6)**. It is paved for the first 2 miles, then gravel. You will reach Sawtooth National Forest Access at mile 4. Continue on this road as far as you'd like but then return to Highway 75 and turn right. Follow 2.7 miles and turn right on Bullion Street.

Just after crossing the Big Wood River, turn left at the Lions Park. Stay left and continue past Lions Park. Park here and explore the Croy Creek Preserve. Follow the well-maintained trail through cottonwoods and aspen heading south for a short ways. You will come to **"Bow Bridge" (7)**. Cross the bridge and follow the trail (right) to find "Heart Tree." Several heart shaped rocks have been left here. When you cross Bow Bridge you are in the Draper Preserve. Return to your vehicle or, after crossing Bow Bridge, follow the trail through

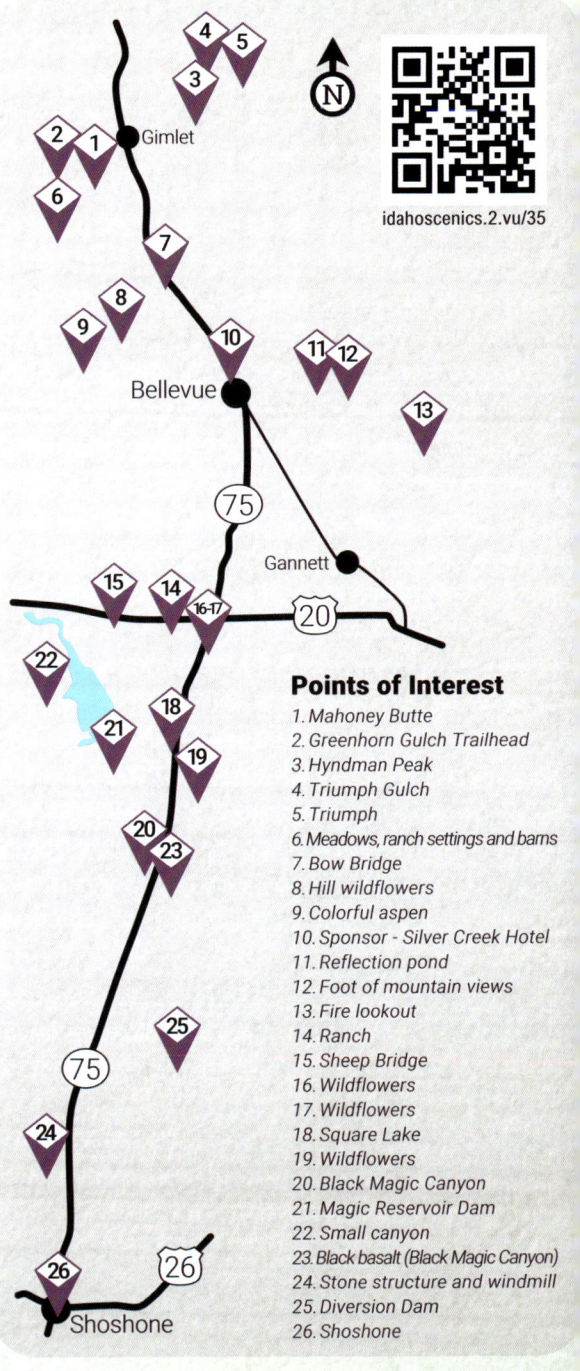

idahoscenics.2.vu/35

Points of Interest
1. Mahoney Butte
2. Greenhorn Gulch Trailhead
3. Hyndman Peak
4. Triumph Gulch
5. Triumph
6. Meadows, ranch settings and barns
7. Bow Bridge
8. Hill wildflowers
9. Colorful aspen
10. Sponsor - Silver Creek Hotel
11. Reflection pond
12. Foot of mountain views
13. Fire lookout
14. Ranch
15. Sheep Bridge
16. Wildflowers
17. Wildflowers
18. Square Lake
19. Wildflowers
20. Black Magic Canyon
21. Magic Reservoir Dam
22. Small canyon
23. Black basalt (Black Magic Canyon)
24. Stone structure and windmill
25. Diversion Dam
26. Shoshone

Directions Continued

wetlands for some texture and close-up photography as it loops back to the parking lot. Return to the main road and turn left. The road from this point is called Croy Creek Road. In 2 miles, turn left onto Colorado Gulch Road. Shortly after the turn, find a parking area on your right. In the spring, it is well worth exploring by hiking a short way up the **hill (8)**. Some years the lupine is outstanding as are the views. Return to Croy Creek Road and turn left. In 1.5 miles, turn right on Bullion Gulch Road. This mile or so side trip is recommended in the fall for **colorful aspen (9)** right next to the road. Return to Croy Creek Road and retrace your route to Hailey and Highway 75 and turn right. In .5 mile turn right on Cedar Street and immediately turn left on to Broadford Road for a scenic four-mile drive to Bellevue. Turn left on Highway 75 and travel .3 mile to our route sponsor, **Silver Creek Hotel (10)** on your left.

Silver Creek Hotel is the Wood River Valley's newest boutique hotel. Locally designed, built, owned, and operated, they're proud to offer guests the most comfortable and convenient stay possible right on the doorstep of the most majestic ski resort in Idaho and just minutes from world famous fly fishing, camping, world class dining, hiking, music festivals, art galleries and more. Choose from queen, king, or suite rooms. Each of their 56 rooms features a down comforter, free cable, fridge, & coffee maker, and microwave. Relax by the year-round heated pool and take a dip in the hot tub while enjoying mountain views.

From Broadford Road and Highway 75, turn right and then left on Pine Street (there's a post office on the corner). Pine Street leads you out of town, and changes to Muldoon Canyon Road. You will pass through the E-Da-Ho Ranch (private property). In 3.3 miles, note the **reflection pond (11)** on the right as you pass grassy meadows mixed with patches of cottonwoods and aspen. In about 1 mile, there are views of the **foot of the mountains (12)** bordering the road on the south. In 2.5 miles you will be at a 'Y' intersection. If you turn right at the 'Y' onto Sharp's Canyon Road, you will climb as you go up to Bell Mountain. After about 2 miles you will reach the **fire lookout (13)**. This is a recommended drive, but note the

Directions

disclosure about a fire in the summer of 2018. You will find wonderful vistas and seasonal wildflowers. Return to Bellevue and turn left on Highway 75 heading south.

Continue on Highway 75 for 9 miles to the intersection of Highways 75 and 20 and turn right. Stay on Highway 20 heading west and go about 2 miles to an area called Stanton Crossing. There's a photogenic **ranch (14)** on the south side of highway. Use caution if stopping for photos. Continue another 2 miles and watch for a sign for Sheep Bridge and turn left on a dirt road. Park at the wide dirt area or, if driving a high clearance vehicle, you can drive down into the draw and park. **Sheep Bridge (15)** is a wooden structured bridge used for sheep to cross the Big Wood River. Return to the intersection of highways 20 and 75 and turn right. In 1 mile, use the pullout on the left to take in the view of the valley looking north. In the spring you may also observe **wildflowers (16)**. In about .2 mile, there is a faint dirt road on the left as you top Timmerman Hill. Climb the small rise on foot for more **wildflowers (17)** and an even nicer view of the valley and mountains to the north.

Continue traveling south for 4 miles. On your right will be a gravel road that drops down to **Square Lake (18)**. The lake is visible from the highway. The best viewing and photography time is spring and early summer; this is a favorite stop for migratory birds and sage grouse with a nice backdrop of snow-covered peaks. This 'lake' dries up later in the season. Return to the highway and continue south.

Watch for an access road marked Picabo Desert Road in 2 miles. In the spring and early summer, **wildflowers (19)** can be found along this dirt road. Travel this road only when weather permits. Return to the main highway and turn left (south).

In 3 miles, turn right at the access marked West Magic Reservoir on the left. You will find a parking area and kiosk describing **Black Magic Canyon (20)** on your right shortly after turning off the highway. Park here and explore the basalt rock walls of the Big Wood River channel. This is a recommended stop for interesting and abstract photography, but precautions need to be taken (see notes and cautions).

Continue on West Magic Road to Magic Reservoir. After the first mile or so, you will find a couple of wooded access areas to the Big Wood River to explore. In a little over 5 miles turn right and go 1.5 miles to **Magic Reservoir Dam (21)**. Visit here when water is being released. Return to West Magic Road and turn right and continue 2 miles. Stay right

Photography Tips

It's recommended to use your circular polarizer for much of what you will be shooting on this route. It will help with color saturation on flowers and trees, and will take the reflection shine off your water shots and when shooting the black basalt rocks. Get down low when exploring Black Magic Canyon and try using your wide-angle lens, then zoom in close with your telephoto lens for intimate abstract photos.

Directions Continued

on West Magic Road and continue traveling north where the road changes to Lava Point Road. Travel through a small **canyon (22)** and enjoy views of the reservoir. Retrace your route and turn left at the intersection marked West Magic and tour the town.

Another access to Black Magic Canyon can be found directly across the highway. Drive the gravel road along the riverbed to find a bridge crossing and the road marked Old Highway 93. Park here and explore more of the beautiful polished **black basalt (23)**. Return to the highway and continue traveling south for about 12 miles.

Turn right on 620 North Road and travel 1 mile. On a slight rise, on the right is a **stone structure and windmill (24)**. Return to the highway and turn right. In 1 mile turn left on 520 N Road heading east to explore another section of Black Magic Canyon, our favorite section. This option is not recommended in wet conditions. In 3 miles before the road makes a curve to the left, it changes to the 3 Mile Road East (350 E). Continue another 3 miles where the road curves again. Turn right onto a two-track dirt road. Travel 2 miles and cross a wooden bridge, then park in the wide area. You will be at the **diversion dam (25)**. Explore in either direction from the dam for exquisite swirled rock formations. Climbing down into the canyon is accessible only certain times of year when the water is turned off (see notes and cautions).

Return to the highway, turn left and continue south to the historic railroad town of **Shoshone (26)**. Explore the pleasant town with its historic buildings and rail station.

This Route's Sponsor

Silver Creek Hotel
721 N. Main Street
Bellevue, ID 83313
(208)725-8282

See page 274 for coupon

Up Next: Routes 34, 38, or 40

Lost River, White Knob and Pioneer Mtns

Route 36 ◇ ----------▶ Mackay to Challis or Sun Valley

This Route at a Glance:

Estimated Driving Time: 5 hours

Highlights: Mountain views

About This Route: We'll start with sunrise over the Lost River Valley from high in the White Knob Mountains, then cross the Valley for up close views of the Lost River Range. After a visit into the Pioneer Mountains for a short waterfall hike, choose your final destination from two options: Cross Trail Creek Summit and descend into Sun Valley (with spectacular views of the valley below), or continue north to Challis where you'll find cabins and maybe some wild horses en route.

Notes and Cautions: All wheel drive required. No low clearance vehicles. Do not attempt this route in wet weather, too early in spring or in winter. 4-wheel drive vehicles may wish to obtain a Mackay Mine tour map in town for an extended tour of the White Knob Mountains.

Directions

From Main Street and Hwy 93 in Mackay, proceed south 2.5 miles on Hwy 93. Turn right on Houston Road. Follow Houston Road for 4.4 miles watching for Lost River Range views and old **log arch gates (1)** framing the mountains. Turn right on Houston Road. In .8 mile turn left on Alder Creek Road In .3 miles turn right on Alder Creek Road. In 1.6 miles turn left. Stay on Alder Creek Road. In 2.4 miles there is a view of a fence with a distant aspen grove and a beautiful **mountain view (2)**. In 4.8 miles stay right. In .9 mile stay right on NF 144. In 1.6 miles there is an **old cabin (3)** near the road. In just over 2 miles you'll find excellent viewpoints looking toward the **Lost River Range (4, 5)**. This is a great sunrise spot. In one mile there is a view site over the town of Mackay. In 1.9 miles turn right. In 1.5 miles stay left onto the pavement. You'll see a river access in .1 mile. In .6 mile, the road curves right onto Main Street. Turn right onto Hwy 93. In one block find **Sammy's Mini Mart (6)** on the left.

Take a break from the road, gas up or just stock up at Sammy's Mini Mart in Mackay. Sammy's features hot meals, including Hot Stuff Pizza and Champ's Chicken, for dine-in or take out. They offer everything from a liquor store to fishing and hunting licenses, snacks and ice and more. Sammy's is perfectly located on Highway 93.

Proceed south on Hwy 93 for 7.5 miles. Turn left on Pass Creek Road and follow it for at least 10 miles through a unique **rock canyon (7)**. Turn around at your leisure. Watch for Road 4300 on the right. Turn right. This quickly turns to Bar Road. For up-close views of the **Lost River Range (8, 9)** and another back road drive, turn right in 6.6 miles just before the dump, on a two-track dirt road along the fence line or follow Bar Road back into Mackay and turn right on Highway 93, then continue at the next paragraph. On the two-track road, stay right in .8 mile. In 1.7 miles turn left at power lines. In 1.5 miles go left. In .4 mile stay straight. In .3 mile turn left at the power lines. In .9 mile turn right then immediately left. In 2.3 miles turn left. In another 2 miles you'll reach a closed but unlocked gate. Close the gate upon leaving. Turn right on Hwy 93.

Continue north on Hwy 93, 5.7 miles from the gate or 9.7 miles from Main Street in Mackay. Turn left on Fish Hatchery Road. In .6 miles as you cross the Big Lost River, you'll have a view of an **old steel bridge and the White Knob Mountains (10)**. In 7.5 miles turn right on Trail Creek Rd. In .8 miles there is an **old cabin (11)** on the corner of 5780 W. Turn around and continue west on Trail Creek Road. In 1.4 miles turn right to find the Old Chilly Cemetery in .2 miles. Return to Trail Creek Road, turning right. Over the next several miles you'll see two-track roads to the left for **river access spots (12)**. In about 10 miles there is a nice roadside river access. The pavement ends in 4.5 miles. In .7

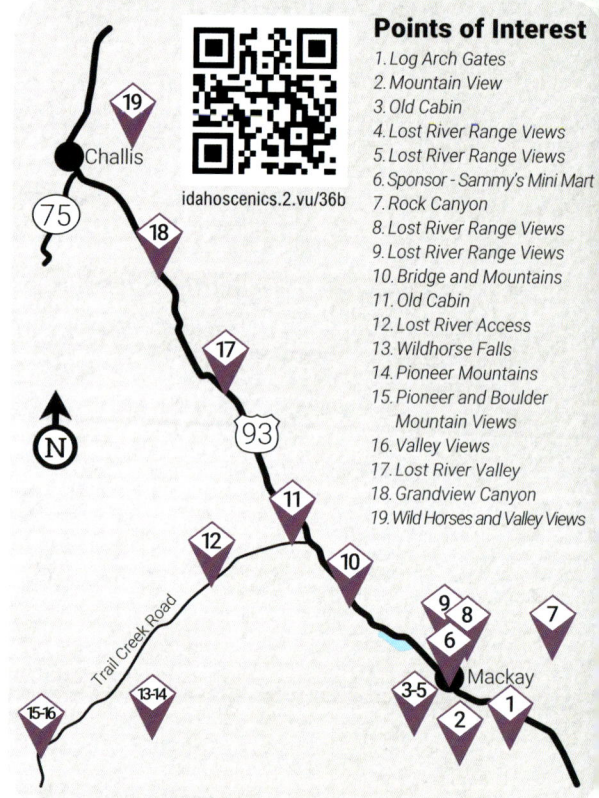

Points of Interest
1. Log Arch Gates
2. Mountain View
3. Old Cabin
4. Lost River Range Views
5. Lost River Range Views
6. Sponsor - Sammy's Mini Mart
7. Rock Canyon
8. Lost River Range Views
9. Lost River Range Views
10. Bridge and Mountains
11. Old Cabin
12. Lost River Access
13. Wildhorse Falls
14. Pioneer Mountains
15. Pioneer and Boulder Mountain Views
16. Valley Views
17. Lost River Valley
18. Grandview Canyon
19. Wild Horses and Valley Views

Photography Tips

This route is most scenic in autumn with a skiff of snow on the mountain peaks and golden aspen in the mountains and cottonwoods along the Big Wood River. A wide-angle lens works well on this route to capture the expansive views. You'll want a telephoto lens if you encounter any wild horses. Wildhorse Falls faces west and is best viewed in the evening light.

Directions Continued

mile turn left on NF 135 signed for Wildhorse Canyon. In 2.2 miles stay right. In 4.5 miles turn left. Arrive at the trailhead for several hikes, the shortest being the gentle walk to **Wildhorse Falls (13)**. Back at the first junction turn left. In .5 mile there's a great view of Wildhorse Creek and the **Pioneer Mountains (14)**. Return to Trail Creek Road. Go left to continue to Sun Valley or right to go to Challis.

Sun Valley Option: Follow Trail Creek Road for 21 miles into Sun Valley. You'll cross Trail Creek Summit and have excellent views of the valley separating the **Pioneer and Boulder mountain ranges (15)**. This would be a great sunset location. Continue watching for pullouts for views as you continue down the **valley (16)**.

Challis Option: Follow Trail Creek Road back 18.7 miles to Old Chilly Road and turn left. At .6 mile there is an old cabin on the left and, in another .9 mile, there is another cabin on the left. In 1.6 miles turn left on Hwy 93. In 2.7 miles turn right on Doublesprings Pass Road to visit the fault site of the 1983 Borah Peak Earthquake. Return to Hwy 93 and turn right. In 7.3 miles there is a small pullout on the left for expansive views of the **Lost River Valley (17)**. In 5.7 miles turn left on Spar Canyon Road. This is a popular area for viewing wild horses. Follow for a few miles and return at your leisure to Hwy 93. In about 5 miles you'll enter Grand View Canyon. In .3 mile there is a pullout on the right for **canyon views (18)**. In 4 miles there is a cabin on the left. In 6 miles turn right on Hot Springs Road; follow it for 2.7 miles, then turn left on Upper Hot Springs. Turn right on Leaton Gulch Road (NF 111). Follow this mildly rough road for 3-4 miles, watching for **wild horses, mountain and valley views (19)**. Return to Hot Springs Road. Return to Hwy 93, turn right and follow into Challis.

This Route's Sponsor

Sammy's Mini Mart
318 W Custer, Mackay, ID 83251

(208) 588-3340
sammysminimartid.com

Up Next: Route 24, 26, or 35

Sawtooth and Boulder Mountains
Route 37 ◇ ----------------------------------▶ Stanley to Ketchum

This Route at a Glance:

Estimated Driving Time: 5 hours

Highlights: Mountains, Lakes

About This Route: Experience sunrise at Redfish Lake with its breathtaking Sawtooth Mountain backdrop. From there, explore the Sawtooth Basin, an area studded with several other alpine lakes, old cabins and mountain views. We'll cross 8,701 ft. Galena Summit, then descend into Hailey, with views of the Boulder and Smoky Mountains flanking us. This is an excellent route for autumn color.

Notes and Cautions: Many of the side roads will be inaccessible in winter and spring. Respect private property. Crossing Galena Summit in winter can be treacherous. Be prepared for winter travel.

Directions

From the junction of Hwy 21 and Hwy 75 in Stanley proceed south Hwy 75, 4.4 miles and turn right on Redfish Lake Road. Watch sunrise touch the peaks above **Little Redfish Lake (1)**. Pull off on the right just past the Mountain View Campground. Walk one of the short trails to the lakeshore. Take the second exit in the roundabout. Park in the Outlet Day-Use Area and walk to the shore for excellent lake and **mountain views (2, 3)**.

Return to Hwy 75 and turn right. In 5 miles there's a hay rake through the fence on the left. In 1.4 miles park at the Williams Creek Trailhead on the left. Carefully cross the highway for fence and **mountain views (4)**. Continue south on Hwy 75. In 2.2 miles turn left on Fisher Creek Road. In 1 mile an **old log cabin (5)** sits beyond a fence on the left. Respect private property. Return to Hwy 75 and turn left. In 1.5 miles an **old cabin (6)** is on the right. In .3 mile turn right on Decker Flat Road (NF 209). Cross the bridge and turn left on NF 315. In .9 mile park near the bridge for photo ops of **Hell Roaring Creek (7)**. Return to Hwy 75.

Turn right, then immediately left on Fourth of July Creek Road (NF 209). In 3 miles park along the road and walk 1/10th mile to the

Points of Interest
1. Little Redfish Lake
2. Lake and mountain views
3. Lake and mountain views
4. Mountain views
5. Old log cabin
6. Old cabin
7. Hell Roaring Creek
8. Boulder and Sawtooth Mtns
9. Aspen
10. Wildflowers
11. Creek crossing
12. Mountains
13. Lake and mountains
14. Cabins
15. Mountains
16. Historic ranger station
17. Scenic viewpoint
18. Titus Lake TR
19. Harriman Trail
20. Boulder Mountains
21. Pioneer Cemetery
22. Boulder Mountain Range
23. Mountains and wildflowers
24. Boulder Mountains
25. Sawtooth National Recreation Area headquarters
26. North Fork Big Wood River
27. Wooden bridge
28. North Fork Big Wood River TH
29. Penny Lake
30. Frenchman's Bend Hot Springs
31. Sponsor - Smoky Mountain Pizzeria Grill

Directions Continued

right (south) for views of Fourth of July Creek and the **Boulder and Sawtooth Mountains (8)**. Continue on Fourth of July Creek Road as far as you want for views of **aspen (9)**, summer **wildflowers (10)**, and **creek crossings (11)**. You will eventually arrive at the trailhead to Fourth of July Lake. Return to Hwy 75 and turn left.

In 3.2 miles turn right on Pettit Lake Road. In .6 mile a small creek crossing makes a nice foreground for distant **mountains (12)**. Follow straight 1.2 miles to Pettit Lake Day Use Area. Here you'll find great views of the **lake and mountains (13)**.

Return to Hwy 75 and turn left (north). Backtrack 2.7 miles to Valley Road on your right. Follow Valley Road for 2.4 miles. There are some **cabins (14)** on the right and another structure on the left in 1.8 miles. Continue to Pole Creek Road in about 5 miles, watching for mountains, old fences and wildflowers in summer. Turn left on Pole Creek Road (NF 197). In .7 mile, park and walk to the south for views of a pond with **mountains (15)** reflecting on a calm day. You'll have a somewhat distant view of the **historic ranger station (16)**. This is also a wildflower area in summer.

Directions Continued

Turn around and follow Pole Creek Road back to Valley Road and turn left, following it 2.3 miles back to Hwy 75 (You will pass a short spur road to the ranger station for close-up views via a short trail). At Hwy 75 turn left. Ascend Galena Summit, reaching a **scenic viewpoint (17)** in about 7 miles. There are several pullouts for views as you descend into the Wood River Valley. Shortly after you start your descent there is a wide turnout on the left and signage for **Titus Lake (18)**. This is a pleasant 3.3 mile out and back hike with great views and a small emerald lake. In 6 miles you'll reach Galena Lodge on the left. Almost directly across from the Lodge starts the 18 mile **Harriman Trail (19)** to the Sawtooth National Recreation Area Headquarters, located eight miles north of Ketchum. The trail follows the Big Wood River as it winds through meadows and wooded areas with outstanding views of the Boulder Mountains.

From Galena Lodge head south on Hwy 75 and turn left in less than 900 feet on NF Road 409, Senate Creek. You'll find an expansive meadow and stream that is beautifully cradled by pine forests and a backdrop of the **Boulder Mountains (20)**. After returning to the highway and continuing south, turn left in less than 1 mile for a **Pioneer Cemetery (21)** a short ways up the hill. Turn left after returning to highway. This stretch of the highway offers several river accesses and viewpoints. Stop at the turnout at Billy's Bridge, 5 miles from the Pioneer Cemetery. At Billy's Bridge, walk a short way for views of the **Boulder Mountain range (22)**.

In less than 3 miles, turn left just before the Baker Creek picnic area. Here you will find more views of the **Boulder Mountains and seasonal wildflowers (23)**. Across the highway you can drive up Baker Creek Road. The trailhead to Baker Lake is about 10 miles. Return to the highway and turn right. For the

Directions Continued

next 7 miles, you will be traveling through an area that is incredibly scenic in all seasons, with the Big Wood River on the right and the **Boulder Mountains (24)** on the left. Take advantage of the turnouts for views of these scenes.

After 7 miles, turn left into the **Sawtooth National Recreation Area headquarters (25)**. Travel on the gravel road past the headquarters and turn off at the first few campsites on your right. Wander the short distance to the tree-lined **North Fork Big Wood River (26)**. Another nice easy accessible stop would be right after you cross the **wooden bridge (27)** over the River. From this point drive a little over 5 miles to the end of NF Road 146 to the turn-around at the **North Fork Wood River Trailhead (28)** but be sure to take the time to visit the various turnouts and riverside camp areas along the way.

Return to the Highway and turn left. In 8 miles you will be in Ketchum. Turn right onto Warm Springs Road. **Penny Lake (29)** is on the left in 3.5 miles. Continue south (left) on Warm Springs Road for 7 miles to **Frenchman's Bend Hot Springs (30)** off to the side of the road. Retrace your route to Ketchum and

Photography Tips

A mid range zoom lens and longer works well along this route on those areas that you just can't get close enough too. We also recommend trying your circular polarizer to bring out the colors and saturation. Find a nice foreground and create a grand vista shot by using your wide angle lens. That is what this route is about...those fabulous vistas of the mountain ranges.

This Route's Sponsor

Smoky Mountain Pizzeria Grill
200 Sun Valley Rd,
Ketchum, ID 83340

(208) 622-5625
www.smokymountainpizza.com

See page 276 for coupon

Directions Continued

Highway 75. Turn right and go .2 mile then turn right on Sun Valley Rd. In one block turn left on Washington Avenue. You'll find this route's sponsor, **Smoky Mountain Pizzeria Grill (31)**, on your left.

Smoky Mountain Pizzeria Grill is a comfortable, casual, dynamic family restaurant conveniently located in the heart of downtown Ketchum. Their extensive menu features unique pizzas and pastas, delicious salads, sandwiches, grilled steaks, hamburgers and more. You can dine inside the restaurant, soak up some rays on the wonderful patio, or take advantage of the fast, friendly delivery service. Don't wait another minute. Grab your friends and family and join the fun at Smoky Mountain Pizzeria Grill.

Up Next: Routes 34, 35, or 38

Little City and the Centennial Marsh

Route 38 ◇----------▶ Gooding to Anderson Ranch

This Route at a Glance:

Estimated Driving Time: 6 hours or overnight

Highlights: Camas Lilies, Rock Formations, Barns, Wildlife

About This Route: Begin your day with sunrise at this lesser known "Little City of Rocks," then drop down into Fairfield, where you'll find old houses, barns, and farmlands backed by the Soldier Mountains. Climb into the mountains for views and a unique aspen grove, then visit the camas marshes for sunset. The fields of camas put on a stunning display of blue in late May. Cap this overnight route with a trip to Anderson Ranch Reservoir, some roadside hot springs, and a drive through the smaller, lesser known Castle Rocks.

Notes and Cautions: A high-clearance vehicle is recommended on the dirt road into Little City of Rocks. Avoid traveling this road during wet weather or winter. Wells Summit is likely inaccessible in winter, and the road can be rough in spots. Bring bug spray to the Camas Marsh. Bring a swimsuit for a soak in the riverside hot pools.

Directions

From Gooding, travel 14 miles north on ID-46. Look for a sign on the west side of the road for Little City of Rocks. There are two entrances; use the northern entrance. It is about 8 miles of dirt road to reach the **Little City of Rocks (1)**. There are unique rock formations and hoodoos, fantastic vantage points, trails and almost 6,000 acres to explore. In the spring, you'll find wildflowers, several small creeks and a few waterfalls. From March-April you may be fortunate enough to observe the male sage grouse strutting to attract the females. This is a fantastic place for your sunrise shoot.

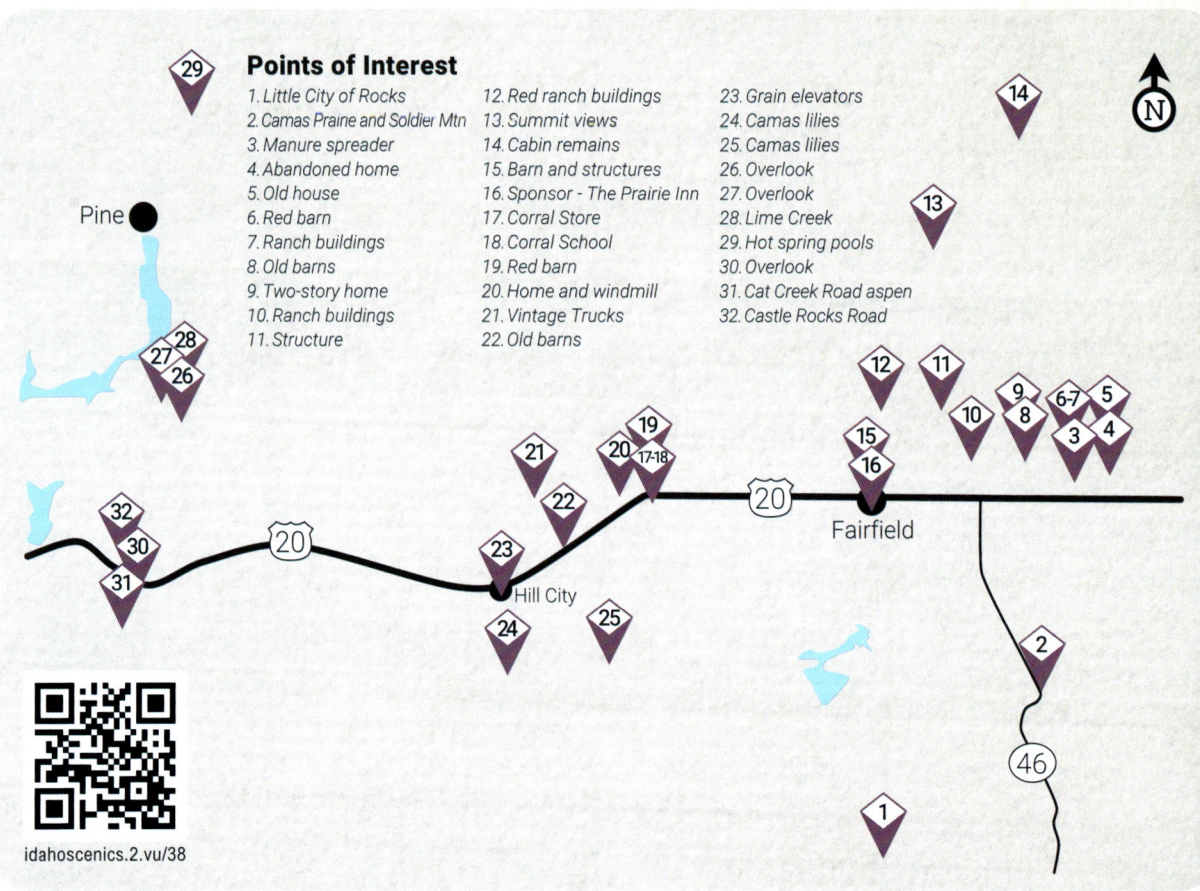

Points of Interest
1. Little City of Rocks
2. Camas Prairie and Soldier Mtn
3. Manure spreader
4. Abandoned home
5. Old house
6. Red barn
7. Ranch buildings
8. Old barns
9. Two-story home
10. Ranch buildings
11. Structure
12. Red ranch buildings
13. Summit views
14. Cabin remains
15. Barn and structures
16. Sponsor - The Prairie Inn
17. Corral Store
18. Corral School
19. Red barn
20. Home and windmill
21. Vintage Trucks
22. Old barns
23. Grain elevators
24. Camas lilies
25. Camas lilies
26. Overlook
27. Overlook
28. Lime Creek
29. Hot spring pools
30. Overlook
31. Cat Creek Road aspen
32. Castle Rocks Road

idahoscenics.2.vu/38

Return to the main road and continue north on Hwy 46. Stop at the overlook in 6 miles for a wide-open view of the **Camas Prairie and Soldier Mountain (2)**, just before dropping down into the valley.

Continue to the junction for US Hwy 20 in 7.5 miles, then turn right (east). In 3 miles, turn left onto 700 East Road. Watch for an **old manure spreader (3)** on the right in 1.5 miles. In .5 mile, turn right at a 'T' onto 200 North and travel 1.5 miles to find an **abandoned two-story home (4)** on the left.

Turn around and head west to 800 East then turn right in one-half mile. Continue north on a road signed 'Dead End'. At the end of the road, find a couple barns on the left and an **old house (5)** on the right side. Re-trace your route, about 1 mile to the

Directions Continued

intersection of 250 North and turn right. A **red barn (6)** will be on your right in .5 mile. Continue another .5 mile and keep right at the 'Y' intersection. There are **ranch buildings (7)** on your right, shortly after the turn. Continue west another 2 miles. There are several pieces of farm machinery and a couple **old barns (8)** on the right (Be respectful of private property). In a quarter mile, turn right onto 400 East Road (road was not shown on Google Maps at the time of print). A lone tree and a **two-story home (9)** sit isolated in one mile, on your left, making for a nice photo op. Turn around and go back to 250 N and continue west. In another .5 mile, you will be driving through an area with **ranch buildings (10)** on both sides. Turn right onto 300 East at the 'T' intersection, then left in 1.5 miles on 400 North. In .5 mile you will see a structure on the right. Drive past a short ways and shoot looking back at the **structure (11)** for the best viewpoint. The foothills in this area are usually filled with yellow lupine in the spring.

Continue heading west 2 miles to North Soldier Road. Turn right and watch for some **red ranch buildings (12)** on the left. In 2 miles, turn right onto a dirt road marked for Wells Summit. This road is a little washboardy in places. Watch for nice mountain views and wildflowers in season. In 5 miles, you'll cross the **summit (13)** and have nice views looking north and south. A wonderful grove of aspen awaits you on the left side of the road after the summit. They are beautiful in the fall. In another 5 miles, turn right at the 'T'. In almost 2 miles, watch for a faint two-track lane on the left. Park here and walk the short distance uphill to find the remains of a **cabin (14)**.

Go back to the main road and re-trace your route to North Soldier Road, turn left toward Fairfield. (Soldier Road makes a slight ¼ mile jog at the stop signed intersection.) Turn right and then turn left. In one mile, turn right on 100 North Road. In .1 mile is a barn and **older wood structures (15)**. Make a U-turn, and then continue south on North Soldier Road to Fairfield.

If taking advantage of our route sponsor's offer, now would be a good time to check in. **The Prairie Inn (16)** is located at 113 East Hwy 20. "We are a clean, comfortable, small town motel where hospitality is our main focus. For the comfort of all, we are totally no smoking and no pets."

If you are visiting in mid-May to mid-June, a great late afternoon or evening shoot would be to head to Centennial Marsh for sunset over the camas lilies and again for sunrise over the marsh.

Directions Continued

From the intersection of North Soldier and Hwy 20, turn right onto the main highway. In 7.8 miles look for the **Corral Store (17)** on your right, then turn right onto the 800 West Road. The former **Corral School (18)** granaries and Corral Store are all within walking distance of each other. Continue north 2 miles. A **red barn (19)** is on the right of the intersection. Then turn left on 200 North Road and go 1 mile, then turn left on 900 West Road and proceed 1 mile. An older white home with blue trim and a **windmill (20)** is located at this intersection. Turn left on 100 North Road. Watch for a reflective pond on your left. In 3 miles the road turns left. You will find **vintage farm trucks (21)** on the right. Turn left on 1200 West Road heading south. In 1 mile, turn left on Harrison Road. In 1 mile, turn right on 1100 West Road and continue .7 miles. There are **old barns (22)** on your left. In another mile you will turn right on Hwy 20. In 2.5 miles at Hill City, turn left at the sign to Centennial Marsh. Some **grain elevators (23)** will be on your right. You can continue on this loop counterclockwise, through the scenic Centennial Marsh. Watch for stream crossings, wildlife and **Camas lilies (24, 25)** in late May/early June.

Retrace your route to Hill City and Hwy 20 and continue west. In 11.3 miles, turn right on

Photography Tips

A variety of focal lengths are recommended for this route. You may want a macro lens for close-ups of camas flowers, or a wide angle to encompass a broad scene of the marsh. Mid-range lenses are useful for many of the buildings. When shooting sunset or sunrise a graduated neutral density filter can be useful to balance the light against the landscape.

This Route's Sponsor

The Prairie Inn
113 Hwy 20, Fairfield, ID
(208) 420-6726
www.theprairieinn.com

See page 276 for coupon

Directions Continued

Anderson Ranch Reservoir Road. Watch for overlook pullouts. Also note the blue bird boxes that line this stretch of the road. There is an **overlook (26)** in 7.6 miles and **another (27)** in 2.5 miles before dropping down to the reservoir. In 1.5 miles, pull off the road to view a pretty little curve in **Lime Creek (28)** In 2.5 miles, a public access area to the reservoir is on the left. Continue on to Pine. Watch for access to the South Fork of the Boise River shortly after leaving Pine. In another 3.5 miles, you will be at Johnson Bridge. In 1 mile there are **hot spring pools (29)** on your right. Continue on and enjoy the quaint town of Featherville before returning to Hwy 20.

At the intersection of Hwy 20 and Anderson Ranch Road, turn right and drive about 3 miles to a **scenic overlook (30)**. Then, in less than a mile, turn left onto Cat Creek Road and drive up this **aspen-lined dirt road (31)** for a mile or so, then retrace your route to Highway 20 and turn left. In two miles turn right at Castle Rocks Road. Here you'll find great views of some unique rock formations, pockets of aspen and **geological wonders (32)**. Return to Highway 20 and either return to Fairfield by going left or continue on to Mountain Home by turning right.

Up Next: Routes 34, 35, or 40

City of Rocks and the California Trail
Route 39 ◇----------------------▶ Albion to Oakley

This Route at a Glance:

Estimated Driving Time: 6 hours

Highlights: Oregon Trail, City of Rocks, Wildflowers, Mountain Lakes

About This Route: You can almost taste what it was like coming west to the unknown: It's an area of rocks, boulders and spires, unique in form and shape, where early settlers left their marks and stories along the way. It's an area of small towns with family ranches and farms that have run for 100 years. Mountain streams, rivers and lakes border this incredible region of rich history.

Notes and Cautions: The Castle Rocks State Park is a fee area. Birch Creek Road at Emery Canyon Road/ City of Rocks Road is closed in the winter at higher elevations. Cell phone coverage is intermittent. Be mindful of private property. The road to Lake Cleveland and Mount Harrison Lookout is closed in winter. The Oakley/Elba Road is impassable in the winter and not recommended in bad weather.

Directions

Start in the quiet town of **Albion (1)**. After exploring the town, former Normal School College campus and painted red church, travel 6.5 miles to the Pomerelle Ski area turn-off on Howell Canyon Road. Go 3 miles to a large turnout on your left. A **trailhead (2)** offers an easy and pleasant hike to Bennett Springs Campground and opportunities for some creek photos.

Back on the road, you'll find a turnout in 1 mile on your right, offering wide open **vistas (3)** of the valley and mountain range. Continue traveling 2 miles to Howell Canyon (NF 549) on the right. Park and access the surrounding views of **spring flowers and fall color (4)**.

Return to the main road and go .5 mile. At the 'Y' turn right for the road to Lake Cleveland and Mount Harrison Lookout (this road is closed in winter). Arrive at the Thompson Flat area, with access to overlooks, in just over a mile. Travel another mile to the turn off to **Lake Cleveland (5)**, a glacier-carved alpine lake in a basin north of Mount Harrison, surrounded on three sides by beautiful granite rock. Before dropping down into the Lake, park on the left and walk a short way up the hill for windswept vistas and **wildflowers (6)** in season.

After leaving Lake Cleveland, turn right and go less than 2 miles to a cutoff on your right onto a dirt road to an overlook area that is a popular **jump-off point (7)** for hang gliders. You'll find a meadow of **wildflowers (8)** in season along this road. Return to the paved road and continue to the **lookout tower (9)** for panoramic views. Retrace your route to the main highway and turn right (south) on Hwy 77.

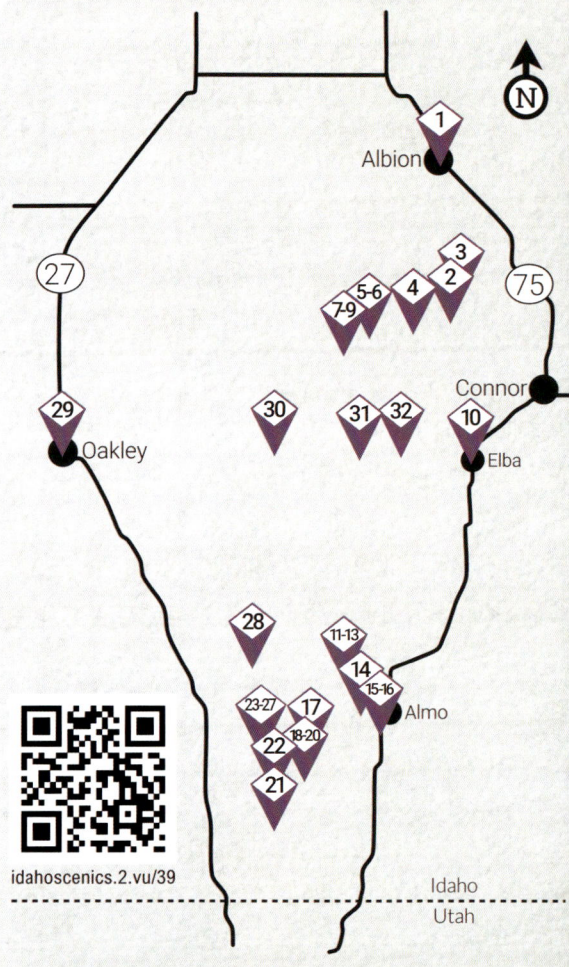

idahoscenics.2.vu/39

Points of Interest

1. Albion
2. Turnout, trailhead
3. Wide-open vistas
4. Spring flowers and fall color
5. Lake Cleveland
6. Wildflowers and vistas
7. Jump-off point
8. Wildflowers
9. Lookout tower
10. Elba
11. Fishing pond
12. Lodge and bunkhouse
13. Stines Creek Trailhead
14. Red structure
15. Tracy General Store
16. City of Rocks Visitor Center
17. Circle Creek Overlook
18. Stone structure
19. Camp Rock
20. Treasure Rock
21. Twin Sisters
22. Elephant Rock
23. Window Arch
24. Bath Rock
25. Turnouts
26. Emery Pass
27. Bread Loaves
28. Aspen trees
29. Oakley
30. Elba Pass
31. Elba Pass
32. Elba Pass

Directions Continued

Travel 5 miles and turn right at the 'T.' In 3.5 miles, take another right. Explore the tiny town of **Elba (10)**. Return to the main road and travel about 10 miles to the turnoff for Castle Rocks State Park on 2800 South Road. Look for the access to the **Fishing Pond (11)** on your left. On a calm day, you can find reflections in the water of the peaks of Castle Rocks. In less than .5 mile arrive at the lodge and bunkhouse. Parking for day-trippers can be found before and after the **lodge and bunkhouse (12)**. Continue to **Stines Creek Trailhead (13)**. Park here for picnic areas and plenty of trails to explore for photos. Early mornings or later in the afternoons are best for photos. Retrace your route to the intersection of 750 East and 2800 South. Turn right on 750 East. Watch for a faded **red structure (14)** on your right. In 2 miles turn left onto the 2980 South Road and go 1 mile to the Elba/Almo Road. Visit your route sponsor, **Tracy General Store (15)**, on your left.

The Tracy General Store, established in 1894, is a great place to visit while in Almo! Stop in and enjoy an old-fashioned milkshake, cone or Italian soda. Their kitchen offers a daily homemade meal in addition to freshly made sandwiches, hamburgers or veggie burgers. Enjoy their delicious homemade cookies! Find basic

Directions Continued

groceries, snacks and drinks at a reasonable cost. Browse their antique displays and learn the history of the Almo Valley!

Continue on the Elba/Almo Road through Almo. Stop at the **City of Rocks Visitor Center (16)** for questions or lodging reservations. In .5 mile, turn right onto 3075 South to the City of Rocks National Reserve. In 3.5 miles, take a right to the **Circle Creek Overlook (17)** for panoramic views. For a short hike, climb the hill on the left for better views. Return to the main road and turn right. The remains of a **stone structure (18)** are on the right in 1.5 miles. Respect private property.

Stop at **Camp Rock (19)** on your left in .5 mile and walk to the back of the rock to see where California Trail Pioneers wrote their names on the rock using axle grease. In .5 mile, on your right is Treasure Rock (20). The scene is much the same as what the California Trail Immigrants would have seen. In .5 mile, turn left at the 'Y' intersection to the **Twin Sisters (21)** on your left and explore the rock features. Return to the intersection and turn left on the main road. **Elephant Rock (22)** is on your left shortly after the turn. Turn right into the campsite #14 (or most any of the campsites) and explore the unique rocks in this area (see photo tips). Return to the main road. In less than a mile, watch for the sign that reads **"Window Arch" (23)**. This is a photo opportunity you won't want to miss. (see photo tips).

Return to the main road and turn right. Follow for 1 mile to **Bath Rock (24)**. Park on the right and access the trails on your right. Winter road maintenance ends here. Continue on the main road for another mile to Bread Loaves taking advantage of the **turnouts (25)** and views. Just before you round the corner to Bread Loaves, stop at the parking area marked **Emery Pass (26)**. There is a pleasant trail on your right. Explore the area around **Bread Loaves (27)**.

From the parking lot, turn left onto Emery Canyon Road (the main road) heading southwest. Go 1 mile and turn right on Logger Spring Road. Continue on this road for about 4 miles. Near the top of the ridge, this road passes through a large grove of **aspen trees (28)** offering wonderful fall color.

Directions Continued

Return to the main road and either retrace your route to Almo or consider one of these late spring through fall options:

Option 1: Continue on to Oakley (29) in 13 miles on the Emery Canyon Road (which changes to Birch Creek Road). The road is closed between the City of Rocks and Oakley in winter.

Option 2: This option is highly recommended, but only available during late spring through late fall. Travel east of Oakley and take the Oakley/Elba Road over Elba Pass (30, 31, 32). It is 20 miles to Elba. You'll find spring wildflowers, wide-open vistas, meadows, aspen, fall color, and the trailhead to Independence Lakes.

Photography Tips

Your polarizer will be of good use to you on this route for wildflowers, water and to lessen the glare off of the rocks. Use your wide-angle lens to include the foreground in your shots, and don't forget your zoom lens to get some compression for drama in your photos. Window Arch is a great place to capture a sun star looking through the arch if shooting in the afternoon. Set your aperture at f16 or f18 to catch the edge of the sun coming through the arch. At campsite #14, try some gentle rock climbing to get photos using the pan holes in the foreground or utilize some great leading lines in your compositions that are to be found in the rocks. Then don't miss a perfect opportunity to shoot back toward **Elephant Rock (22)** with your zoom lens.

This Route's Sponsor

Tracy General Store
3001 S Elba Almo Rd,
Almo, ID 83312
(208) 824-5570

See page 276 for coupon

Up Next: Routes 40, 41, or 43

Waterfalls and Snake River Canyon
Route 40 ◇----------------------------▶ Twin Falls Area

This Route at a Glance:

Estimated Driving Time: 6 hours

Highlights: Water Falls, Deep Canyons, Springs, Rivers, Bridge

About This Route: This route takes you to the iconic Shoshone Falls, the "Niagara of the West." You'll also visit the Perrine Bridge, waterfalls and intoxicating views of the Snake River and Canyon. This is one route you won't want to miss, as you continue to travel country roads for a couple barns and more water features.

Notes and Cautions: Most roads are paved, but the dirt two-tracks listed in several locations for access to the canyon edge are rough and rutted. Do not attempt to drive them in wet weather. The road into Cauldron Linn is rough, narrow and steep with deadly drop offs. Do not attempt in snow or when really wet. Be very careful walking along the basalt riverbanks here, especially when wet. Many canyon view locations are potentially deadly. Choose your footing wisely.

Directions

Start at **Federation Point (1)** on the Snake River Canyon rim located at the intersection of Washington Street North and 4150 North. Park here and follow the paved walking path (Snake River Canyon Trail) east toward the Perrine Bridge. It's a short walk to get some nice images of the bridge and canyon below. Continue walking east on the path or drive south to Pole Line Road and turn left. In .5 mile turn left onto Harrison Street, and park at the end of the road. The Snake River Canyon Trail access is on your left.

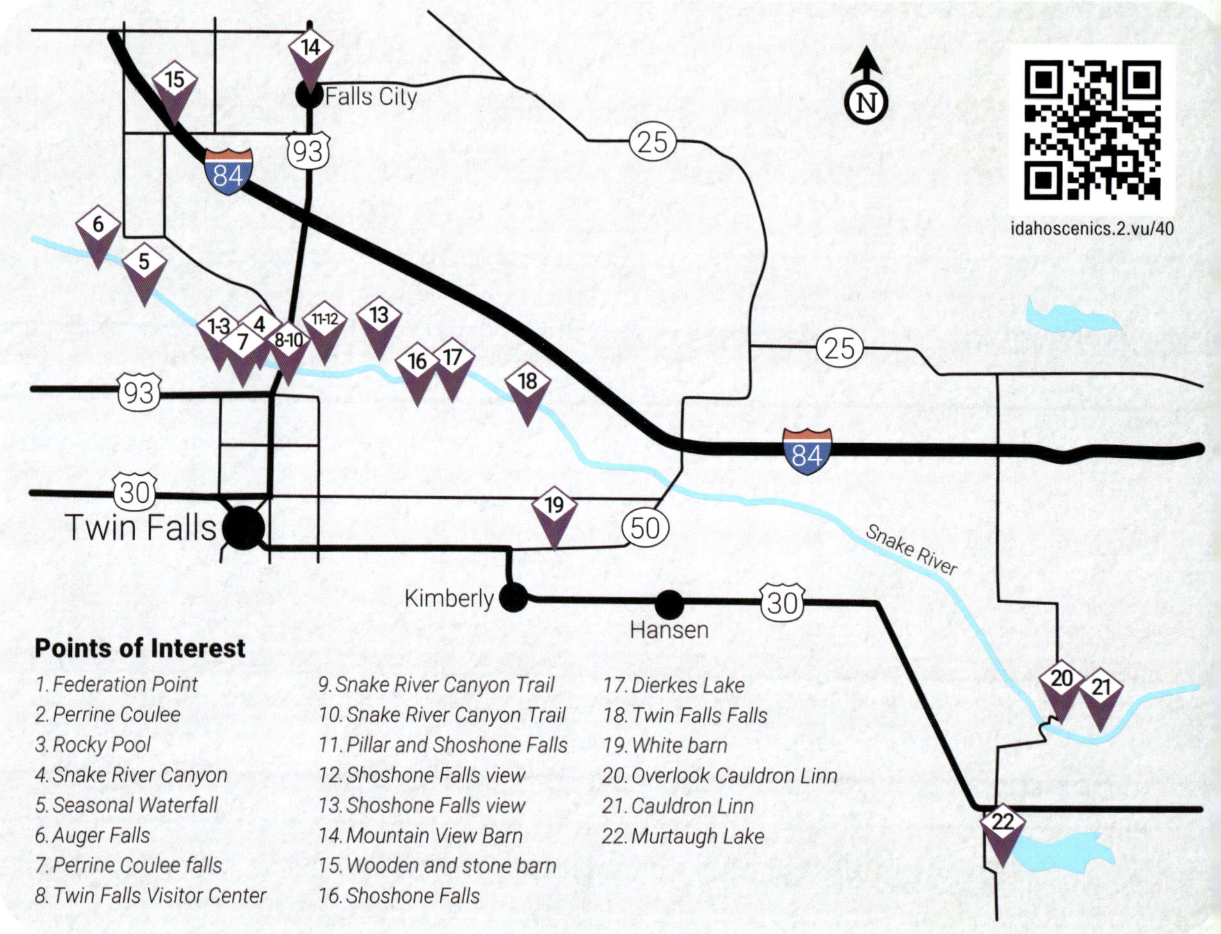
Falls City
Twin Falls
Kimberly
Hansen
Snake River
84
93
25
30
50
idahoscenics.2.vu/40
Points of Interest
1. Federation Point
2. Perrine Coulee
3. Rocky Pool
4. Snake River Canyon
5. Seasonal Waterfall
6. Auger Falls
7. Perrine Coulee falls
8. Twin Falls Visitor Center
9. Snake River Canyon Trail
10. Snake River Canyon Trail
11. Pillar and Shoshone Falls
12. Shoshone Falls view
13. Shoshone Falls view
14. Mountain View Barn
15. Wooden and stone barn
16. Shoshone Falls
17. Dierkes Lake
18. Twin Falls Falls
19. White barn
20. Overlook Cauldron Linn
21. Cauldron Linn
22. Murtaugh Lake

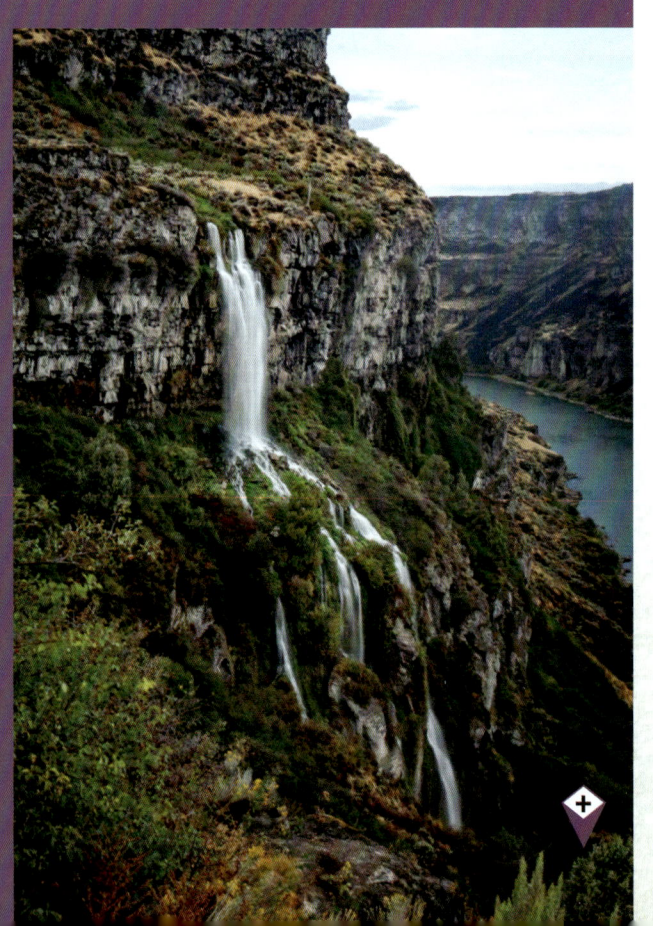

Turn right before crossing the bridge and continue to the canyon rim. This short, easy walk to an overlook area offers a great perspective of the **Perrine Coulee (2)**. Retrace your path and turn right on the walking bridge. Continue on the walking path for another perspective of the Perrine Coulee dropping over the canyon rim into a **rocky pool below (3)**.

Return to Pole Line Road and turn left. In .5 mile turn left on Blue Lakes Boulevard, then left onto Canyon Springs Road, down into the Snake River Canyon. Be cautious, as this road is narrow. At the second hairpin curve turn right to the Centennial Waterfront Park and park in the gravel pullout parking area shortly after making the turn. There is a well-worn path that takes you to the bluff

Directions Continued

above the river for a closer view of the Perrine Bridge. Follow the dirt path to the top of the hill for views looking both up and down the **Snake River Canyon (4)**. After returning to your car, continue driving down to the Centennial Waterfront Park for more views of the Bridge and reflections on the water. Retrace your route back to the stop sign and turn right onto Canyon Springs Road which takes you along the canyon floor past a golf course. The road changes to gravel. Go 2 miles on the gravel road to a parking area where you will find a **seasonal waterfall (5)**. The 3-mile round trip hike to Auger Falls begins here. Hike along the gravel road to **Auger Falls (6)**. Take one of the paths toward the cliffs above the Snake River.

Retrace your route up the canyon grade. When traveling out of the canyon, at the last hairpin turn, pull off in the wide area on your right for another view of the **Perrine Coulee (7)**. Once you are back on the top of the canyon, turn left (at the stop sign) onto Fillmore Street, then turn left onto Nielson Point Place and follow the signs to the **Twin Falls Visitor Center (8)**. Here you will also find more vantage points of the Perrine Bridge and Canyon as you walk east along the **Snake River Canyon Trail (9 & 10)**.

Drive north on Blue Lakes Boulevard across the Perrine Bridge. Turn right onto Shoshone Falls Road in .5 mile (at the stoplight). Go a little over a mile and turn right onto a rutted dirt road (there are several). You'll need a high-clearance vehicle, or walk the short distance to the canyon rim by following a rutted road for views of **Pillar Falls and the Perrine Bridge (11)**. A view of **Shoshone Falls (12)** is seen looking east. Return to Shoshone Falls Road and drive about a mile east. Park in the pullout area just before the private road that drops into the canyon. Follow the power lines to the canyon rim for an outstanding perspective of **Shoshone Falls (13)**, especially during high water. Return to the Highway 93 intersection and turn right.

Travel a short 5 miles and turn left just after crossing the tracks onto 300 South Road, then immediately turn right. You'll appreciate taking a break and visiting the historic **Mountain View Barn (14)**, which houses this route's sponsor.

Grab a cup of coffee and a bite to eat. Mountain View Barn is an historic gathering place for the Magic Valley. They have a restaurant and catering service and an event venue. They host weddings, meetings, reunions, vendor shows, dances, private and public workshops. Special family occasions are celebrated at the barn. The Jerome Farmer's Market takes place in the beautiful yard June through October.

Directions Continued

Return to Highway 93 and turn right. Travel 1 mile and turn right again onto 400 South Road. Follow for 3 miles, then turn right onto 100 E Road. In less than a half mile you will find a nice **wooden and stone barn (15)** among some trees on your right. Retrace your route, backtracking south to Twin Falls. At the intersection of Blue Lakes Boulevard and Falls Avenue turn left and go 3 miles, then turn left onto Champlin Road. Follow the signs to **Shoshone Falls (16)**. The main overlook gives you a wonderful view of Shoshone Falls. Walking west up the Canyon Trail, you will find excellent vantage points as well.

When leaving the falls, take a left at the 'Y' and visit **Dierkes Lake Park (17)**. Then follow the trail on the south side of Dierkes and detour to your right as you near the end of the lake, to visit Hidden Lakes. Continue back to Falls Avenue. Turn left to visit the "falls" of Twin Falls. In 2 miles, turn left on 3500 E. and follow the signs to the **Twin Falls Power Plant (18)**. Return to Falls Avenue and turn left. In 1 mile, turn right onto the 3600 East Road. Go 1.5 miles. There is a **white barn (19)** on your right (3829 E 3600 N). Continue another 1.5 miles to Hwy 30. Turn left (east) and travel 6.5 miles. At the curve, stay straight onto 3700 North Road. Follow this road 4.5 miles and

Photography Tips

The Snake River Canyon rim sites are best shot in either early morning or evenings. After getting the iconic bridge and Shoshone Falls photos, use your telephoto lens to get some more intimate photos of the landscape. If you want to show motion on your water images, use a polarizer and/or neutral density filters. Overcast skies are also good for helping you use slower shutter speeds. At low water times, the exposed rocks at Cauldron Linn are unique and fun to photograph as the water has worn them smooth creating curves and holes.

Directions Continued

urn left onto Archer Street. Follow to Murtaugh Road and turn left. You will drop down into a small canyon draw and make a few hairpin turns before arriving at the top of the canyon on the other side of the Snake River (1900 East Road). On your right will be a faint two-track road. Park here and walk to the canyon edge for a view of the water feature known as **Cauldron Linn (20)**.

Return to the main road and turn left, continuing south for .5 mile to 1475 South. Turn right, go 1 mile and take another right. The road going into the canyon can be rough and is narrow. Optionally, park at the top of the grade, and then walk down. The riverbanks of **Cauldron Linn (21)** (also known as Star Falls) get dangerous in inclement weather. Early morning, overcast days or evenings would be the best time to photograph this site.

To visit Murtaugh Lake, retrace your route to the tiny town of Murtaugh and 4500 E Road. Turn left and go 1 mile to Hwy 30. Turn right and then immediately turn left onto 4475 E Road. In less than 1 mile, you will arrive at the first access to **Murtaugh Lake (22)**. We prefer the second entrance for photos, which is just around a curve at 1 mile. With the backdrop of Mount Harrison and Cache Peak, shooting easterly in early morning or sunset will make for a nice photograph.

This Route's Sponsor

Mountain View Barn
392 E 300 S, Jerome, ID 83338
(208) 969-0784
mountainviewbarnidaho.com

See page 276 for coupon

Up Next: Route 41 and Route 42

Rock Creek Canyon and the South Hills

Route 41 ◇----------------▶ Hansen to Magic Mountain

This Route at a Glance:

Estimated Driving Time: 2 hours

Highlights: Canyon, Creeks, High Country Desert, Ski Area, Wildlife

About This Route: Not far from busy streets, this reddish basalt canyon corridor is a wonderful treasure well worth exploring. Multiple trails, waterfalls, shaded creeks and hoodoo rock formations line the canyon before opening up to quaking aspens, pines and a ski/snowmobiling area. Wildlife includes deer, elk, moose and an area to watch hummingbirds feed. You can follow the rim of the mountains and drop down into small ranch- and farm-based communities.

Notes and Cautions: There is no winter maintenance on the optional dirt road side trips. Watch for cattle on the road as it is open range. The road going up Rock Creek Canyon is winding with several blind corners. There is no cell phone service in most areas once you start up the canyon.

Directions

Start in Hansen at the **T and T Café (1)**, our route sponsor, located just off Hwy 30 when you head south on 3900 E. "We pride ourselves on being one of the warmest and welcoming restaurant in the area." T and T Cafe is a family owned and operated, friendly breakfast and lunch stop right on your route. Stop in for their famous biscuits and gravy, homemade French fries, fresh ground coffee or our daily specials. Try a cinnamon roll or a slice of freshly baked pie. Breakfast and lunch served seven days a week plus dinner is available on Fridays and Saturdays.

Head south on 3800 E. There is a **red barn (2)** on the left in 1 mile. Visit the **Rock Creek Station and Stricker Homesite (3)**. From Hansen, go 5 miles south, then turn west on 3200 N. This station was once the center of activity for the Oregon Trail, the Keltic Freight Road and Overland Stage Route. Return to the 3800 E Road and continue south.

Continue south 4 miles, then turn right onto Cherry Springs Road. In .5 mile, park on the right at the wide spot in the road, then walk south for a nice **panoramic view (4)** of the small valley.

Return to Rock Creek Canyon Road. Continue south one mile. On your right there are some nice **ranch structures (5)**. As you travel up the canyon, take advantage of any of the campground turnouts for some creek images, starting with the **Schipper Campground (6)** in 5 miles. The Harrington Fork Picnic Area is 2.5 miles farther, with multiple accesses, views of Rock Creek, and a trailhead for **Harrington Fork (7)**. In 1.5 miles, you will find another campground area with easy access to **Rock Creek (8)** and a view up the canyon. Continue 2 miles to **Third Fork Camp Area (9)**, which offers trailhead accesses on both sides of the road. Cross the bridge on the west side for a short hike to a view looking up the canyon.

Continue south approximately 4 miles. Park on the right in a designated parking area signed **"Ross Falls" (10)**. A one-third mile hike up the side of the hill leads to a waterfall.

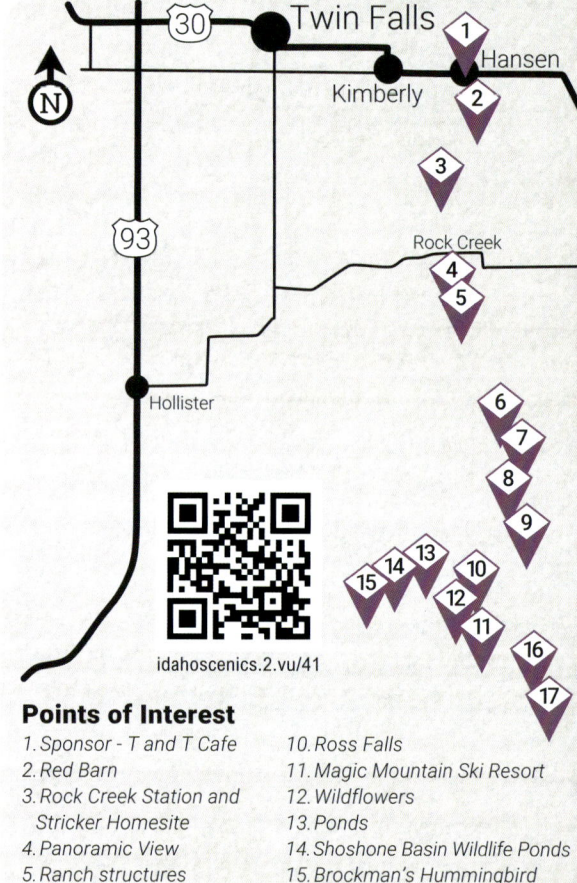

Points of Interest
1. Sponsor - T and T Cafe
2. Red Barn
3. Rock Creek Station and Stricker Homesite
4. Panoramic View
5. Ranch structures
6. Schipper Campground
7. Harrington Fork
8. Rock Creek
9. Third Fork Camp Area
10. Ross Falls
11. Magic Mountain Ski Resort
12. Wildflowers
13. Ponds
14. Shoshone Basin Wildlife Ponds
15. Brockman's Hummingbird Feeding Station
16. Valley views
17. Monument Peak overlook

Arrive at **Magic Mountain Ski Resort (11)** in 2 miles. For seasons other than winter consider these options:

Option 1: To the right of the resort, watch for the sign for Magic Mountain Road. This road will take you over the hill to Shoshone Basin

Photography Tips

Rock Creek Canyon is in the shade until mid-morning and then again late afternoon. This is great for water shots. There are plenty of opportunities to use your macro, mid-range zoom or wide-angle lens. A polarizing filter is great for reducing glare or accentuating reflections in the calm spots of water. It also helps slow your shutter speed.

This Route's Sponsor

The T and T Cafe
195 Rock Creek Rd,
Hansen, Idaho 83334
www.thetandtcafe.com

See page 276 for coupon

Directions Continued

and Rogerson. It is a 25 mile one-way trip, but worth the drive in good weather with several photo options including **wildflowers (12)** and wide open vistas. . Watch for moose near the **ponds (13)** around the 7-mile mark. The **Shoshone Basin Wildlife Ponds (14)** are a mile farther. **The Brockman's Hummingbird Feeding Station (15)** is at Mile 9 from Magic Mountain. Stay on Magic Mountain Road, which changes to Shoshone Basin Road. Turn left at the corrals at mile 20.3. You'll reach US 93 at mile 25.3, near the town of Rogerson. This road is not recommended to travel in wet weather or the winter. This route ties in well with Route 42.

Option 2: After leaving Magic Mountain, stay on Rock Creek Road, following signs to Oakley. The pavement ends in 1 mile near Diamondfield Jacks. At mile 4.6, pull off for panoramic views of the **valley (16)**. At mile 5.5 you will come to a sign for Monument Peak on your right. This **overlook area (17)** is nice for wide vistas.

Return to Rock Creek Road/Oakley Road and either return to Hansen or turn right and continue another 23 miles to Oakley. This is wonderful drive in the late spring for wildflowers or fall before the snow flies. You'll drop down the mountain into the backside of the quaint town of Oakley, famous worldwide for its quarried stone and historic gingerbread homes. This route option ties in well with Route # 39.

Up Next: Routes 39 or 42

Salmon Falls Dam and Three Creek Rd

Route 42 ◇-------------------------▶ Rogerson to Castleford

This Route at a Glance:

Estimated Driving Time: 6 hours

Highlights: High desert, Historic dam, Canyon, Reservoirs

About This Route: This route takes you along miles of open sage-covered desert, rolling hills and canyons rich in western history. From near the Nevada border, head west from the small town of Rogerson to a reservoir and dam well over 100 years old. Ranches dot the desert, as do small groves of aspen and mountain mahogany where the hills rise up to snow-capped mountains. Take a side trip or two for more intimate views of the diverse landscape. The Centennial Trail starts along this route.

Notes and Cautions: Mostly paved roads or good gravel. Side trips are gravel or two-track dirt roads. China Creek Road is gravel and not maintained in the winter and is not recommended in bad weather. Be aware, traffic is scarce here, and there is limited cell service available. Please respect private property.

Directions

Rogerson is 15 miles north of Jackpot, Nevada and 24 miles south of the Highway 93/30 Junction near Twin Falls, Idaho. When you near the town of Hollister, watch for two old silos on the west side of the road. One is in Hollister, the second is further south just out of town. Start your trip with an early morning stop at this route's sponsor, **Helen's Place in Rogerson (1)**. Grab some breakfast, a cinnamon roll or a sandwich to take with you while you explore. Friday night specials are worth coming back for. This is where you will also get the local fishing report.

11

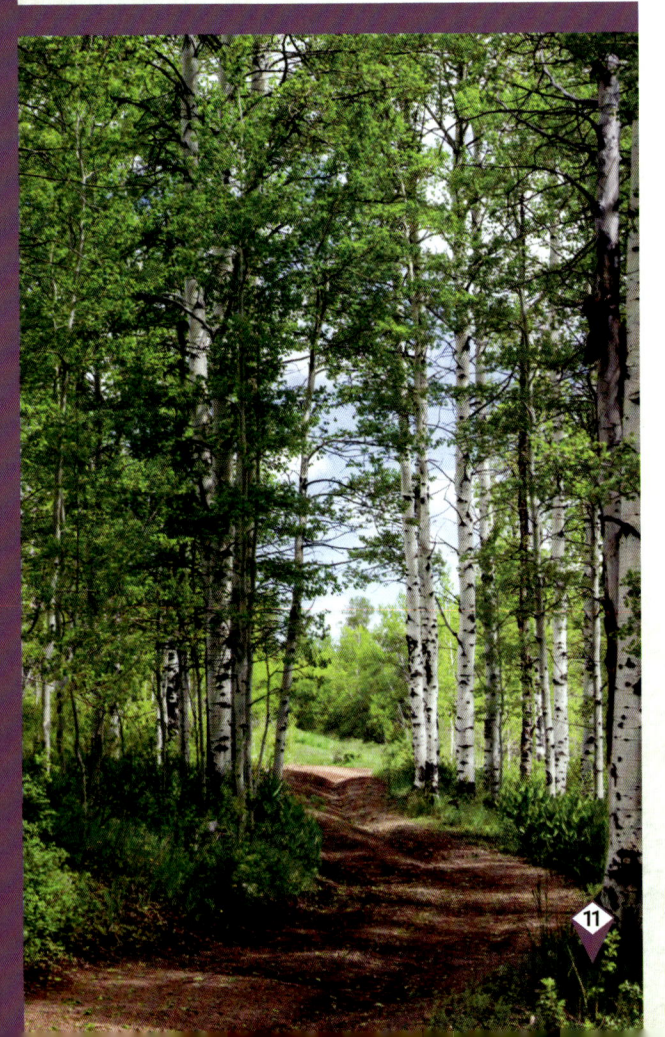

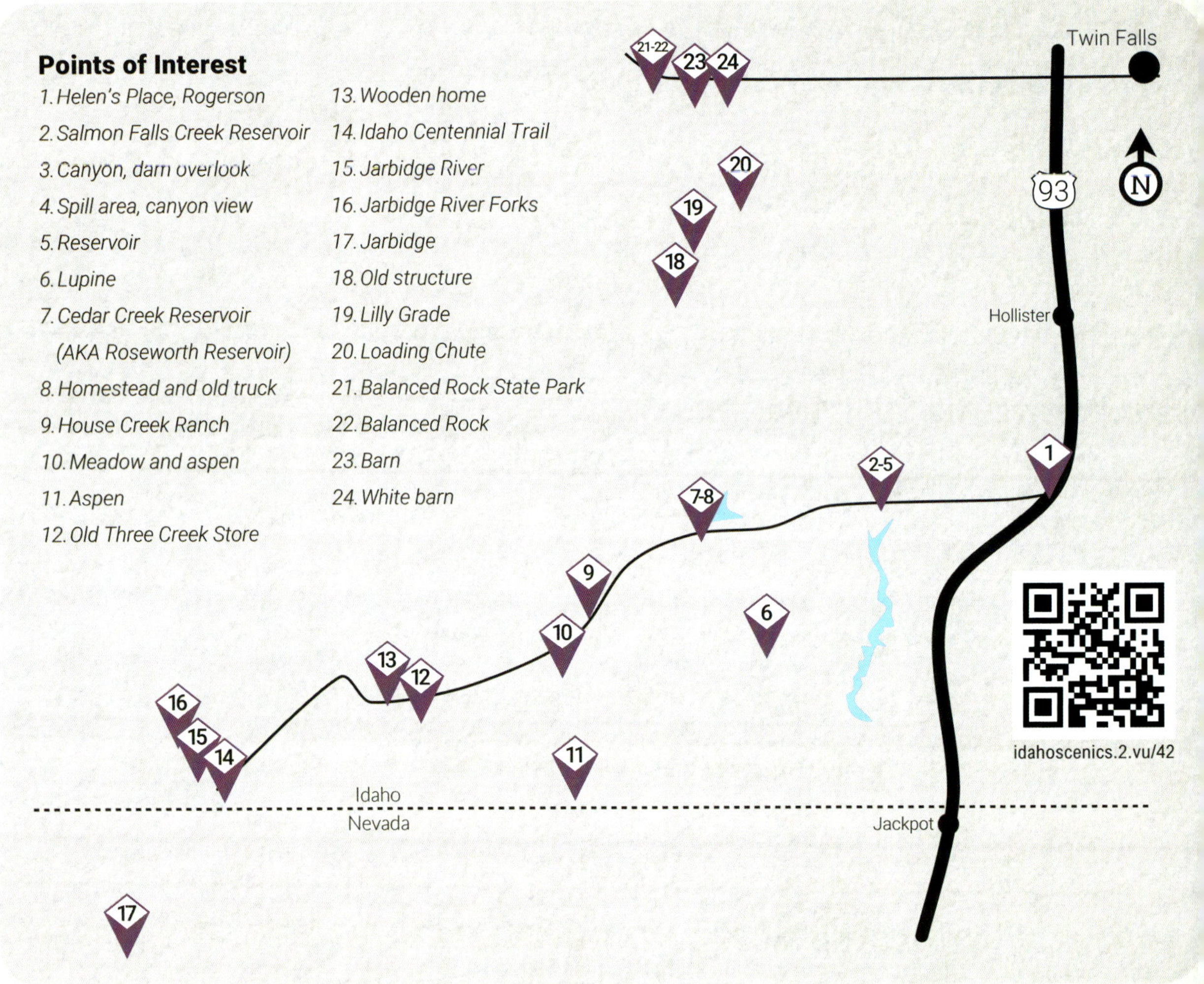
Points of Interest
1. Helen's Place, Rogerson
2. Salmon Falls Creek Reservoir
3. Canyon, dam overlook
4. Spill area, canyon view
5. Reservoir
6. Lupine
7. Cedar Creek Reservoir (AKA Roseworth Reservoir)
8. Homestead and old truck
9. House Creek Ranch
10. Meadow and aspen
11. Aspen
12. Old Three Creek Store
13. Wooden home
14. Idaho Centennial Trail
15. Jarbidge River
16. Jarbidge River Forks
17. Jarbidge
18. Old structure
19. Lilly Grade
20. Loading Chute
21. Balanced Rock State Park
22. Balanced Rock
23. Barn
24. White barn
Twin Falls
93
N
Hollister
Idaho
Nevada
Jackpot
idahoscenics.2.vu/42

Take the 1520 N Road west for 7.9 miles to Salmon Falls Dam. Stop at Lud Drexler Park on your left (day use fees). Park here and walk over to the rim of the canyon for a great view of the back side of the 100-year-old dam and the **Salmon Falls Creek Reservoir (2)**. Camping and fishing are available here.

Go back to the main road (now called the Three Creek Road or Jarbidge Road) on a single-lane road across the dam. Parking is available on the far end for good photo

Directions Continued

opportunities and a better view of the size of the dam and depth of the **canyon (3)**.

There is a two-track road with a gate on your right, just after this parking area. You'll need a high-clearance vehicle on this road. At the Y, park at the top of the grade (on the right). For viewing when they release water from the **dam (4)**, walk the 4x4 road to the left.

Go .5 mile and turn left (south) to explore the west side of the reservoir. This would be an excellent place to park for a sunrise photo with reflections in the **reservoir (5)**. Return to the main road and continue west for 1.7 miles. Turn left (south) onto China Creek Road. Spring is the best time to visit this area. Watch for wildlife. Desert wildflowers are found along this road with an abundance of **lupine (6)** around mile 8. A little farther, there are corrals, a loading chute, and a creek crossing. There are two-track dirt roads travelling toward the back side of Salmon Creek Reservoir and canyon. Return to main road.

Go west 6.7 miles and turn right to **Cedar Creek Reservoir (7)** which is a popular fishing area. Return to the main road and continue west less than a mile. As you drop down into the draw on the right side, there is an abandoned homestead structure and a

Directions Continued

well-aged rusted **truck (8)**. This is where Cedar Creek flows into the Cedar Creek Reservoir. Be respectful of private property.

Continue west for 6 miles. You will drop down a rise into the beautiful **House Creek area (9)**. After crossing House Creek, the 17 Mile Road is on your right in about .5 mile. This road passes through open range cattle country, sage-covered rolling hills, and beautiful wildflowers in the spring.

Stay on Three Creek Road for 1.5 miles, past the 17 Mile Road turnoff. Turn right on the gravel road signed Lime Creek and Wilson Creek. Take the two-track dirt road on your left in 1 mile. Here you will find a hidden meadow of **aspen (10)** and a small creek running through it. Return to the Lime Creek/Wilson Creek Road and turn left. This road traverses the top of rolling hills for miles dispersed with small groves of **aspen(11)**.

Return to the main road and continue west on Three Creek Road, passing a few working ranches and creeks. In 3.5 miles, cross Three Creek and arrive at the 7 Triangle Ranch. The stone structure on your right houses the **Old Three Creek Store (12)**.

Top a small rise in 1.5 miles and arrive at the historic Three Creek School on your left. A lone **wooden home (13)** sits in a field to the right. Just west of the school, turn right at the turnoff to the Pole Creek Ranger Station in 16 miles. This is a rough gravel road. Be sure to have plenty of gas, as there are no gas stations. Campsites and trailheads are available to the Humbolt Wilderness Area.

Return to Three Creek/Jarbidge main road. Continue west, passing more ranches, open meadows and sage covered hills. In about 10.3 miles arrive at the beginning of the **Idaho Centennial Trail (14)** before dropping down in to the town of Murphy Hot Springs, built on both sides of the East Fork of the **Jarbidge River (15)**.

Continue 15 miles to the tiny former mining town of Jarbidge, Nevada. This road makes a bend at Jarbidge Forks at the main **Jarbidge River (16)** in 2.7 miles. The road is narrow and can be rough. Travel approximately 12 miles to **Jarbidge (17)**

Photography Tips

Sunrise would be well-spent at the Salmon Dam area with mid-range zoom or wide-angle lens. A wide angle to telephoto zoom might be your best bet along most of the route. You might try getting a sun star at Balanced Rock by just catching the corner of the sun on the edge of the rock and by using a small aperture.

Directions Continued

then return to Three Creek/Jarbidge Road and travel east approximately 39 miles to the 17 Mile Road on the north side.

Take the 17 Mile Road Turnoff to Castleford by turning left. In 17 miles, there is a **structure (18)** just north of the intersection for the 17 mile road and 2600 North Road. Turn onto the 2600 Road and continue for 1 mile, and turn left (north) onto 700 East. Continue for 6.5 miles and drop down into the Deep Creek Canyon known as **Lilly Grade (19)**. About midway down the grade, there is a pull off on your right with an old wooden **loading chute (20)**, along with great views of the canyon on this road. You'll arrive in Castleford in another 4 miles. Continue 1 mile north of Castleford and turn left on 3700 N Road through a unique canyon in 3 miles. Explore **Balanced Rock State Park (21)** before continuing north to **Balanced Rock (22)** on your right. Take the short trail leading up to the base of Balanced Rock for the best view and photo opportunities. After leaving Balanced Rock, return to the 3700 N Road at the top of the grade in 1.8 miles. In 1 mile, there is a **barn (23)** on the north side of the road. In another mile, turn left onto 800 E Road and photograph a **white barn (24)**. Return to 3700 N Road and continue another 10 miles to the town of Buhl, watching for more barns.

This Route's Sponsor

Rogerson Service
1506 N 2300 E Rd,
Rogerson, ID 83302
(208) 655-4277

See page 276 for coupon

Up Next: Route 43, 45, or 46

Thousand Springs and the Snake River

Route 43 ◇----------------------▶ Buhl to Hagerman

This Route at a Glance:

Estimated Driving Time: 6 hours

Highlights: Springs, Fossils, The Oregon Trail, Snake River

About This Route: Explore old barns near the town of Buhl before heading down into the Snake River Canyon. Follow its winding path into the Hagerman Valley, the "banana belt" of the Magic Valley. Visit the beautiful Snake River, finding waterfalls, springs, orchards, an historic bridge, a wildlife refuge, and Ritters' Island among the outstanding attractions here.

Notes and Cautions: Park carefully along roadways and be respectful of private property. State Park areas have fees. Box Canyon Nature Preserve offers a trail that goes down into the canyon. Trail is steep at times and can be slick. Also be careful of stinging nettle in the summer months. There is limited cell phone use in a few locations. In the remote desert areas, be cautious of snakes in the warmer months.

Directions

This route starts with a short tour of some local barns near Buhl. Travel east of Buhl on Hwy 30. In approximately one mile, there is a **white barn with red trim (1)** on the north side of the highway. Park on the 1600 E Road for photos. Travel 1 mile to the 1700 E. Road on your right. Travel .5 mile for a **barn (2)** on your right. At the intersection of 1700 E and 4000 N, you will find the **Kunze-Sandmeyer barn (3)** on the southeast corner. Staying on the 4000 N Road, travel 1 mile. There is a **white barn (4)** in a field on your left. Turn right onto 1600 E for .5 mile to find **barns (5)** on both sides of the road. Retrace your route and turn right on the 4000 N Road. Go west .5 mile to the **Nehemian Barn (6)** on your left. At the next intersection, 1500 E, turn right (north) into the town of Buhl. 1500 E Road becomes Clear Lakes Grade. In 5 miles, park in the wide area just before the **bridge (7)** on the west side of the road. Stay on the shoulder and walk toward the bridge for nice shots of the Snake River. Then return south 1/8 mile and turn west at River Road. (In the spring, you have the option of going right (east), 4.5 miles one way, to see **fruit orchards (8)** in bloom and then, later in the season, the fresh fruit stands are open. Retrace your route to Clear Lakes Grade Road and turn left, then immediately right onto River Road). Going west on River Road will take you on a 7.5-mile, gentle scenic drive along the Snake River.

Turn right on Hwy 30. Travel a little over 2 miles to 1000 Springs Resort on your right, which is directly across the river from **Minnie Miller's barn (9)** on Ritter Island. You will be in a good location for viewing and photographing the barn across the Snake River. Continue on Hwy 30 for another 1.5 miles. Just before crossing the Snake River Bridge, turn left onto Bell Rapids Road. In 1 mile arrive at a nice park area and the historic iron **Owsley Bridge (10)** on your right. Continue on Bell Rapids Road 2.8 miles to **Snake River Overlook (11)** where you see the layers in the side of the bluffs where the famous Hagerman Horse fossils were found. Continue 3 miles to a parking area and the

idahoscenics.2.vu/43b

Points of Interest

1. White barn with red trim
2. Barn
3. Kunze-Sandmeyer Barn
4. White barn
5. Barns - both sides of road
6. Nehemian Barn
7. Bridge with river views
8. Fruit orchards
9. Minnie Miller's Barn
10. Owsley Bridge
11. Snake River Overlook
12. Interpretive Trail
13. Hagerman Wildlife Management Area
14. Red barn
15. Sponsor - Papa Kelsey's Pizza and Subs
16. Malad River
17. Failed canal system
18. Devil's Washbowl
19. Thousand Springs Preserve
20. Box Springs Nature Preserve
21. Niagara Springs Wildlife Management Area
22. Niagara Springs
23. Crystal Springs

Directions Continued

Oregon Trail overlook. Here you'll find great panoramic views of the hills and a .5-mile **interpretive trail (12)**. Or hike the 3-mile Immigrant Trail that follows the original Oregon Trail.

Return to Hwy 30 and travel 1.5 miles northwest to the Hagerman Wildlife Management Area. This is a great birding area with **migratory birds (13)**. Return to Hwy 30. There is a red barn framed by a **white fence (14)** along the road coming into Hagerman. As you travel through town, stop on the left (west) for lunch at our route sponsor.

Papa Kelsey's Pizza and Subs, 130 S. State Street. **Hagerman Papa Kelsey's (15)** is a pleasant, family-friendly restaurant, which offers a huge variety of delicious pizzas and subs on famous homemade bread and crusts. They also serve Farr's ice cream, specialty sodas, and Rich's giant cookies, as well as salads, burgers, wraps, fingersteaks, fries, tots, kids' meals and more. Check them out on Facebook at PKSHagerman. You can dine in or take out.

While in Hagerman visit the life-size sculptures of a herder, sheep and his dog and take advantage of the easy accesses to the Snake River on the west side of Hwy 30 (State Street) as you drive through town.

These areas are well maintained and well-signed. Just watch for the public access signs instructing you to turn left (west).

After exploring Hagerman, return to the highway and continue traveling north. From Hagerman go 1.7 miles north on Hwy 30 and turn right, just before you cross the bridge. Travel a short ways to an Idaho Power facility. Here you will find views of the glacier blue **Malad River (16)**. Retrace your route to Hwy 30, and turn right. Then directly after crossing the bridge over the Malad River, turn left on River Road. Travel 5 miles, then turn left to cross the Bliss Bridge over the Snake River. (You will see the bridge spanning the River on your left.) Now you are on Shoestring Road. In 1.5 miles, stay right at the 'Y'. Travel another 8 miles to a **failed irrigation system (17)** on the right. This wooden canal structure winds its way across the hillside and lends itself well to photography. Return to Hwy 30 by retracing your route and turn right toward Hagerman. In less than 2 miles turn left onto Justice Grade, (E 2500 South Road).

Directions Continued

Travel east on E 2500 S, 2.5 miles to Richie Road, then left 1.75 miles to Malad Gorge State Park. After entering the park, turn right and travel to the parking lot near the bridge next to the freeway. While it is best viewed in the spring or high water months, walk across the bridge for photos. You will be about 150 feet above Malad River, which plunges into **Devils Washbowl (18)**. The river travels 2.5 miles before joining the Snake River.

From Malad Gorge State Park, travel south on Richie Road 6 miles to the Hagerman Hwy (E 2900 S Road), then turn left. Go 1 mile. Turn right (south) on 1300 E for 3 miles to the entrance (on right) for Ritter Island State Park and **Thousand Springs Preserve (19)** with historic dairy barn, springs, kayaking opportunities and endless photo ops. Return to 1300 E Road, turn left and then turn right onto 3200 South Road. Go 2 miles and turn right onto 1500 E Road.

Continue traveling south a little over 1 mile then turn right (west). You will be on a lane that takes you to a parking area for **Box Springs Nature Preserve (20)**. Here you will find a viewing area looking down into Box Springs. The spring water is pristine green blue. (To hike farther, the total round trip is about four miles. Stay along the canyon rim

Photography Tips

The best time of day is early or late for the waterfalls, but it is photogenic at any time. You may want to use your polarizing filter. During the brighter part of the day, a neutral density filter will come in handy as well for water shots. Use a telephoto lens to isolate and photograph the failed canal system outside of Hagerman.

Directions Continued

until you find the trail that takes you down into the canyon. Follow the trail and you will reach a close-up view of an outstanding, 20-foot glacier-blue waterfall. Stay on the trail as it takes you to a secluded crystal-clear swimming hole. Retrace your route or continue on as follows.

Stay on the trail, which makes a loop along the Snake River, then winds up a road to the top of the canyon, then returns to the parking area.)

Return to the main road and continue south (right) onto 1500 E for 1 mile, then turn left on 3500 S (changes to Bob Barton Hwy). Go east 5 miles (staying right at a 'Y' intersection) and turn right onto Rex Leland Hwy (1900 E). Go approximately 3 miles to Niagara Springs Wildlife Management Area and Niagara Springs State Park. Turn hard right at the bottom of the grade to the **Wildlife Management Area (21)**. Park in the wide gravel parking lot and walk across the footbridge. You will find a small reflective pond and picnic tables. Trails will allow you to explore along the river at your leisure. Return to Niagara Springs Grade and turn right. Just before Niagara Springs State Park, you will pass a spring-fed waterfall, **Niagara Springs (22)**, on your left. There is a parking area and viewing deck here. Continue a little over a mile to **Crystal Springs (23)** on your left. Spring water coming out of the canyon walls makes a perfect backdrop for this small pond. Retrace your route and park at the top of the canyon grade in the pullout areas to enjoy sunset.

This Route's Sponsor

Papa Kelsey's Pizza and Subs
130 S. State Street
Hagerman, ID

(208) 837-6680
www.papakelseysofhagerman.com

See page 278 for coupon

PAPA KELSEY'S PIZZA & SUBS

Up Next: Routes 40, 44, or 45

Southwestern Region

Route

44. Bruneau Dunes and Owyhee Backcountry
45. Silver City and the Owyhee Mountains
46. Reservoirs and Canyons of the Boise Mts
47. Owyhee Foothills and Leslie Gulch
48. Payette River and the Sawtooths

Morning light at the Oolite Interpretive Area on route 44.

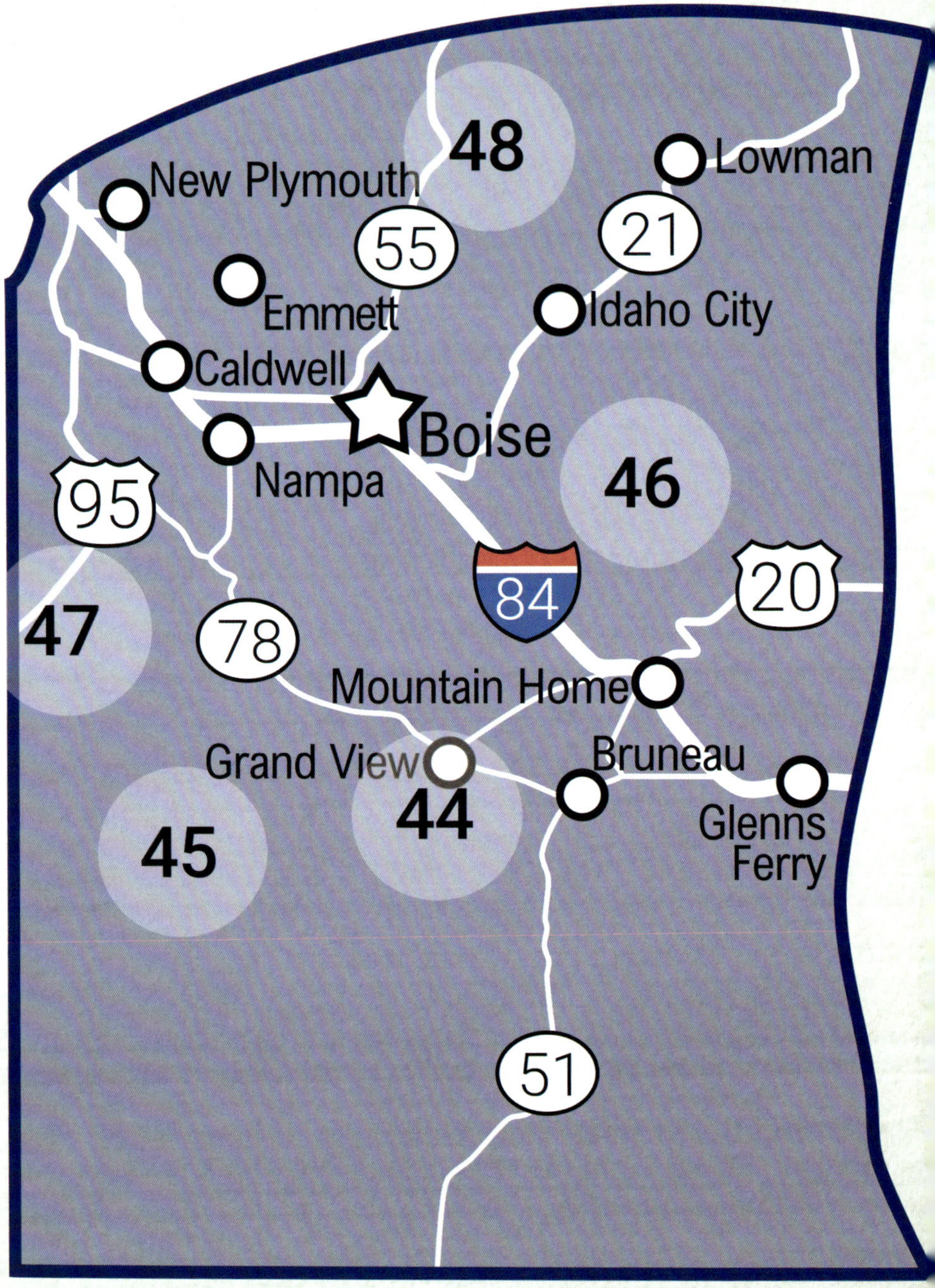

Welcome to Idaho's Southwestern Region

These routes feature the Owyhee Mountains and desert as their main geographical features, with historic mining towns and towering sand dunes, deep river-cut gorges and sagebrush deserts. Photogenic Silver City is a classic ghost town that once was a center of gold and silver mining. To the north, the Boise Mountains dominate with showy spring wildflower displays and deep canyon views to pique your interest. The Owyhee Range was one of the last areas explored in the lower 48 states, with Bruneau Dunes, featuring the tallest free-standing sand dunes in North America. The South Fork of the Payette River, Boise and Snake Rivers are all magnificent scenic attractions.

A calm stretch of the Payette River near Banks, route 48.

Snake River canyon on an early fall evening, route 45.

Bruneau Dunes and Owyhee Backcountry

Route 44 ◇------------------▶ Bruneau to Grand View

This Route at a Glance:

Estimated Driving Time: 6 hours

Highlights: Sand Dunes, Desert Scenery, and Basalt Canyons

About This Route: We begin by watching sunrise at Bruneau Sand Dunes. We'll visit Bruneau Canyon, then explore the beautiful Owyhee Mountains, the Oolite Interpretive Area, a pioneer cemetery and the Owyhee Backcountry Byway. With unforgettable vistas of spring wildflowers and desert sage, with abundant rock formations and deep river gorges, you'll want to explore this area again and again.

Notes and Cautions: There are no gas stations or cell phone service on Mudflat Road in the Owyhee Uplands Backcountry. Do not travel on these roads in inclement weather. Trout Springs Road is narrow due to overgrowth. Be very careful of the cliff edges of Bruneau Canyon.

Directions

Start at the **Bruneau Sand Dunes (1)** for sunrise, then head to the town of Bruneau. Turn left at the Bruneau One Stop, our route sponsor. Welcome to the **Bruneau One Stop (2)**; A locally owned cafe and convenience store serving breakfast, lunch and dinner 7 days a week. When you work up an appetite on your scenic drive, stop in and enjoy some food or check out their other offerings.

Continue on Hot Springs Road, which changes to Clover Creek Road, for 18 miles to the **Bruneau Canyon Overlook (3)**. Return to Highway 78. Travel 4.5 miles on Highway 78 and take a right at Jack's Creek West for a nice setting looking across **C.J. Strike Reservoir (4)**.

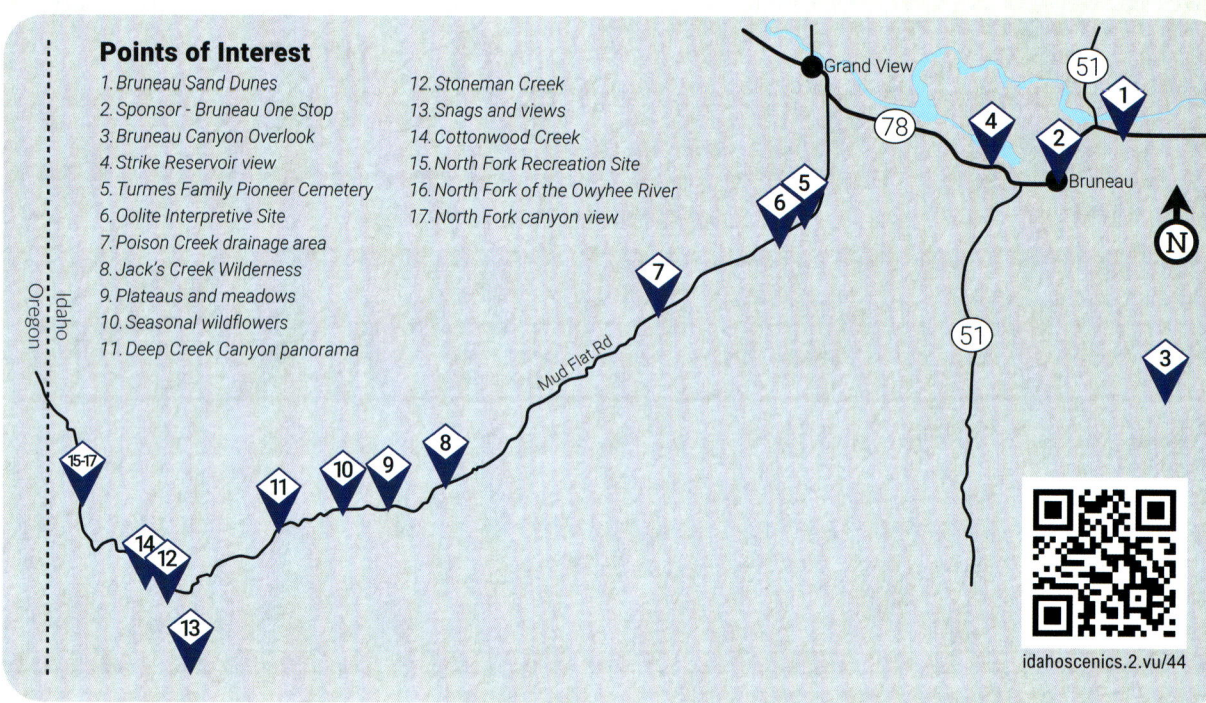

Points of Interest
1. Bruneau Sand Dunes
2. Sponsor - Bruneau One Stop
3. Bruneau Canyon Overlook
4. Strike Reservoir view
5. Turmes Family Pioneer Cemetery
6. Oolite Interpretive Site
7. Poison Creek drainage area
8. Jack's Creek Wilderness
9. Plateaus and meadows
10. Seasonal wildflowers
11. Deep Creek Canyon panorama
12. Stoneman Creek
13. Snags and views
14. Cottonwood Creek
15. North Fork Recreation Site
16. North Fork of the Owyhee River
17. North Fork canyon view

idahoscenics.2.vu/44

Return to Highway 78 and continue another 13.5 miles west to Mudflat Road and turn left, travelling 8.5 miles to the **Turmes Family pioneer cemetery (5)** on your right, a short ways up the hill. Stone buildings and corrals of the Turmes Ranch will be on your left. Continue 1 mile to the **Oolite Interpretive Site (6)** and hike the half mile trail to the top of the ridges for great views and interesting rock formations. The hike, which is not strenuous, is highly recommended.

In approximately 12 miles, climb the **Poison Creek drainage area (7)**. Pull off for photo ops of the wide-open expanse of the Little **Jacks Creek Wilderness (8)**. In the spring you will find wildflowers dispersed over the **plateaus and meadows (9)**. 18 miles past Poison Creek, you will pass the Mudflat Administrative Site, followed by meadows with **seasonal wildflowers (10)**. The road winds through some great rock formations

In 8 miles, park at the Deep Creek Bridge and take the easy hike up the hill on your left for a panorama of the **canyon (11)**. Continue west on Mudflat road about 4 miles to **Stoneman Creek (12)**. In the fall the beaver ponds create nice reflective pools. Continue on Mudflat Road another

Photography Tips

Shoot the Dunes early or late for the best results. Try to get there after a rainstorm or high winds, for sweet untracked dunes for prime shooting. The Owyhee desert is full of intricate design and details if one can take their time to look. Recommended lenses are telephoto and mid-range telephoto. If you want to capture some wildflowers, be sure to have your macro lens. Set your shutter speed high enough to stop any motion the flowers might have, or get creative with some intentional movement.

This Route's Sponsor

Bruneau One Stop
45251 ID-51, Bruneau, ID 83604
(208) 845-2511

See page 278 for coupon

Up Next: Routes 43, 45, or 46

Directions Continued

10 miles to the Juniper Mountain turnoff, on your left at the kiosk. Follow the two-track dirt road up the mountain for views of the valley and Juniper Mountain, then to a junction for Trout Springs Road for fantastic **snags and views (13)**.

Return to Mud Flat Road and turn left. In less than a mile you will reach **Cottonwood Creek (14)**. Continue another 10 miles and just before dropping down into the canyon, park and take a short walk up the hill for a panoramic view looking north of the canyon. You'll arrive shortly at the **North Fork Recreation Site (15)**, a perfect opportunity for water images and foliage along the slow-moving **North Fork of the Owyhee River (16)**. Travel up the north side of the canyon grade and take advantage of another view of the North Fork of the Owyhee looking down into the **canyon (17)**. You can continue 31.3 miles on to Jordan Valley, Oregon, then to on to Boise, Idaho.

Silver City and the Owyhee Mountains

Route 45 ◇ ------------------------------▶ Oreana to Melba

This Route at a Glance:

Estimated Driving Time: 6 hours

Highlights: Historic Town, Cemeteries, Petroglyphs, and Canyons

About This Route: Along this route, we explore the historic mining town of Silver City that was built in the high desert Owyhee Mountains; a beautiful stone church that was built in the late 1800's; and a former iron railroad bridge spanning the Snake River. The back roads take us through fertile farm ground to open barren desert and spectacular, photogenic views of the Snake River and its basalt canyon.

Notes and Cautions: There are no gas stations in Silver City, and no winter road maintenance. The first 8.5 miles of Silver City Road are paved before becoming gravel and washboard. Always respect private property.

Directions

We begin this route 17.1 miles northwest of Grand View junction on Highway 78. Turn left onto Oreana Loop Road (Note: There are two turn-offs for Oreana. Use the easterly exit.) In 2 miles on your left is the **Our Lady, Queen of Heaven Church (1)**. Built in 1883, it originally served as a general store for Oreana. A small **pioneer cemetery (2)** with a backdrop of the Owyhee Mountains is a short way south of the church.

Return to the main highway and continue west on Highway 78. In 9 miles, turn left on the road signed Silver City. The road is narrow with only a few turnouts. Watch for cattle. Use the turnouts on the high areas for panoramic vistas of the **Owyhee Mountains (3)**. Creeks may be dry later in the year. Wildflowers are abundant in season.

Silver City (4), set in the high desert of the Owyhee Mountains, is a small former mining town rich in history and photo opportunities. Photograph the **cemetery and old vehicles, (5)** open stores, shops, a small park and a café. Return to the main highway and turn left. You will be traveling through the small town of Murphy, which features an historic museum, in 14.8 miles.

Continue 10 miles on Highway 78 and turn right at the 'Y' intersection onto Highway 45. Continue on Highway 45 for 1 mile to Walter's Ferry Crossing (Western Heritage Scenic Route). Dan's Ferry Service (6), Melba, our route sponsor, will be on your right. Stop in for supplies and a good meal.

Dan's Ferry Service is a convenience store and gas station that provides cold drinks, a small deli, and non-ethanol fuels to locals and visitors from all over the state. They are located along Idaho's Western Heritage Historic Byway, adjacent to the Snake River and the 1860s Walters' Ferry River Crossing. Gas up, grab a snack, then walk down the hi to enjoy the nature trail, museum building and view the original Ferry Service site tha linked Boise to the Silver City mining tow and on to San Francisco.

In 1.5 miles, turn right onto Ferry Road, the right again on Hill Road in another mile. Hi Road becomes Warren Spur Road. Take right onto Sinker Road in 2 miles, an

Points of Interest
1. Oreana Our Lady Queen of Heaven Church
2. Pioneer Cemetery
3. Owyhee Mountains
4. Silver City
5. Cemetery and old vehicles
6. Sponsor - Dan's Ferry Service
7. Guffey Railroad Bridge
8. Petroglyphs Trail
9. Dedication Point
10. Scenic Views

idahoscenics.2.vu/45

Photography Tips

A wide-angle lens will be nice for the panoramic views of the Owyhee Mountains, and again when viewing the canyon rim at Celebration Park. Sunset and evening shots would be great at Dedication Point in Celebration Park. A multi-focal length zoom lens would work well for exploring Silver City.

Directions Continued

ontinue 3 miles to Guffey Railroad Bridge nd Celebration Park. The **Guffey Railroad Bridge (7)** is in Idaho's only archeological ark. The bridge allows foot and horse ccess between the south and north sides f the Snake River. Hike across the bridge nd tackle the **Petroglyphs Trail (8)** for ncient rock engravings.

eturn to Warren Spur Road and turn right. urn left at the 'T' intersection. In 3.7 miles, rn right onto McDermitt Road and, in 1 ile, turn left onto Victory Road. Go 2 miles another 'T' intersection and turn right on Swan Falls Dam Road. Stop at **Dedication Point (9)** in 4 miles. A short walk to the canyon rim takes you to a panoramic view of the Snake River and canyon on the right. Continue on to the Historic Swan Falls Dam. Before dropping down into canyon, take advantage of pullouts to get the best **scenic views (10)**. Sunset or late afternoon would be a good time to visit. Self-guided tours through one of the buildings are available certain times of year. Retrace your route and follow the signs to Kuna, then to the interstate, or go back to Highway 78 and go to Nampa.

This Route's Sponsor

Dan's Ferry Service
1984 Hwy 45 So.
Melba ID, 83641
(208) 495-2507

See page 278 for coupon

Up Next: Routes 44 or 47

Reservoirs and Canyons of the Boise Mtns

Route 46 ◇------▶ Lucky Peak Reservoir to Blacks Creek

This Route at a Glance:

Estimated Driving Time: 4 hours

Highlights: Reservoirs, Canyons, Wildflowers, Waterfalls

About This Route: Impressive springtime views and features make this a delightful journey. In late April, you'll find wonderful wildflower displays to complement the deep river canyons that feed the reservoirs at the start of this trip. Spring waterfalls and a couple of old barns cap this lovely route.

Notes and Cautions: Much of the 37 miles around the reservoirs is very rough dirt road. This winding route is potentially dangerous, with many steep drops. Be extremely careful when viewing from any of the canyon edges. All waterfalls are likely seasonal and are best viewed in spring. This route is not accessible in winter.

Directions

From I-84 in Boise take Hwy. 21 northeast about 13 miles to FS Rd. 268 (also known as E. Spring Shores Road), which becomes Arrowrock Road. Follow for 37 miles, taking in the views over these **two reservoirs (1,2)**. There's a nice little campground called Willow Creek along the N.F. of the Boise River, after passing the end of Arrowrock Reservoir. It looks like a great place for a picnic and maybe a photo op of the riverbend and rapids. In another mile turn right onto FS Rd. 213 (also known as Long Gulch and Slide Creek Road). As you cross these mountains there's many patches of aspen that would make for a nice drive in autumn. There's a **creek (3)** and then a **barn (4)** with a mountain backdrop in 16.5 miles. In 2.5 miles take a break at the **Y-Stop Country Store and Restaurant (5)**, our route sponsor on the left.

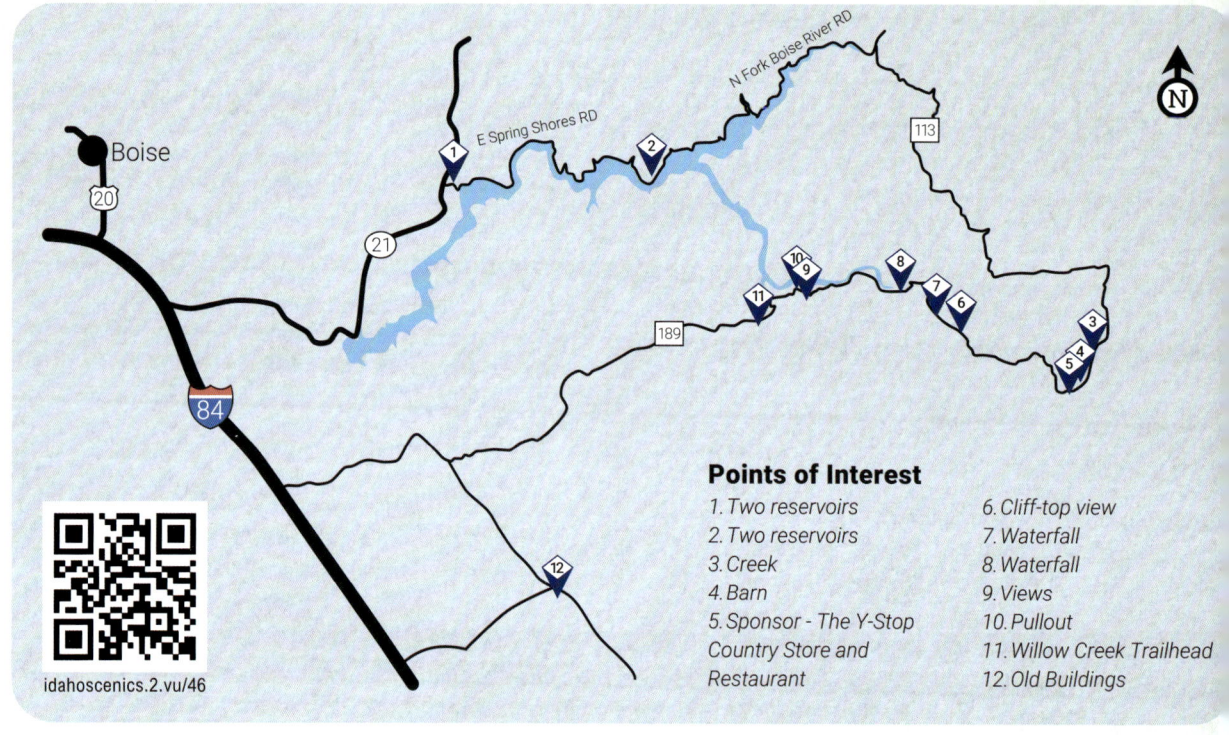

Points of Interest
1. Two reservoirs
2. Two reservoirs
3. Creek
4. Barn
5. Sponsor - The Y-Stop Country Store and Restaurant
6. Cliff-top view
7. Waterfall
8. Waterfall
9. Views
10. Pullout
11. Willow Creek Trailhead
12. Old Buildings

idahoscenics.2.vu/46

The Y-Stop Country Store and Restaurant was founded in 1999 near the little town of Prairie Idaho. They have a quaint little Country Store and Restaurant nestled in the Mountains North East of Boise, Idaho... The Country style store offers gifts, snacks, groceries, ice cold beer, gas, propane and a full liquor store. The Restaurant focuses on providing good quality food and hospitality to every guest at every meal, each and every day. Stop in and enjoy a great selection of comfort foods. The Y-Stop believes in treating strangers like friends and friends like family.

Just ahead you'll reach a Y junction fo Smiths Prairie and Blacks Creek Road Turn right on Blacks Creek Road an follow it for 4.7 miles. Watch for a two track path on the left going toward th canyon edge. Park along the road an walk. Here's a great **cliff-top view (6** looking back up the canyon. In anothe mile you'll find a pullout on the left for bird's-eye view of a **waterfall (7)**. There' another waterfall tucked into the canyo that you'll want to see. To view it, wal towards the main canyon rim about 20 feet and look upstream. You'll encounte

Photography Tips

Late April and early May will reveal wildflowers in the Blacks Creek area. Run this route backwards for best sunrise views over Blacks Creek. A wide to mid range lens is best for this route, as well as a macro lens for wildflowers. A telephoto lens would be best for two of the more distant waterfalls. Use a polarizing filter to make the clouds pop, and accentuate any reflections in the water.

Directions Continued

nother **waterfall (8)** about two miles arther, which is viewed from the oadside below. In 1.5 miles there is a avern in the rock across the river with et another waterfall.

ou'll see great **views (9)** to the north as you each the top of the grade. This area can be mazing with wildflowers in late April/early lay. There's a good **pullout (10)** at the top, n the right. In 2 miles is **Willow Creek railhead (11)**. Stretch your legs with a hike along Willow Creek. It is about 1 mile to reach the reservoir. Continue on Blacks Creek Road for 11.7 miles. At the paved junction with Mayfield (also known as Foothill Rd and Slater Flat Rd.), go left. In 6.8 miles look for a few **scattered buildings (12)** which remain from the community of Mayfield. Retrace your route a short distance to the intersection of Indian creek Rd. and turn left. Stay on Indian Creek Rd until it becomes Mayfield Road. The I-84 interchange #71 is just ahead.

This Route's Sponsor

The Y-Stop Country Store and Restaurant

1260 W. Long Gulch Road,
Prairie, Idaho
(208) 868-3249

See page 278 for coupon

Up Next: Routes 45, 47, or 48

Owyhee Foothills and Leslie Gulch

Route 47 ◇ ------------------------------▶ Marsing to Homedale

This Route at a Glance:

Estimated Driving Time: 4-5 hours

Highlights: Rock Formations, Canyons, Wildflowers, Waterfall

About This Route: Although the unique rock formations in Leslie Gulch and the Succor Creek Recreation area are in Oregon, they're accessed through Idaho. We'll start with sunrise overlooking the Idaho Owyhees, then proceed to viewing the pinnacles and canyons of Leslie Gulch and Succor Creek. Wildflowers proliferate in the spring, and autumn colors decorate the banks of Succor Creek in the fall. Top it off back in Idaho with a short hike to a desert waterfall to cap this gorgeous route.

Notes and Cautions: Once off the highway, this route is very bumpy. Roads in the Owyhees should never be attempted in wet weather. Do not be caught in Leslie Gulch in a rainstorm, as this canyon is prone to flash flooding. Be very careful at some of the cliffside overlooks for Succor Creek. Watch for rattlesnakes when hiking. Take a picnic lunch, as there will be no services until you reach Homedale.

Directions

From Marsing, travel west 2 miles on Highway 95 to the intersection of highways 95 and 55. Stay left on Highway 95 and continue south 9.8 miles to a **scenic overlook (1)** on the left. Enjoy a sunrise view here overlooking the Snake River Plain south of Boise.

Continue 3.5 miles to a dirt road on the left. This BLM access road travels into the Owyhee foothills. Follow it for a couple of miles through unique **rock formations (2)**. Return to Highway 95 and turn left. There is a **cabin (3)** on the left in 1 mile. Continue on Highway 95 for 4.7 miles, then turn right on McBride Road. In 7 miles there's a neat **old house (4)** in a horse pasture. You are now in Oregon. In 4 miles turn right on Succor Creek Road, then turn left on Leslie Gulch Road in 1.7 miles. This 14-mile road dead-ends at the **Owyhee Reservoir (5)**. The attraction is the gulch itself and the amazing **red rock formations (6)** along the route. In spring there can be an abundance of **wildflowers (7)**. There are many hiking opportunities where even more treasures await you. Return to Succor Creek Road, watching for **lupine (8)** in the spring on the highlands on your way out. Turn left on Succor Creek Road.

Watch for a pullout on the right in just under 9 miles. Here you can walk to the cliff edge for views of **Succor Creek (9)**. In .2 mile there's another view spot for **creek vistas (10)** from above. In .5 mile turn right into the **Succor Creek Campground (11)**. Take a hike of a mile or so along the creek trail for beautiful creekside views, then continue on Succor Creek Road by turning right from the campground. Enjoy the **creekside drive (12)** through the canyon for the next few miles. 15.5 miles from the campground, turn right (east) onto Oregon Highway 201. You'll cross back into Idaho in 1.8 miles and be traveling on Highway 19, reaching Homedale in less than 5 miles. Turn left on N. 1st Street W and find this route's sponsor, **The Bowling Alley, LLC (13)**, on the right in ½ block.

The Bowling Alley, LLC has been serving Homedale since 1958. Their full-service

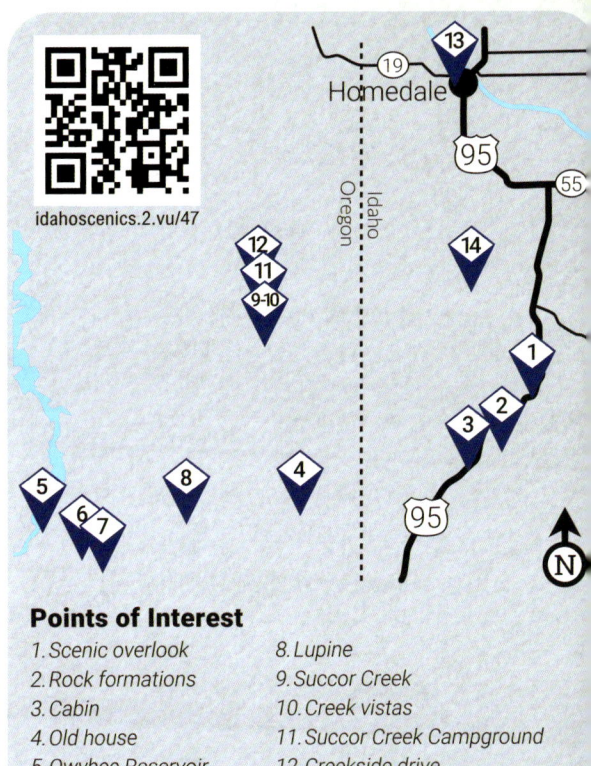

idahoscenics.2.vu/47

Points of Interest
1. Scenic overlook
2. Rock formations
3. Cabin
4. Old house
5. Owyhee Reservoir
6. Red rock formations
7. Wildflowers
8. Lupine
9. Succor Creek
10. Creek vistas
11. Succor Creek Campground
12. Creekside drive
13. Sponsor - The Bowling Alley, LLC
14. Scenic waterfall

Photography Tips

Visit this route in spring for the wildflowers in Leslie Gulch or autumn for golden color along Succor Creek. Both are great color contrasts with the red rock found in the area. You'll want a wide angle for the great roadside views in Leslie Gulch in addition to a telephoto for more distant rock formations or close-ups. A polarizing filter will help accentuate the colors. Arriving at Jump Creek Falls in the late afternoon should put the waterfall in shade and help slow your shutter speeds. Keep that polarizing filter on here.

This Route's Sponsor

The Bowling Alley, LLC
18 W 1st St, Homedale, ID 83628
(208) 337-3424

See page 278 for coupon

Directions Continued

estaurant offers home-cooked meals from scratch, including breakfast, lunch and dinner beginning at 6:30 a.m. Try their specialty, the very best fingersteaks in Idaho! They have a 50-seat banquet room available; please call ahead to schedule your group. The bowling center features open bowling and leagues, with eight lanes providing a vintage feel.

Return to Highway 19 and go left (east). In 1 block turn right on S. Main Street. In .6 mile turn right (south) onto Highway 95. In 3.9 miles turn right onto S. Jump Creek Road. Follow S. Jump Creek Road 5.8 miles to the trailhead for Jump Creek Falls. This .6-mile hike takes you into Jump Creek Canyon with the reward of a **scenic waterfall (14)** at the end. Watch for wildflowers in the spring and autumn color later in the year. Return to Highway 95 and go left back to Homedale or Boise via Marsing.

Up Next: Routes 45, 46, or 47

Payette River and the Sawtooths

Route 48 ⟡┄┄┄┄┄┄┄┄┄┄┄┄┄┄┄┄┄┄┄┄┄┄┄┄► Emmett to Stanley

This Route at a Glance:

Estimated Driving Time: 7 hours

Highlights: River, Canyons, Hot Springs, Mountains

About This Route: We start this route in the farming community of Emmett and travel over 120 miles to Stanley Lake. Along this route you'll have the opportunity to soak in hot springs, hike, experience breathtaking river, canyon and mountain views, follow the South Fork of the Payette River along the Wildlife Canyon Scenic Byway (the Banks-Lowman Road), and photograph Stanley Lake at sunset, with iconic Mt. McGown Peak as a backdrop.

Notes and Cautions: Start early for this lengthy route. You may need a recreation pass for parking at Banks Beach, which is a fee area. Take your swimsuit and water shoes and enjoy two hot springs on this route. Highway 21 is sometimes closed in the winter over Banner Summit, as well as the side trips to Grandjean and Stanley Lake.

Directions

From the junction of Highway 16 and Washington Street in Emmett, proceed north on Washington Street 3.2 miles and turn left on Black Canyon Road There is a big **red barn (1)** on the left. Make a u-turn and stay straight on Black Canyon Highway. In 3.4 miles turn right on Plaza Road. Cross the bridge and park on the left. A short walk toward the river will give you views of a small falls and **Squaw Peak (2)** above the Payette River.

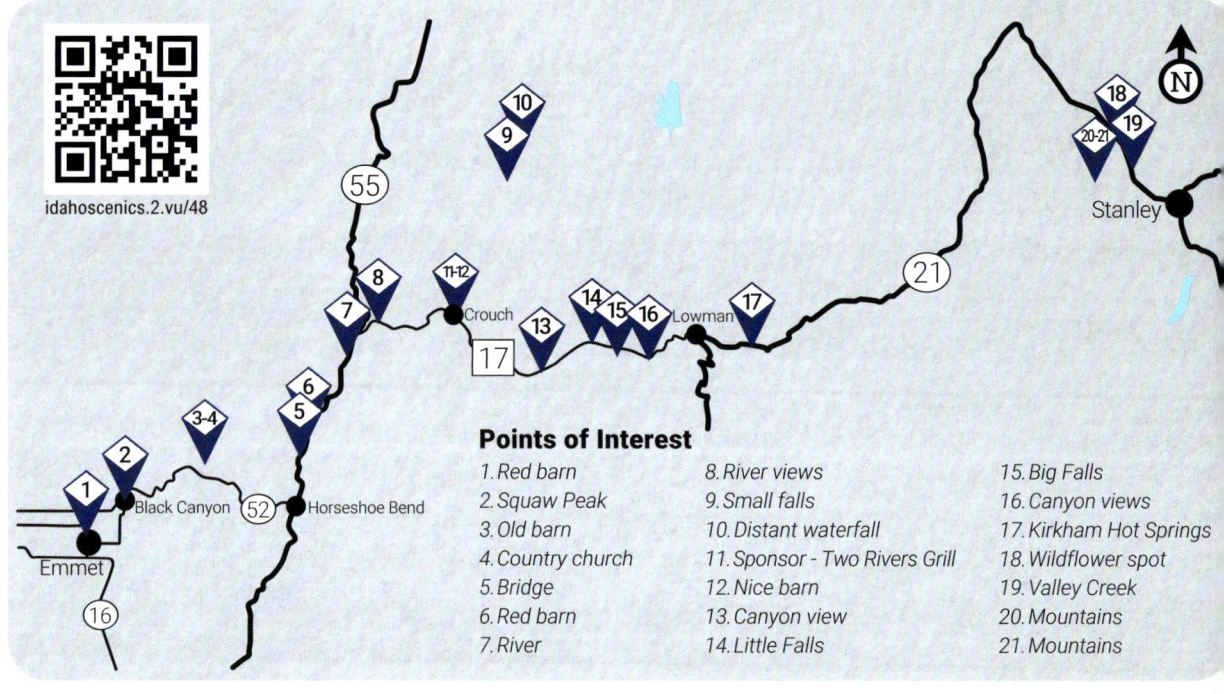

idahoscenics.2.vu/48

Points of Interest
1. Red barn
2. Squaw Peak
3. Old barn
4. Country church
5. Bridge
6. Red barn
7. River
8. River views
9. Small falls
10. Distant waterfall
11. Sponsor - Two Rivers Grill
12. Nice barn
13. Canyon view
14. Little Falls
15. Big Falls
16. Canyon views
17. Kirkham Hot Springs
18. Wildflower spot
19. Valley Creek
20. Mountains
21. Mountains

Return to the highway and turn right (east). In .4 mile there is a barn on the right. In .5 mile turn right into Wild Rose Park for views of the dam from below. In 3.4 miles you'll reach Triangle day use area for recreational access to Black Canyon Reservoir. In 2.6 miles there are some old tractors. In another 1.2 miles turn left (north) on the Sweet-Ola Highway. In 1.7 miles turn left on Butte Road. There is an **old barn (3)** on the left. Make a u-turn, then turn left on Sweet-Ola Hwy. There is a **country church (4)** on the right. If you got an early start and like country churches, continue north on Sweet-Ola Highway to the community o Ola in about 14 miles. You'll find anothe lovely church on the right as your ente the community. Make a u-turn and retrac your route back to Black Canyon Highwa (Hwy 52) enjoying the scenery and severa other barns en route.

Turn left on Hwy 52. In 3.3 miles there i river access on the right. In 3.3 mile there is a nice farm with a barn on the left In .8 mile you'll reach the junction o Highway 55. Turn left. In 4.3 miles there is a pullout on the right for a view of the **bridge (5)**. In another 1.3 miles there is

Directions Continued

distant view of a **red barn (6)**. Banks Beach is on the left in In 7.7 miles. This is a pretty view of the **river (7)** and also a popular swimming location. In one more mile, turn right on Banks-Lowman Road. You'll find numerous pullouts on the right for **river views (8)** and access. In 8.4 miles turn left (north) on S. Middle Fork Road. Make your way through town following the Middle Fork Road. In about 2 miles from the highway junction there is a barn with a painted quilt on the end. There are more barns and an old homestead on the right in 2.4 miles. There is a red barn 2.1 miles farther. You'll find numerous river access points, but watch for one on the left 7.4 miles past the red barn. You should see steam rising across the river. This is the access to Rocky Canyon Hot Springs. When the river is running low enough, wade across the river and enjoy these hot pools above the Middle Fork of the Payette.

Continuing up the canyon, you'll see **small falls (9)** along the route. In 5 miles stay straight on Middle Fork Road (NF 698). Continue 2.2 miles and turn around at the bridge. As you head back down Middle Fork Road measure 1.6 miles, where a small pullout on the right, high above the canyon, will provide you with views of a

Directions Continued

distant waterfall (10) cascading into the deep ravine. Be very careful at this unfenced viewpoint. Back in town turn left on Old Crouch Road and find this route's sponsor, **Two Rivers Grill (11)**, immediately on your right.

Two Rivers Grill offers fine dining in the heart of Garden Valley. This unique mountain destination serves up fresh fish, steaks, pasta, salads and burgers. Enjoy lunch on their outdoor patio. Try their baby back pork ribs, rib eye steak and pan-fried crab cakes. They offer a full bar and a friendly atmosphere.

Follow Old Crouch Road across the bridge. You'll see a **nice barn (12)** to the right, as you turn the corner just across the bridge. Respect private property and shoot from the road. In .9 mile turn left on Banks-Lowman Highway. In 8.1 miles a pullout on the right provides a **canyon view (13)**. The Danskin Boat Access is 2.4 miles farther. In 2.6 miles, there is a small pullout on the right for views of **Little Falls (14)** on the Payette. You'll pass great canyon views and in 2.3 miles a small pullout on the right for views of **Big Falls (15)**. Another great **canyon view (16)** comes up in 1.5 miles. In 6.8 miles turn left on Highway 21.

Photography Tips

You'll want a wide-angle lens and a polarizing filter at Stanley Lake if you're lucky enough to get a calm lake scene with reflections. Stanley Lake is a great place to be as the sun goes down. It sets to the right of the peaks most times of the year, casting a golden glow onto the peaks. A telephoto lens is useful for a couple of the barns and the waterfall north of Crouch.

This Route's Sponsor

Two Rivers Grill
(208) 462-3770
1049 Old Crouch Road
Garden Valley, Idaho. 83622

Up Next: Routes 26, 35, or 37

Directions Continued

n 4.3 miles turn right to visit **Kirkham Hot Springs (17)**. Then return to Highway 21 and turn right. In 8.5 miles, turn right on NF 531. Cross the river, then turn right and arrive at Lowman Nature Ponds. Return to Highway 21 and turn right. Travel 37.5 miles, watching for scenic views. Turn right into the Park Creek Overlook. This can be a **great wildflower spot (18)** in early summer. 2 miles further a pullout on the left provides views over the meadows to the north and **winding Valley Creek (19)**. In .4 mile turn right on Stanley Lake Road (NF 455). In 3.1 miles turn left into Stanley Lake Campground, then right toward the overlook day-use area. Enjoy the last light of day touching the **mountains (20, 21)**. Return to Highway 21 and go right, arriving in Stanley in 4.7 miles. See route 26 for an excellent lodging option.

A Day in the Life
Exploring Idaho's Backroads

Story and Photos by Linda Lantzy
First published in Idaho Magazine, June 2019.

As I descend the steep, winding road into the Pittsburgh Landing area of Hells Canyon, the temperature starts to climb. Even on this gray, drizzly spring day in late April, it is warming into the 70s at only 9 A.M. Coming around a corner, the vehicle passes over a dead rattlesnake in the road, and my knee instinctively shoots up to hit the steering column. Now fully alert, I make a mental note to be very careful when walking. The road continues to drop into the canyon, and I see another snake but this time don't flinch.

Surrounded by rugged peaks with a few patches of snow remaining, I'm in awe. The golden petals of arrowleaf balsamroot in bloom catch my eye and I am hopeful for a break in the rain and a chance for photographs. Reaching a "Y" in the road, I clock my mileage, scribble it into my notes, and instinctively go left. The road ahead traverses a bluff above the mighty Snake River and my inclination is to continue rather than drop down to the water right away.

Excitement builds as this two-track stretches before me through a field of green grasslands. It is so beautiful, even on this stormy day. Completely forgetting the snakes, I pick a spot that affords a view upstream of the river. I park and walk about a hundred feet through waist-high grass to the edge of the bluff for a quick look. This is a great spot, and I retreat to my car to grab my gear.

Heading back to the river vantage point with tripod and camera in hand, there in the path I just made through the grass is a four-to-five-foot rattler, coiled and ready to strike. I freeze in my tracks. There's nobody here but me. No cell phone service. The nearest hospital would be Grangeville, approximately forty slow miles away. Ever so slowly, I back away, remembering my caution to myself, and thinking how lucky I am. But there will be no river photograph from this spot.

From the safety of the trailhead parking area at the end of the road, I make my photographs of the river and canyon. It is bittersweet, but will suffice. A lone tree in the field also catches my eye. Still a little shaken from my previous stop, I don't venture any closer to it. Back in the safety of the vehicle, I sit for a few minutes and listen to the soft pitter-patter of rainfall against the windshield. I love my life.

It's hard to leave this place and it seems incredible that this is the first time I've seen it. As the road climbs out of the canyon, I vow to come back again. Ascending the Pittsburgh Saddle and then descending back onto the Salmon River side, I pass several roads it would be great to explore, but those must wait for another day. I stop for an old barn, with a tree full of apple blossoms nearby. It shows its age, a weathered gray testament to the long life it has had. I am happy to document its existence. I stop again for some purple lupine along a fence with a backdrop of the Gospel Hump Wilderness. It would be much too early in the season for a visit there, but the thought of sleeping in my vehicle on a cold night last autumn and then watching the sunrise above the Upper Gospel Lake brings a smile.

Forty-five minutes later, I turn south on Highway 95. At this point it's about 10 A.M. and I've already been on the road for eight hours. The morning had started no differently than most of the mornings on such a trip—my 2 A.M. departure from Coeur d'Alene was not exactly planned. Like most nights before a trip, I couldn't sleep, so why not start driving? While I didn't exactly relish the prospect of driving at night, the possibility of watching sunrise in a new location several hours south of my place spurred me on—and driving in the dark kept me alert for wildlife.

Several hours after leaving home, the surroundings started to lighten as I headed south of Lewiston, and I tried to calculate where my location would be about thirty minutes before sunrise. My hope was to make it through the Winchester Canyon and be somewhere on the highlands between there and Grangeville. I could now see lots of clouds in the sky, maybe too many for a good sunrise. Still, as I passed Cottonwood, I took a road to the left, having no idea what I'd find, if anything. The sky was starting to look more promising and I could see distant rain squalls. Any kind of foreground would be welcome: a barn, a farm implement, a fence line running towards the sunrise. But luck was not on my side this morning. With just a touch of color in the sky, I noticed a curve in the green furrows of winter wheat. That would be my sunrise location.

I bought gas at Grangeville and after crossing White Bird Summit, pulled off at one of the upper viewpoints. The view here never disappoints. Today wisps of mists hung in the valleys between distant peaks, and the landscape was a verdant green. The old highway follows many twists and turns as it crosses the White Bird Battlefield. Slowing for cattle on the road several times, I continued my descent. Reaching a switchback that gives a view of hillsides carpeted in the yellow of arrow-leaved balsamroot, I paused. At the base of the hill, I turned away from the highway.

This wandering of mine is not aimless, by the way, it has a purpose. Like almost all my trips in the last year, this one is about exploring new areas, revisiting familiar places, and taking notes. The fourth notebook is almost filled, and my travels are almost complete.

On the way back to Highway 95 from Hells Canyon, I traversed the hillsides until the road ascended into the Nez Perce National Forest. Here there was a viewpoint I had discovered on a previous exploration, which overlooks the Skookumchuck Drainage and the Seven Devils Mountains. I clocked the mileage, admired the view, and then followed a different route back to Highway 95. The drive along Skookumchuck Creek is gorgeous this time of year. The cottonwood trees lining the creek are just budding and the trees have taken on a lime-green appearance. There were many spots where I stopped to admire the rushing water before it joins the mighty Salmon.

Now that I'm back on the highway as it snakes along side the Salmon River, my mind wanders to the rattlesnake, and I involuntarily shiver. It brings up memories of other adventures the year held for me. There was the time I stood on a bridge over the Pahsimeroi River with billowy white clouds in the distance, until a skunk came out of the bushes about twenty feet away and headed straight towards me. I barely made it back into the vehicle before he came around the back of my rig. But for the most part, that beautiful summer day was filled with wildflower vistas and complete solitude in the Pahsimeroi Highlands.

One crisp autumn day, the views from Granite Mountain Fire Lookout in eastern Idaho were amazing and the evening light bathed the lookout in a warm glow. Along the way up there, I had stopped beside the road to view a young bull moose across a deep ravine. While I should have been at a perfectly safe distance, he became very agitated and suddenly charged, sending me running the short distance back to the vehicle. I laugh about it now, but my heart sure was beating then.

A Day in the Life - Continued

As I continue south, I make a stop at a market in Riggins to peddle some calendars. They buy a dozen. Then I watch for a business that would make a good sponsor for one of my routes. I pull into the café near the south end of town where I've eaten several times, and it's always been a good experience. At first, calling on businesses was a very difficult thing for me, but over time I've gotten better and my confidence has grown. It has given me experience that I am now glad to have had. I ask for the owner and, luckily, she is nearby and hears my request.

"Hi, my name is Linda. I'm a landscape photographer out of Coeur d'Alene and I'm writing an Idaho guidebook geared towards the photographer or sightseer, and filled with photography. There are forty-eight driving routes around the state and what we're doing is having one business sponsor each route. I have three routes that either begin or end in Riggins and we'd like to bring you some extra business. Do you think this is something you might be interested in?" Kim says yes and I give more details. She follows up with some typical questions I receive from potential sponsors, including if the book will mention the rafting, fishing and hunting the area has to offer? I have to explain that this isn't the type of guidebook I'm writing. Customers come into her café, and she asks me to call her in a few days. I leave feeling fairly confident she'll say yes.

At New Meadows, I turn right. I attempt to drive the road into Meadow Lake but find the snow is still too deep. I take measurements up the Middle Fork of the Weiser River, document some barns and an old truck near Cambridge, and visit Mann Creek Reservoir. I think about how this project has had an effect on me and my life. There's been good and bad. The bad is I've become so consumed with the project itself and the documentation aspects that I have let some of my creativity go. I found myself passing up a great photo op several times, merely because it wasn't on one of my routes. I need to refocus my creative vision.

Some of the good things about this project have been the actual need to travel, getting to visit many areas of the state that I had not been super-familiar with, finding new places and things. I've felt a definite purpose to my work, my confidence has been bolstered, and my communication skills have improved with all the writing I have done. I've also strengthened a friendship with photographer Shari Hart, my partner on the project.

By mid-afternoon, I must nap. Parked on the side of a country road lined with lupine and arrowleaf balsamroot, I drift off feeling contented with my accomplishments for the day—and the year, for that matter. It's time for this project to reach conclusion.

A Hike to Mt. Harrison
Wandering in solitude with camera and hounds

Story and Photos by Shari Hart

It had been a few years since I wandered to this area in spring. My hiking partners got older and couldn't go with me on what once was a tradition. I anxiously looked forward to continuing the tradition with the 'New Kid,' Asher B, sharing a place I love, in this small envelope of time between the snowmobilers and summertime campers.

While I was driving, I impatiently checked the time and told my companion we should have left sooner. As I topped the hill before dropping down into the Albion Valley, worries about not being there earlier dissipate. Not totally, because it's all about the light for a photographer. But one doesn't always have to be there for the golden hours to enjoy the experience and create nice images. Inclement weather and overcast days are perfect as well. On this day, we compromised with some nice clouds and a light breeze.

The small town of Albion looks like something out of the Saturday Evening Post and a Norman Rockwell painting, with its well-kept homes and buildings. We drive slowly on the main road, stopping on the edge of town for a homemade cinnamon roll.

Continuing on our way, my mind goes back to all the previous wanders with my hounds, with my camera slung over my shoulder. I felt a bit nostalgic, missing my two four-legged friends. But the one-year-old pup beside me wonders just where we are going and when he'll be able to get out of the van.

This is what I love best about photography-the solo wanders with my canine companions, who were always content to come along. The comfortable rhythm of walking in silence, where volumes are spoken in subtle body language or eye contact, allowed me to get lost in thought and enjoy what was around me. My loyal companions checked in frequently and waited while I set up for a photo or paused for a break. In turn, I waited while they explored a new smell or completed their inspection of a hole.

My thoughts return to the present, as we drive past the ski lodge on Mt. Harrison. Though it is late spring, there is still enough snow at the higher elevations to find a gate across the road blocking vehicle access to the area. Excited to have not seen anyone else with the same intention as me and my pup, I gather my camera bag and tripod. We are off on the first adventure up Mt. Harrison for Asher B.

It is an easy hike up the road, even as we encounter some decent snow drifts now and again. Not in any hurry, I pause for photos, enjoy the antics of my young pup and take deep breaths of the wonderful pine-scented air. After taking a few side trips just to see 'what is over there,' we find ourselves on the windy ridge above Lake Cleveland. The panoramic views are gorgeous, with wildflowers just beginning to show. The clouds race across the sky like ships in the ocean, their shadows pausing briefly along the valley floor and distant hills. My pup rolls and runs in the snow with youthful exuberance, bringing a smile to my face and a camera to my eye. We eat our snacks in blissful companionship before wandering the short half-mile down to Lake Cleveland. The lake is tucked in the folds of granite walls. Ice still covers a good portion of its surface, and drifts cover the accesses along its southern shores and across the main road. We settle for enjoying the outlet portion of the lake, as Asher braves the ice-cold water in the shallow portions.

All too soon, it is time to hike up the grade and wander our way back to the van. We are going back down the mountain with more that we came with. I have photographs of our time there that will bring back good memories and smiles. While I regret the hike is almost over, plans run through my head for another visit before the snow is gone, and where we should go next.

"Which of the photographs is my favorite? The one I'm going to take tomorrow."
- Imogene Cunningham

Behind The Scenes
Images from the making of this book

Coupons

The following coupons and special offers from our sponsors are available for your one time use. Please remove the page at the spine and cut out individual coupons or have your coupon stamped at time of use. Not all routes have coupons.

The Rusty Moose Tavern and Grill — Route 2

Free Small Cheese Bread

with any large pizza purchase at regular price.

7211 Main St, Bonners Ferry, ID 83805

(208) 267-1950

Moose Knuckle Burgers and Brews — Route 3

Buy one burger, get one **50% off**

Discount taken on the lesser priced item

10 Cavanaugh Bay Rd, Coolin, ID 83821

(208) 443-2222

Hotel Ruby Sandpoint — Route 4

20% off

477255 US-95, Ponderay, ID 83852

(208) 263-5383

- Based on availability
- Coupon must be presented upon check-in
- Cannot be combined with other offers or discounts
- Coupon has no cash value

Evans Brothers Coffee Roasters — Route 5

Free 12oz Drink

with purchase of bag of beans
No limit on bags/drinks. Coupon to be used once.

524 Church St. Sandpoint, ID 83864

(208)-265-5553

Michael D's Eatery — Route 6

Buy one burger, get one **50% off**

Discount taken on the lesser priced item

203 E Coeur D'Alene Lake Dr, Coeur d'Alene, ID 83814

(208) 676-9049

Route 26 offers impressive views of the Sawtooth Range

Route 7 — SERVING SMILES, ~~ONE SCOOP~~ TWO SCOOPS! AT A TIME

BUY ONE DOUBLE SCOOP WAFFLE CONE, GET ONE **FREE***
*Equal or lesser value, no cash value

HARRISON Creamery & Fudge Factory

YAY, TWO SCOOPS OF YOUR FAVORITE FLAVORS FREE! a $5.25 Value!

@harrisoncreamery • 206 S. Coeur D'Alene Ave • Harrison, Idaho • 208-689-9241

The Snake Pit — Route 8

10% off
Your Total Bill

1480 Coeur D'Alene River Rd,
Kingston, ID 83839

(208) 682-3453

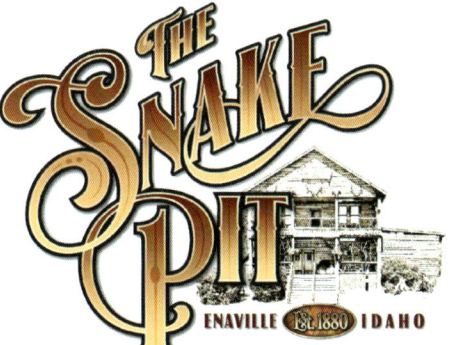

Main Street Bistro and Espresso — Route 9

15% off
one large pizza

806 Main Ave, St Maries, ID 83861

(208) 245-5539

The Pie Safe Bakery and Kitchen — Route 12

One Free Cookie
with purchase

307 Main St,
Deary, ID 83823

(208) 877-1200

THE PIE SAFE BAKERY & KITCHEN

Shari Hart — Wind & Sage Photography

20% off photographic prints
View selection at windandsagephotography.com and email for pricing and discount

"Photography is a way of feeling, of touching, of loving. What you have caught on film is captured forever... It remembers little things, long after you have forgotten everything."

— Aaron Siskind

Late winter atmosphere above Box Canyon on route 43

Hearthstone Bakery and Tea House — Route 13

One Free Cookie

with purchase

502 Main,
Kamiah, ID 83536

(208) 935-1912

The Grangeville Super 8 — Route 14

Awarded the #1 Quality Super 8 in all of North America

- Affordable Prices
- King and Queen Suites
- Indoor Pool and Spa
- Exercise Room
- Free Breakfast
- WiFi
- Guest Laundry

At the junction of Hwys. 13 and 95
(208) 983-1002

super8idaho.com
Reservations (866) 786-6835

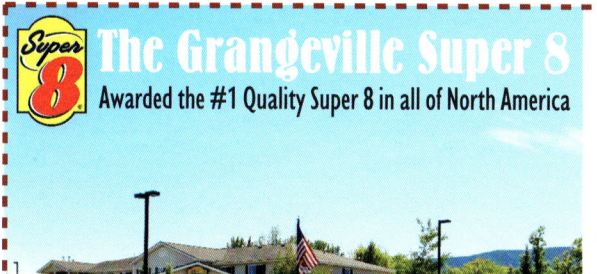

River Dance Lodge — Route 15

$20.00 Off Any Cabin Rental

excludes glamping accommodations

7743 Highway 12
Kooskia, ID

(866) 769-8747
Weekends: (208) 926-4300

Syringa Cafe — Route 15

Buy 1 entree, get the other **50% off**

Discount applied to the lower cost item

7743 Highway 12
Kooskia, ID

(208) 770-2517

Hearthstone Lodge — Route 16

FREE Tour of the Lodge

Highway 12, Milepost 64
Kamiah, ID

(208) 935-1492

White Bird Summit Lodge — Route 17

10% off Lodging

Book direct with Terri

2141 Old White Bird Hill Road
Grangeville, ID

(208) 983-1802

River Rock Cafe — Route 18

10% off Your Order Total

1149 Main St
Riggins, ID

(208) 628-3434

The old Stock Creek School near Cottonwood can be seen on route 14.

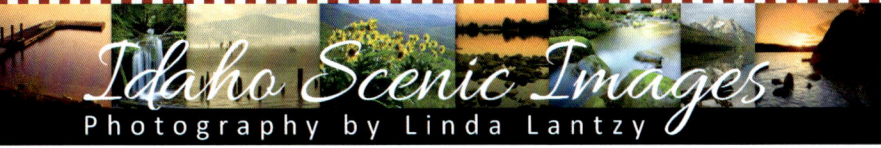

Photo Critique Services

From composition to lighting, to use of lines, color, balance, tension, and layering. Effective use of light and shadows...angles and perspective...focus and depth of field... even lens choice. These elements can make or break your landscape image.

Let me offer some guidance on your landscape photos. You'll receive a in depth analysis of your images...what you did right, and how you can improve.

idahoscenics.2.vu/critique

Gramma's Restaurant Route 21

10% off
Meal of Your Choice

224 N. Main St
Cascade, ID

(208) 382-4602

Idaho's Finest Collection of Barn Images

Learn more at: **IdahoScenics.com**

Awesome Burger Route 22

10% off
Your Order Total

10 W Central Blvd,
Cambridge, ID 83610

(208) 257-3636

The Village at North Fork Route 23

20% off One Item
at the North Fork Adventure Company

Must present coupon to the manager on duty.

208.865.7001
2046 Highway 93 N
North Fork, ID 83466

Taking a Spark of Inspiration; Forging it into Something Special

If you like this book, check out lenziforge.com to view my latest projects and offerings. I specialize in publishing and page layout services, and serve clients remotely across the country. If you seek professional design services, check out my portfolio and contact me to see how we can make your vision a reality.

$40 off Design Services
When you mention this ad. One time use. New Clients Only.

www.lenziforge.com

Long Creek flows through wildflowers in the Bitterroot Range on route 16

Rise & Shine Espresso
Route 25

Purchase a Breakfast Burrito
Recieve 20% off any drink

900 Shoup St,
Salmon, ID 83467

(208) 303-1001

Idaho Scenics Calendars

Free Shipping
on up to 3 regularly priced calendars
Shipped within the continental USA

Visit Idahoscenics.com and
send an email mentioning your coupon.

(208) 667-3325 www.idahoscenics.com

Connie's Restaurant & Saloon
Route 27

Free Slice of Fruit Pie
with any meal(s) purchased over $19.95 before sales tax.

4130 Quakie Lane
Island Park, Idaho

(208) 558-6987

Big Hole Bagel
Route 28

10% discount
One time use and no other restrictions. No cash value.

285 N Main
Driggs, ID

(208) 354-2245

Snake River Roadhouse
Route 29

1 Free Appetizer
up to a $10.00 value with purchase of 2 entrees

2998 Swan Valley Hwy,
Swan Valley, ID 83449

(208) 483-2000

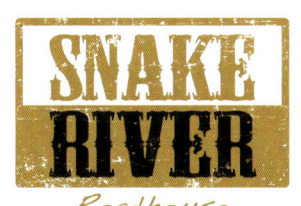

Cedar Bay Marina Rv Park and Cafe
Route 30

Pay 1 night full hookup ($45), get
2nd night for $30.00
OR
Pay 1 night dry camp, get
2nd night for $15.00

3429 Hwy 34
Henry, ID

(435) 730-6140

Order breakfast, lunch or dinner and receive a
Free Drink and Single Scoop Ice Cream

3429 Hwy 34
Henry, ID

Cafe Phone
(208) 574-2208

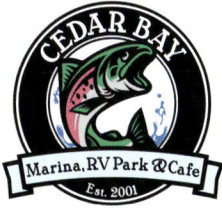

Dramatic Skies over Lake Coeur d'Alene seen along route 6

Ken Levy Media

Award-winning professional editorial services for
News Outlets • Magazines • Businesses • Non-Profits

www.KenLevyMedia.com

KenLevyMedia@gmail.com

(208) 371-4254

Cody's Gastro Garage
Route 32

Free Drink
with food purchase. Not valid for take-out.

Open 7 days a week, 3 meals a day

48 S. Main
Paris, ID

(208) 540-0273

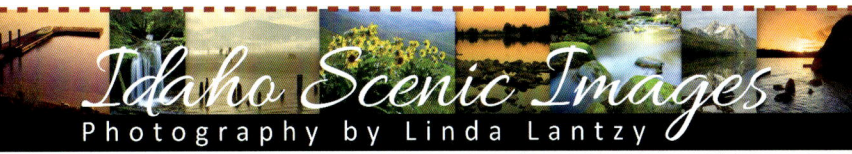

Premier Landscape Photography

- Art Prints
- Licensing
- Education

(208) 667-3325
www.idahoscenics.com

Idaho Scenic Images Scholarship opportunity

Idaho Scenic Images is pleased to announce the presentation of a yearly educational scholarship to one Idaho high school senior or collage undergraduate who demonstrates a passion for the outdoors and shows promise in the field of fine art landscape photography.

idahoscenics.2.vu/scholarship

Silver Creek Hotel
Route 35

$10.00 off Nightly Rate

721 N Main St,
Bellevue, ID 83313

(208) 725-8282

Photographic prints from Idaho Scenic Images

20% off Your Order
With Minimum Purchase of $20

Select from thousands of images

Visit **idahoscenics.2.vu/prints**
enter coupon code: **IDAHOGUIDE**

A winter view of the Smoky Mountains at sunrise along route 37

Smoky Mountain Pizzeria Grill — Route 37

One free order of Brie Kisses
Limit one per table, must present at time of order
With purchase of Entrée, Dine In Only

200 Sun Valley Rd,
Ketchum, ID 83340

(208) 622-5625

The Prairie Inn — Route 38

10% off one night stay

Good towards one room only, subject to availability. No Smoking and No pets.

115 Hwy 20 E
Fairfield, ID

208.420.6726

Tracy General Store — Route 39

One Free Tracy General Store **Cookie!**
Home made and freshly baked!

3001 Elba-Almo Rd
Almo, ID

(208) 824-5570

Mountain View Barn — Route 40

Buy one get one ½ off Lunch Special

392 E 300 S
Jerome, ID

(208) 969-0784

COFFEE SHOP • SPECIALTY SHOPS • EVENTS & WEDDINGS

T and T Cafe — Route 41

Buy One Biscuits and Gravy **Get One Free**

195 Rock Creek Rd,
Hansen, ID 83334

(208) 423-5110

Rogerson Service and Helen's Place — Route 42

Free Cinnamon Roll and Cup of Coffee or Cocoa
with a $20.00 fuel purchase

1506 N 2300 E Rd
Rogerson, ID 83302

(208) 655-4277

A calm day along route 22 reveals reflections in OxBow Reservoir

Papa Kelsey's Pizza & Subs — Route 43

Free Medium Drink with One Whole Sub Purchase

Offer good with this coupon only. One per customer. Not valid with any other offer or any other location.

130 S. State
Hagerman

(208) 837-6680

PAPA KELSEY'S PIZZA & SUBS

Bruneau One Stop — Route 44

10% off Food Purchase from the Cafe

45251 ID-51, Bruneau, ID

(208) 845-2511

Bruneau, Idaho
ONE STOP
Local Supply
OWHYEE COUNTY
COLD BEER · HOT COFFEE
Long Ropes

Dan's Ferry Service — Route 45

Free 44 oz. Fountain Drink or **large cappuccino** when combined with any other purchase.

1984 Hwy 45 So.
Melba ID, 83641

208-495-2507

Dan's Ferry Service Est 1992

The Y-Stop Country Store and Restaurant — Route 46

Buy one meal at regular price, get a second meal of equal value at **Half Price**

1260 W Long Gulch
Rd Prairie, Idaho

(208) 868-3249

THE Y-STOP Country Store and Restaurant

The Bowling Alley, LLC — Route 47

One Free Slice of **Homemade Pie** or **Any Dessert** of your choice!
With purchase of any meal.

18 W 1st St,
Homedale, ID

(208) 337-3424

The Bowling Alley — Eat + Drink + Bowl

Discovering Idaho Facebook Group

Join the **Discovering Idaho's Scenic Drives and Backroad Treasures** Facebook group for book updates and to share photos from your Idaho travels!

idahoscenics.2.vu/fb

Idaho Scenics Publishing

Check out our other products

We're always working on exciting new products. Here are some of our current offerings available for purchase at Idahoscenics.com:

- *Barns of Idaho - Sentinels of Yesteryear*
- *Greeting Card and Post Card Sets*
- *Full size and mini Idaho Calendars*
- *Custom greeting cards for business, Gifts, and More!*

In Fall 2021, you'll also find our latest book: **"*Incredible Idaho - Journey through the Gem State*"** on our website and in your local book store.

Your great idea, our expertise

In addition to our own titles, we're offering our publishing expertise t[o] those who want to avoid the hassles of learning the in and outs o[f] publishing and continue devoting their time to creative endeavors.

We will handle ISBN purchasing and registration, design work, printin[g] and delivery to your door. Then we will list your finished project on ou[r] website with direct link to your eCommerce website. (You will house th[e] product and handle all marketing, orders and delivery)

If you'd like an estimate for your art/photography based project, pleas[e] give us a call at (208) 667-3325 or visit: idahoscenics.2.vu/publish

Visit Idahoscenics.com to purchase these great products and many more!

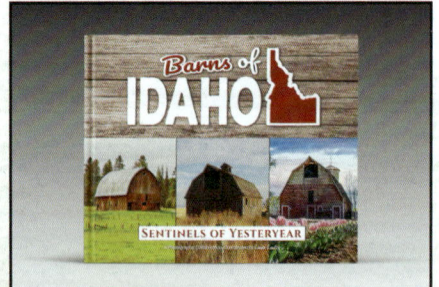